Beyond Words

What is language, really? Where did it come from, and how did we figure it out? How do babies go from babbling to speaking full sentences? Why can some people juggle multiple languages, while others wrestle with one? How does language work, and what happens when it doesn't? With sharp insight and a sense of humor, Stollznow dives into the strange and endlessly fascinating world of language and the mind. From animal communication to AI, wild children to word slips, and first words to last, this book takes you deep into the science of psycholinguistics, where nothing is ever simple, and everything speaks volumes. Packed with pop culture, real-life cases, and eye-opening experiments, *Beyond Words* reveals how we learn, use, and lose language, and what it all says about being human. If you've ever fumbled for a word or feared forgetting your own name, this thoughtful, surprising book is for you.

Dr. Karen Stollznow is a linguist, researcher, and podcaster. She's the author of *Bitch: The Journey of a Word*; *On the Offensive: Prejudice in Language Past and Present*; *Missed Conceptions: How We Make Sense of Infertility*; and *Language Myths, Mysteries, and Magic*. Karen is a Host of Monster Talk and a Visiting Scholar at the University of Colorado Boulder.

Beyond Words

How We Learn, Use, and Lose Language

Karen Stollznow

University of Colorado Boulder

Shaftesbury Road, Cambridge CB2 8EA, United Kingdom

One Liberty Plaza, 20th Floor, New York, NY 10006, USA

477 Williamstown Road, Port Melbourne, VIC 3207, Australia

314–321, 3rd Floor, Plot 3, Splendor Forum, Jasola District Centre,
New Delhi – 110025, India

Cambridge University Press is part of Cambridge University Press & Assessment,
a department of the University of Cambridge.

We share the University's mission to contribute to society through the pursuit of
education, learning and research at the highest international levels of excellence.

www.cambridge.org
Information on this title: www.cambridge.org/9781009587433
DOI: 10.1017/9781009587389

First published 2026

A catalogue record for this publication is available from the British Library

Library of Congress Cataloging-in-Publication Data
Names: Stollznow, Karen author
Title: Beyond words : how we learn, use, and lose language / Karen
Stollznow, University of Colorado Boulder.
Description: Cambridge, United Kingdom ; New York, NY : Cambridge
University Press, 2026. | Includes bibliographical references.
Identifiers: LCCN 2025042062 (print) | LCCN 2025042063 (ebook) |
ISBN 9781009587396 hardback | ISBN 9781009587389 ebook
Subjects: LCSH: Language and languages | Psycholinguistics
Classification: LCC P112 .S76 2026 (print) | LCC P112 (ebook)
LC record available at https://lccn.loc.gov/2025042062
LC ebook record available at https://lccn.loc.gov/2025042063

ISBN 978-1-009-58739-6 Hardback
ISBN 978-1-009-58743-3 Paperback

For my son, Blade, who has taught me more about language than any book ever could, and for my parents, who gave me language and showed me what it means to lose it.
With all my love, this is for you.

Contents

Acknowledgments   *page* viii

   Introduction: The Mysteries of Language   1

1 What Is Language?   10

2 Where Did Language Come From?   41

3 How Do We Learn Our Mother Tongue?   70

4 How Do We Use and Understand Language?   100

5 How Do We Lose Language?   132

6 How Do We Learn Other Languages?   162

   Conclusions: In Other Words   195

Further Reading   202
Index   217

Acknowledgments

My deepest thanks to Matthew Baxter, my partner in life and language, for your unwavering support, good humor, and sharp editorial eye. To my son, Blade Stollznow, thank you for reminding me every day why words matter and for inspiring more chapters than you know.

I'm also incredibly grateful to the brilliant team at Cambridge University Press for believing in this book and helping bring it to life. Special thanks to Becky Taylor and Izzie Collins for your guidance, encouragement, and thoughtful care throughout the publishing process.

I'm indebted as well to my copy-editor, Sue Browning, whose skill and insight made this a stronger book.

A special thanks to Ken Feder, Gary Goldberg, Stuart Hayes and Mark Newbrook for lending their expertise and insight.

Introduction
The Mysteries of Language

Beyond Words is a book driven by big questions.

What exactly is language, and where did it come from?
How do we learn our first language, and what happens when we try to learn another?
How do we use and understand language in everyday life?
And how, sometimes, do we lose it?

This book began as an exploration of psycholinguistics. What's that, exactly? (No, it's not the study of psycho linguists or linguistics for psychos.) It's the science of how we learn, use, understand, and sometimes lose language. A fusion of linguistics and psychology, psycholinguistics examines the intricate relationship between language and the human mind. The linguist Thomas Scovel once described it as a window into how the mind works. It's a field with many roots, stretching across disciplines, and as linguist Jean Aitchison put it, it's like a hydra, the many-headed creature of Greek myth. Cut off one head, and more appear.

Many of the big questions we've touched on fall under the banner of psycholinguistics. But pretty quickly, it became clear that this journey couldn't be boxed into just one field. The questions driving this book inevitably lead us across the wider landscape of linguistics. Alongside core psycholinguistic topics, we dip into what language *is* (that's descriptive linguistics), where it came from (evolutionary and historical linguistics), how language shapes and is shaped by society and culture (sociolinguistics), and the deep connection between language and the brain (neurolinguistics). These threads are woven together to paint a richer, more complete picture of how language really works. This book unravels the mysteries of language, its origins, diversity, use, and loss, and shows how language gives us a unique window into the human mind.

As we'll see, the story of language science is full of surprising twists and turns and fascinating characters, colorful, curious, and sometimes controversial, who have shaped its growth across history.

Our capacity for language has fascinated humankind for millennia. Some of the earliest reflections on language and the mind come from ancient Egypt, one of the first civilizations to develop writing. Around 1700 BCE, a scribe compiled a catalog of head and spinal injuries in a document now known as the Edwin Smith Surgical Papyrus (named after the American collector who later purchased it). The text is thought to preserve medical knowledge dating back even further. Remarkably, it includes what is believed to be the first recorded case of aphasia, a language disorder that affects a person's ability to speak or understand speech. Case 20 describes a patient who, after a head injury, "speaks not at all, although he is conscious." Despite these early observations, the Egyptians didn't think much of the brain. In fact, they removed it during embalming, assuming it served no purpose. (Embalmers likely used hooks to liquefy and extract the brain before burial.) Instead, they believed the heart was the seat of thought, emotion, and consciousness.

The Greek physician Hippocrates was one of the first to argue that the brain, not the heart, was the true center of thought, sensation, and language. Around 400 BCE, he wrote *On the Sacred Disease*, a treatise on epilepsy that offered an astonishingly modern view of the mind. "Men ought to know," he wrote, "that from nothing else but the brain come joys, delights, laughter and sports, and sorrows, griefs, despondency, and lamentations ... and by the same organ we become mad and delirious ... and by this same organ we speak." Drawing on his observations of patients who had suffered head trauma, from battle wounds, chariot accidents, or falls, Hippocrates noted how injury to the brain often led to disrupted or lost speech. His ideas stood in sharp contrast to the dominant view of the time, which held that language loss was a supernatural punishment. Instead, Hippocrates proposed something radically different: that speech, emotion, and even mental illness had physical, biological roots in the brain. It was an idea far ahead of its time, and one that would eventually shape the entire field of language science.

The Greek philosophers were the first to write extensively about language, especially Plato, who, like Hippocrates, believed that the brain was the seat of intelligence. In *The Republic*, Plato pondered the meaning of words, most famously through his Allegory of the Cave. In this thought experiment, prisoners are chained inside a cave, able to see only the shadows of objects cast on a wall by firelight. As "sign-bearers" name the objects, animals, plants, and everyday items, the prisoners mistakenly associate the names with the shadows rather than the real things. Plato's point was that language represents the world indirectly: The words we use are often tied more to our perceptions than to reality itself. Understanding, then, is an act of the mind. As we'll see, Plato returned to questions of language in other writings too, notably in *Cratylus*, a dialogue exploring whether names are arbitrary labels or somehow intrinsically linked to the things they represent.

The early history of psycholinguistics was filled with philosophical speculation, but if we trust the historians, there were also a few questionable attempts at experimentation. These early "studies" wouldn't stand a chance with modern ethics committees. In each case, infants were raised in extreme isolation, with caretakers either instructed not to speak or unable to communicate verbally. The goal? To discover what language, if any, children would develop on their own. The accounts vary. According to Herodotus, the Egyptian Pharaoh Psamtik I (seventh century BCE) claimed the children began speaking Phrygian, an ancient language of Anatolia (modern-day Turkey).

During the Middle Ages, Holy Roman Emperor Frederick II reportedly conducted a similar experiment, though tragically, all the infants died. In the fifteenth century, King James IV of Scotland is said to have tested the same theory by raising children on the remote island of Inchkeith. Supposedly, they emerged speaking Hebrew, though this strains credibility. A century later, Mughal Emperor Akbar the Great of India tried a version of the experiment too. While he failed to uncover a "natural language," there's some suggestion the children may have developed a rudimentary form of sign language, perhaps modeled on gestures used by their caretakers.

In the modern era, a quirky cast of characters contributed to the story of language and the mind, none of whom would have called themselves "linguists," but all of whom helped shape the field in their own way. Take Wolfgang von Kempelen, an eighteenth-century Austrian inventor and something of a showman. He was a pioneer in speech synthesis, creating one of the earliest "speaking machines" designed to mimic human speech, an ancestor of today's Siri and other voice assistants. Kempelen's device was the first working model of the vocal tract, using bellows as lungs and a vibrating reed to simulate the voice box, channeling sound through a chamber that acted as the mouth. Played like a musical instrument, it produced childlike sounds and eerily spoke simple words like "mama" and "papa." It could even utter short phrases such as "You are my friend – I love you with all my heart" and "Come with me to Paris."

In 1791, Kempelen published *Mechanismus der menschlichen Sprache* ("Mechanism of Human Speech and Language"), a detailed examination of human speech's origins, its sounds, and the organs behind them. A genius with a flair for the dramatic, Kempelen was also a bit of a trickster. His most famous invention, the "Chess Turk," was a turbaned automaton that seemingly played chess against opponents. But it was all smoke and mirrors. A hidden human chess master controlled the moves from inside the cabinet, baffling audiences and even besting greats like Napoleon Bonaparte and Benjamin Franklin. It's likely that Kempelen's speaking machine was created to add a haunting voice to his mysterious chess player, blending science with spectacle.

Cognitive science also plays a key role in our story. In the nineteenth century, German physiologist Franz Joseph Gall pioneered the study of brain anatomy and was an early advocate of brain localization, the idea that specific parts of the brain are responsible for particular mental functions, including language. (Gall is perhaps best remembered for inventing phrenology, the now-discredited practice of reading personality and mental traits by feeling bumps on the skull. For example, he believed that people with bulging eyes had better memories for words.) While phrenology was debunked, Gall's research laid important groundwork for understanding how language is localized in the brain.

Soon after, French physician Paul Broca proposed a connection between brain regions and language loss, though he knew that only direct anatomical evidence, not feeling skull lumps and bumps, could prove it. When a patient with speech loss died, Broca's postmortem examination uncovered an egg-sized lesion in the left frontal lobe, now famously called Broca's area, confirming his theory. About a decade later, German neurologist Carl Wernicke encountered a patient with fluent but nonsensical speech and poor comprehension. After the patient's death, Wernicke identified a lesion in the temporal lobe. This led him to propose a second key language area of the brain, now known as Wernicke's area, linked to understanding, rather than producing, language. These landmark discoveries were vital for understanding brain injury, dementia, Alzheimer's, and other conditions that affect language abilities.

The emergence of language is another fascinating chapter in this story. Philosopher Jean-Jacques Rousseau was an early voice in exploring how we acquire language. In his influential book *Emile, or On Education*, Rousseau argued for a "natural" approach to childhood learning, favoring observation and experience over rote drills in reading and writing. He encouraged parents and teachers to pay close attention to children's development. *Emile* stirred controversy for its progressive religious views: The Church denounced it, copies were publicly burned, and the book was banned in both Paris and Geneva. Still, its impact on developmental psychology has endured, inspiring later thinkers like Jean Piaget.

Rousseau's work also influenced philosopher Dietrich Tiedemann, who began a detailed diary tracking the development of his son Friedrich over his first thirty months, with special attention to the child's emerging language. This style of diary study gained popularity after Charles Darwin published his own account, sometimes affectionately dubbed "The Daddy Diaries," about the development of his son William. Darwin didn't stop there. In *The Expression of the Emotions in Man and Animals*, he examined animal communication, and in his wider evolutionary work, he speculated about how human language itself may have evolved.

In the previous century, British judge William Jones made a surprising discovery. While studying Sanskrit, he noticed that many words bore striking similarities to their counterparts in Greek and Latin, even though the people who spoke these languages lived thousands of miles apart. These resemblances couldn't be coincidental, he thought. The languages must have "sprung from some common source." This idea sparked the concept of a proto-language, an ancient linguistic ancestor from which multiple languages have evolved. It also reignited a much older question: How did the earliest humans begin to speak in the first place?

One line of thinking holds that language is innate, a built-in capacity of the human mind shaped by our evolutionary development. That idea found a strong proponent in Darwin's cousin Francis Galton, who believed that intelligence and talent, including the faculty for language, were inborn traits. He's the one who coined the now-famous phrase "nature versus nurture." (Unfortunately, Galton was also a proponent of eugenics. In fact, he originated this term too, and was the movement's founding figure.) On the other side of the argument, seventeenth-century philosopher John Locke described the human mind as a *tabula rasa*, or blank slate, at birth, shaped by experience and environment. Of course, this debate stretches back even further. Plato emphasized inborn knowledge, while his student Aristotle championed the role of learning and observation. In one form or another, we're still wrestling with those same questions today.

The nineteenth century marked the beginning of psycholinguistics as its own field. Dutch physiologist Franz Donders was a pioneer in mental chronometry, a method that measures how long it takes for people to process information mentally. Using a phonautograph, the earliest known device for recording sound (which he whimsically dubbed the "understanding-swiftness-writer"), Donders measured the time it took to identify sounds, colors, and numbers. Today, this approach remains fundamental in research, helping scientists track how long it takes us to produce speech or recognize words. For example, eye-tracking technology reveals the intricate ways our brains process written and spoken language. Interestingly, this technology has also found a place outside the lab, in marketing, where it tests how consumers respond to advertisements and product packaging.

In 1879, Wilhelm Wundt became the first person to call himself a "psychologist" and established the very first psychology laboratory in Leipzig, Germany. For Wundt, psycholinguistics was as much about the mind as it was about language. His influential book *Die Sprache* ("The Language") unified many psycholinguistic ideas, covering child language acquisition, language use and comprehension, and even sign language. Because of this, Wundt is often called "the Father of Psycholinguistics."

He shares that title with psychologist Jacob Kantor, who first introduced the term "psycholinguistics" in his 1936 book *An Objective Psychology of Grammar*. Ironically, both Kantor and his one-time colleague B. F. Skinner championed behaviorism, an opposing theory that claims children learn language through imitation, practice, and reinforcement. Skinner's best-known work, *Verbal Behavior*, argued that kids pick up language because parents reward the "right" ways to speak and discourage the wrong ones. (Though it's worth noting that his research was largely based on experiments with rats and pigeons.)

The book's premise famously prompted linguist Noam Chomsky to write a scathing rejoinder. He argued that no amount of conditioning could explain the infinite creativity and systematic nature of human language. This clash brought new attention to the nature versus nurture debate, with Chomsky firmly on the nativist side. He proposed that humans are born with an innate ability to acquire language, a specialized mental faculty unique to our species. His ideas helped usher in the "cognitive revolution," a new focus on internal mental processes like language learning, comprehension, and production. It also introduced the concept of the mind as an information processor, something like a computer.

Chomsky's impact on linguistics is hard to overstate. He famously distinguished between "competence," our internal knowledge of language, and "performance," or how we actually use that knowledge in real-world speech. This echoed an earlier distinction made by Swiss linguist Ferdinand de Saussure between *langue*, the structured system of language, and *parole*, the act of speaking.

These are just a few of the key players we'll encounter throughout the chapters ahead.

Modern technology has revolutionized psycholinguistics. The field has taken off with the rise of neuroimaging techniques like PET scans (positron emission tomography), fMRI (functional magnetic resonance imaging), and TMS (transcranial magnetic stimulation), which allow researchers to watch the brain in action, lighting up as we read, listen, or speak. Tools that once seemed like science fiction now offer real-time insights into the inner workings of language in the brain.

These tools have revealed that language isn't stored in one tidy spot in the brain, it's distributed across a network of regions. For instance, words related to tools, like *hammer* or *shovel*, activate areas involved in both recognizing the object and controlling the physical motions used to operate it. Meanwhile, the modern boom in artificial intelligence has opened new frontiers. AI is now used to simulate human language processing, from virtual assistants like Siri to autocorrect, translation tools like Google Translate, and large language models such as ChatGPT.

As we've seen, psycholinguistics has a rich, and at times, turbulent, history. It's a field shaped by ideas and insights, but also by fads, fallacies, and fierce rivalries. Born at the intersection of theory and experiment, psycholinguistics has been influenced by a diverse cast of doctors, teachers, linguists, philosophers, psychologists, cognitive scientists, and other curious minds, each bringing their own perspective to the question of how language and the mind intersect.

But this history isn't just about scientific breakthroughs. It's also about real people and real stories. In this book, we explore remarkable case studies of so-called "feral" or wild children, like Genie, who reveal what happens when language development is disrupted. We meet individuals who have lost language due to injury or illness. Figures such as the Russian revolutionary Vladimir Lenin, left nearly speechless by a series of strokes, or the poet Charles Baudelaire, whose strokes left him with the single phrase, *"Cré nom!"* (French for "holy shit!").

There are eccentric characters too, like the Reverend Spooner, whose verbal slips earned him linguistic immortality, and true polyglot savants who speak a dozen languages or more. We also look beyond the human species, to signing gorillas, scent-trailing ants, color-communicating chameleons, and dancing honeybees, and ask: Where is the line between communication and language?

Psycholinguistics, and the fields that surround it, give us profound insight into our humanity by exploring how we learn, use, and lose language, our most defining trait.

These are questions that captivate many, not just scientists. The subject can often feel weighed down by terminology and jargon, but this book doesn't assume any prior knowledge of linguistics. *Beyond Words* breaks it all down in an accessible, engaging style, written in a friendly, conversational tone. You might say it's "linguistics without tears" (or headaches).

This book takes us down plenty of rabbit holes. It's packed with astonishing research and surprising discoveries. It's about fierce debates and contentious topics that have fascinated us since ancient times, and still do today. It's a book of big questions, and big answers, some of which inevitably lead to even more questions. And that's perfectly fine. There's a lot we don't know yet, but there's also plenty we do.

Rather than a many-headed hydra, perhaps this topic is better seen as a vast jigsaw puzzle, with countless pieces, each representing a different facet of language and the mind. Our task is to understand not only the individual parts, but how they all connect. The puzzle isn't finished yet, but its image is slowly coming into focus, drawing us ever closer to the heart of what it means to be human.

What we do know is this: Language is weird, but wonderful. It's intricate and inventive, confusing and complex, mysterious, and above all, it's deeply multifaceted.

Language is beyond words.

1

What Is Language?

Before we can explore how we learn, use, and lose language, we first need to define what it is, and what it isn't. Over the centuries, many have attempted to describe language. Aristotle stated, quite simply, that language is sound with meaning. Swiss linguist Ferdinand de Saussure, a pioneer of modern linguistics, described language as a storehouse of word-images in the minds of community members. He also emphasized its social dimension, calling it "a sort of contract signed by the members of a community."

Austrian philosopher Ludwig Wittgenstein likened language to a game, an ever-evolving tool of communication between individuals and across societies. Early linguist Edward Sapir defined language as "a purely human and non-instinctive method of communicating ideas, emotions, and desires by means of a system of voluntarily produced symbols." Renowned linguist Noam Chomsky describes language as a natural part of the human mind, an innate computational system we use to create and interpret thought.

These wordy definitions, however, don't always capture how speakers themselves experience their language. In her Nobel Prize acceptance speech, celebrated African American writer Toni Morrison put it this way: "We die. That may be the meaning of life. But we do language. That may be the measure of our lives."

In the sketch "Language Conversation," from the British comedy *A Bit of Fry & Laurie*, Stephen Fry launches into an extravagant and joyful definition of language – leaving Hugh Laurie looking thoroughly perplexed.

> Language is my mother, my father, my husband, my brother, my sister, my whore, my mistress, my checkout girl. Language is a complimentary moist lemon-scented cleansing square or handy freshen-up wipette. Language is the breath of God. Language is the dew on a fresh apple. It's the soft rain of dust that falls into a shaft of morning light as you pluck from an old bookshelf a half-forgotten book of erotic memoirs. Language is the creak on a stair. It's a spluttering match held to a frosted pane. It's a half-remembered childhood birthday party. It's the warm, wet, trusting touch of a leaking nappy, the hulk of a charred panzer, the underside of a granite boulder, the first downy growth on the upper lip of a Mediterranean girl. It's cobwebs long since overrun by an old Wellington boot.

Speaking on behalf of Mr. Fry, his message is clear: Language is everywhere. It's at the heart of how we live, how we connect, and how we make sense of the world. Language is beautiful and flexible. It belongs to all of us. It's what allows us to understand one another – or not. Yet because we use it so naturally and effortlessly in our daily lives, we often take it for granted. We rarely pause to ask the fundamental question: what *is* language?

This is a straightforward question, although the answer is far more complicated, and intriguing, than it first appears.

Four Hundred Words for Snow

A very basic definition of language is that it is a means of communication – but it's much more complex than that. Communication involves sharing messages between people, whether through talking with friends, making a phone call, sending a text, or writing a letter. It can also include nonverbal cues, such as facial expressions like a smile or frown, and gestures like nodding "yes," waving "hello," or giving a thumbs up. Nonverbal communication extends to sounds, too – laughing, coughing, crying, screaming, moaning, groaning, and other meaningful vocalizations. Verbal communication, meanwhile, involves speaking or writing to convey thoughts, ideas, and emotions. Language is just one of many tools for communication. Like the old saying about bourbon and whiskey – all bourbon is whiskey, but not all whiskey is bourbon – we can say that all language is communication, but not all communication is language. More specifically, language is a system of communication made up of spoken, signed, or written symbols.

Both symbols and signs communicate information to us, although they are distinct from one another. A sign is a natural signal or indicator of something. For instance, smoke is a sign of fire, clouds can signify rain, and sneezing may be a symptom of an oncoming cold. Communication, however, involves intention, which differentiates it from informative signs. A sneeze is a sign that may mean someone has a cold; telling someone that we have a cold is communication. We use symbols to communicate. A symbol represents a concept. For example, the word *dog* denotes the animal we call a "dog." It stands as a name or symbol for the domesticated carnivorous mammal with fur, four legs, and a tail, that barks, howls, and growls – a well-loved house pet.

Language is symbolic; it is made up of symbols like these. Symbols take the form of words, sounds, gestures, or pictures used to convey thoughts or ideas. A red heart can symbolize love, while a skull and crossbones mean danger. Numerals are symbols for numbers, letters of the alphabet symbolize sounds, and personal names represent people. Symbols are subjective, while signs are objective. There is a cause-and-effect relationship between a sign and its meaning – a direct link between the two. Symbols, on the other hand, have a subjective link to their referent.

Symbols are arbitrary. Words are arbitrarily related to what they represent. This means there is no natural or causal relationship between the words in a language and their meaning. For example, English *dog*, German *Hund*, French *chien*, and Spanish *perro* all refer to the same canid creature, *Canis familiaris*, although nothing about these words inherently indicates this animal. The word we use for a dog could be any word at all. Furthermore, words have meaning only in relation to other words. A dog is a dog because it is not a cat, a mouse, or a kangaroo.

A small set of words are related to their sounds, such as onomatopoeic words that imitate noises, like *splash, swish,* and *smash.* This is known as sound symbolism. However, we know there is no consistent pattern or relationship between these words and their sounds across languages, because the corresponding words differ. *Splash* is *Spritzen* in German, *swish* is *frufrú* in Spanish, and *smash* is *fracas* in French. Just because we hear onomatopoeic words a certain way in English doesn't mean speakers of other languages hear them the same way. (We'll delve deeper into this topic in the next chapter.) Words are arbitrary because they are labels that stand for things. For instance, there is nothing about a book that intrinsically makes it a "book." We simply call it that because English speakers have agreed on the label so we can talk about written or printed texts.

Language is conventional too. Language works because everyone (more or less) agrees on what words mean and how to use them. Language is a social agreement, it is culturally formed, learned, and used. Each language is a big group project created and used by people in a particular country, city, village, or social group. Within a speech community, words carry shared meaning, which is the same for everyone so that people can understand each other. One person couldn't just suddenly decide to refer to dogs by the nonsense word *borkleflaps* instead, then expect everyone else around them to know what is meant by that word, and to use it themselves. Nobody voted on the choice of *dog,* but we all understand the word because we've heard it used that way over and over again.

Language is a shared system, a cultural handshake, that is shaped by the community to which it belongs. It also serves as a powerful expression of identity. We have multiple identities, whether these are social, ethnic, racial, gendered, national, or professional. A single person can be many different things, such as a doctor, a woman, a surfer, an Australian, and much more, depending on the groups with which they identify. Speakers can assert these various identities through their language choices.

Language reflects thought as well. Language begins with our thoughts and feelings, it's how we package and express them to the outside world. While most academics would agree that language is an embodiment of thought, whether or not language mirrors the mind is a contentious issue that still invites fierce debate. An early theory of language and the mind is linguistic relativity. This is the idea that language shapes the thoughts of its speakers. (It is also called the Sapir-Whorf hypothesis, which was first advanced by Edward Sapir and later developed by Benjamin Whorf.)

A commonly cited example of linguistic relativity is the trope that "Eskimo" has many different words for "snow" because snow is important to their culture and way of life. ("Eskimo" has largely been replaced by Inuit, which is the preferred and respectful term for many Indigenous peoples of the Arctic.) This theory goes back to a fleeting observation made by the anthropologist Franz Boas while he was on an expedition to Baffin Island in Northern Canada during the 1880s. It's believed that the Inuit have some 50 words for snow (just like the title of the Kate Bush album), while other sources say their vocabulary for snow-related terms might be as high as 400 different words. This suggests that the Inuit people are capable of thinking about snow in ways that other cultures can't. It is a pervasive urban myth, however, because Inuit languages *don't* contain an extraordinarily large number of terms for snow. They simply don't need that many words. Moreover, the ones they use can be expressed in other languages. For example, *qaniy* is "falling snow" in English, while *apun* translates to "snow on the ground." (We'll circle back to this topic soon.) English also has specific snow-related words, such as *sleet, slush, flurry*, and *blizzard*.

The extreme version of this theory is that if a language doesn't have the words to express certain ideas, then its speakers can't conceptualize them. The twentieth-century philosopher Ludwig Wittgenstein once said, "the limits of my language mean the limits of my world." A literary example of this is found in George Orwell's dystopian novel *1984*, in which the restricted vocabulary and grammar of Newspeak makes it impossible for people to speak about or even think of rebelling against the oppressive, totalitarian government.

The idea that language determines our view of the world has been largely discredited, although it is generally accepted that, at least in some ways, language influences our thinking. Guugu Yimithirr, spoken by Aboriginal people in Far North Queensland, was the first Australian Indigenous language to be written down, and the one that gave us the word *kangaroo*. Guugu Yimithirr is interesting because it uses compass directions instead of relative terms to describe spatial orientation. That is, speakers refer to the position of things based on cardinal points (north, south, east, west), not in relation to themselves (left, right, front, back). For instance, instead of asking "Can you move to my right?" they might ask "Can you move to the west?" In place of saying "the cup is to your left," they may say "the cup is north of your hand." To some extent, people who speak different languages see the world in unique ways.

The Building Blocks of Language

As we can see, defining language is complicated. If we review our definition so far, we can say that language is a system of communication that is made up of symbols. But language isn't just about words, it's a social adventure and a way we share what's going on in our minds. Though for language lovers (aka linguists), the definition gets even more granular. Linguists zoom in and break down language even further into its foundational building blocks. Language is often described as a discrete system, that is, a set of smaller segments such as sounds and words that are linked together to create bigger ideas in phrases and sentences. Language is made up of these different levels of language, that is, the sounds we hear (called phonemes), the rules that keep everything organized (grammar or syntax), and the meanings behind it all (semantics). (Heads up: this section is full of information we'll use throughout the book. Feel free to revisit it as often as you like.)

Sounds

Phonemes, or individual sounds, form the building blocks of spoken language. The name comes from the Greek *phōnēma* for "sounds," which we've repurposed into modern English words such as *telephone* and *symphony*. Phonemes are sounds, like the /d/ in *dog* and the /k/ in *cat*, although these sounds are not to be confused with letters. Letters are symbols that represent sounds. There are twenty-six letters in the Latin or

Roman alphabet, while there are about forty-four phonemes in English. These comprise consonants and vowels, including sounds that aren't represented by single letters, such as the 'ch' in *chair* and the 'sh' in *share*. For language scientists, these sounds have their own symbols in the International Phonetic Alphabet (IPA), in which 'ch' looks like /tʃ/ and 'sh' is written as /ʃ/.

The IPA represents all of the sounds in the world's languages. While there are about forty-four sounds in English, there is a wide range of sounds found across other languages. The Pirahã language (pronounced pee-da-han, not like the notorious fish), spoken by the Indigenous people living in a remote part of the Amazon rainforest in Brazil, may have as few as ten phonemes. Hawaiian has a small inventory too of only thirteen sounds. On the other end of the scale, West !Xoon, a dialect of the Taa language spoken in Namibia, has the most sounds in the world with as many as 164 consonants. West !Xoon contains lots of consonant clicks, like many other languages found in Southern Africa and East Africa. The closest we have to clicks in English are the *tut tut* and *tsk tsk* sounds used to express disapproval, or the *clip-clop* sound we make with our tongues to imitate a trotting horse.

People perceive sounds differently across languages. Think about the ways /l/ is pronounced in the word *level*. When we say this word, the first /l/ is pronounced with the tongue touching just behind the upper teeth, while the second /l/ is made slightly higher in the mouth. When a phoneme has subtle variants like this, they are called allophones. Sounds that are clearly distinct in English may not be so apparent in other languages. It's well known that Japanese speakers have difficulty differentiating between /r/ and /l/. For example, they may pronounce *light* as "right." There is also the mocking mispronunciation of English as "Engrish." This confusion happens because these two sounds are allophones of the same phoneme in Japanese. That is, they aren't perceived as distinct sounds, so they're often heard as being the same.

Make no mistake, there are some sound distinctions that are unfamiliar to English-speakers' ears too. For instance, Thai distinguishes between two different /p/ sounds. One is aspirated or said with a puff of air, while the other is unaspirated or said without a puff of air. (You can feel the difference by placing your hand in front of your mouth – there's a noticeable burst of air when you say "pot" but not when you say "spot.") These are completely different sounds to Thai ears and using the wrong one affects meaning. So, Thai language learners might make errors like confusing the aspirated *phaa* "to bring" with unaspirated *paa* "to throw."

Even among speakers of the same language, we don't all hear or produce sounds in the same way. In casual speech, some people drop sounds in a word (a process known as elision). For example, "don't know" may become *dunno* and "want to" can sound like *wanna*. This makes speech faster and more fluid, and in some cases, it also reflects accents. In the musical *My Fair Lady* (based on George Bernard Shaw's *Pygmalion*), Eliza Doolittle, a Cockney flower girl, famously drops her h's, referring to Professor Henry Higgins as "'Enry 'Iggins." Omitting sounds is common as a poetic device too, as seen in the US national anthem the "Star-Spangled Banner," with the line, "O'er the land of the free and home of the brave."

In contrast, sometimes extra sounds are added (which is called epenthesis). For instance, *athlete* is sometimes pronounced as "athelete," and *something* as "sompthing." Back to *My Fair Lady*, Eliza Doolittle adds an extra sound to *lovely*, singing "Wouldn't It Be Loverly" in her strong East London Cockney accent. Sometimes, sounds within a word are rearranged, to make pronunciation easier. Linguists call this switcheroo "metathesis" – when sounds swap places. Common examples include saying "expresso" instead of *espresso* or "aks" instead of *ask* (we'll come back to this one soon). A different kind of variation is found in the pronunciation "nucular" for *nuclear*, infamously used by US presidents Dwight Eisenhower, Bill Clinton, and George W. Bush.

Not all sounds combine together in all languages either. Each language has its own set of rules, called phonotactics, that determine which sound sequences are allowed. For instance, Polish has the word *szczęście* meaning "happiness," although the sound combinations of 'sz' and 'cz' aren't permitted at the start of words in English. Similarly, English allows word-initial clusters like 'str-' (as in *street*), which might be difficult or even unpronounceable in other languages. These patterns of possible (or impossible) combinations are part of what gives each language its distinctive rhythm and sound. Another striking example is the word *psychology* in English. It begins with a consonant cluster 'ps', but the 'p' is silent. Although in Greek, the language the word comes from, both sounds are pronounced, English doesn't allow this sound combination at the beginning of native words, so the first sound is dropped. This shows how these rules influence not just how words are formed, but how borrowed words get reshaped to fit the rules of English.

Words (and Parts of Words)

Words, and word parts, form the next level of language. Phonemes combine to form words, also called morphemes, the smallest units of meaning. Some morphemes stand alone as words in their own right, such as verbs, nouns, and adjectives like *drive, red,* and *car.* Other morphemes are bound and cannot stand alone. These are parts of words that need to be attached to free-standing words, including prefixes like *pre-* at the beginning of *preschool* and suffixes like *-ish* and *-ness* tagged onto the end of *childishness.* These morphemes can't exist independently and must be attached to words. They may be small, but they pack a lot of meaning. For example, *walked* consists of two morphemes, *walk,* which signifies the action, and *-ed,* which shows that the action took place in the past.

Pigs also contains two morphemes, *pig,* which refers to a swine, and *-s,* which indicates plurality, that there is more than one of them. Morphemes that can stand alone are known as root words, while those that must be attached to roots, such as inflections, convey grammatical information like tense, number, or possession. Though some words are deceptive. They look like they might be composed of multiple morphemes, like *father* and *pumpkin,* although we can't break them down any further, into *fat* and *her* or *pump* and *kin,* because these segments don't relate to the actual meaning of the word.

We can build some really big words by tacking morphemes onto each other. A well-known example is *antidisestablishmentarianism,* often cited as one of the longest words in the English language. (It certainly contains a lot of morphemes.) This daunting word can be broken down into smaller parts: *anti-* meaning "against," *dis-* "to deprive of," *estab-lish,* (here referring to the Church of England), *-ment* "the act of," *-arian* "a person who," and *-ism* meaning "the ideology of." Words can also be combined to create compound words. This happens when two or more individual words are joined together to form a new word that acts as one unit, such as *foot + ball = football.*

As we know from the trope above of "400 words for snow," Inuit languages use compounding. They add elements to a root word for "snow," for example, *sikurluk* means "melting ice." This would be like us perceiving the phrase "packed snow" as a single word: "packedsnow." Through compounding, speakers of Inuit languages can generate countless words for snow ... or grass, or coffee, or anything else, for that matter. German is replete with compound nouns too, including extremely long ones like the 63-letter long word *Rindfleischetikettierungsüberwachungsaufgabenübertragungsgesetz.* This translates to "the law concerning the delegation of duties for the supervision of cattle marking and the labelling of beef." In his humorous essay "The Awful German Language," Mark Twain pokes fun at the complexity and length of German words, quipping that some "are so long that they have a perspective." He added, "These things are not words, they are alphabetical processions. And they are not rare; one can open a German newspaper at any time and see them marching majestically across the page – and if he has any imagination, he can see the banners and hear the music, too."

In addition to forming compound words, English has a variety of ways to create new vocabulary. One common method is simply borrowing from other languages. These so-called loanwords include *psychology* from Greek, and more recently, *emoji* from Japanese, and *sriracha* from Thai (derived from the coastal city of Si Racha in Thailand). Of course, we never give back these borrowed words. As the popular meme puts it, "English doesn't 'borrow' from other languages: it follows them down dark alleys, knocks them over, and goes through their pockets for loose grammar and valuable vocabulary." English has drawn extensively from French, especially after the Norman Conquest of 1066. Some ten thousand French words entered the language during that time, many of which remain in use today, from *restaurant* and *brunette*, to *garage* and *government.*

We can also invent entirely new words. It's rare to create new grammatical words, such as conjunctions like *but* and *or*, and prepositions like *up* and *down*, though it does happen occasionally. For instance, in recent years we have seen the introduction of new non-binary pronouns like *xe* and *xem* as well as *co* and *cos*. We often coin new words, or neologisms, especially when it comes to adjectives, nouns, and verbs. These parts of speech are productive, meaning that we can invent new ones for emerging concepts, such as *covid, selfie, unfriend,* or *blockchain technology*. New words are popping up all the time. A popular trivia question is: How many words are there in the English language? While estimates suggest there are over one million words, there is no exact count. One reason for this is that the English lexicon keeps expanding at an astonishing rate.

Grammar

Collectively, these segments serve as the building blocks of language. Sounds are strung together to form words. Words, and parts of words, are then assembled into coherent thoughts through phrases and sentences. These larger units of language are governed by grammar, or syntax, the set of rules that structures a language. Sentences typically consist of a subject, verb, and object, and they express statements, questions, or exclamations. To convey meaning clearly, these elements must follow a specific, prescribed order.

In English, the standard word order is subject-verb-object (SVO), as demonstrated by the title of The Beatles song, "She loves you." English shares this word order with languages as diverse as Hebrew, Chinese, and Swahili. In contrast, languages like Japanese and Turkish follow a subject-object-verb (SOV) pattern, which would rearrange the song title to "She you loves." These two orders are the most common patterns found across the world's languages. Some languages, like Fijian, use the much rarer verb-object-subject (VOS) order, which would render the title as "Loves you she." Others, such as Irish, Welsh, and Māori, favor a verb-subject-object (VSO) pattern, resulting in "Loves she you." Latin is notable for having what's known as free word order, meaning the subject, object, and verb can appear in any sequence. However, each word must be inflected (that is, changed) to indicate its grammatical role in the sentence.

The sentences we create using these rules can be as short and simple as "Run!" or as long and complex as needed. Most language is recursive, meaning sentences can be nested within other sentences. We can repeat grammatical structures over and over, just like that. A fun example appears in *Ferris Bueller's Day Off*, when Ferris's economics teacher calls out his name monotonously during roll call, "Bueller? Bueller? Bueller?" Finally, a fellow student pipes up with, "Um, he's sick. My best friend's sister's boyfriend's brother's girlfriend heard from this guy who knows this kid who's going with the girl who saw Ferris pass out at 31 Flavors last night."

We can find examples in literature as well. In P. G. Wodehouse's *Thank You, Jeeves*, the somewhat dim-witted and idle-rich Bertie Wooster hatches a plan for his "gentleman's gentleman" to dispatch a letter to an acquaintance. Wooster describes the scheme as Jeeves taking "a letter from you to her and then one from her to you and then one from you to her and then one from her to you and then one from you to her and then one …" before he is politely stopped in his tracks.

Words are both productive and creative, and so are sentences. As long as they abide by the rules of grammar, speakers can generate an infinite number of unique sentences to express a wide range of meanings. Chomsky illustrated this feature of language with his famous example: *Colorless green ideas sleep furiously*, a sentence that is grammatically correct, although nonsensical. This point is also cleverly demonstrated in the same episode of *A Bit of Fry & Laurie* mentioned at the beginning of this chapter. In the sketch, Stephen Fry's pompous character tells a nonplussed Hugh Laurie, "Our language, hundreds of thousands of available words, frillions of possible legitimate new ideas, so that I can say the following sentence and be utterly sure that nobody has ever said it before in the history of human communication, 'Hold the newsreader's nose squarely, waiter, or friendly milk will countermand my trousers.' One sentence, common words, but never before placed in that order."

Meaning

These quirky examples demonstrate that we can distinguish between grammatical and ungrammatical sentences, even when they don't make any logical sense. As Chomsky shows, it's grammatically possible to construct a sentence like *Colorless green ideas sleep furiously*. While it follows the rules of syntax, it lacks coherent meaning. In contrast, rearranging the same words into *Furiously sleep ideas green colorless* violates grammatical rules and feels jarring. This distinction highlights the role of semantics, the branch of linguistics concerned with meaning. Whether we're talking about morphemes, words, phrases, or entire sentences, semantics helps us understand how language constructs, conveys, and sometimes confuses meaning among speakers and listeners.

The common phrase "It's just semantics" often implies nitpicking or trivial argument, but in reality, semantics is fundamental to communication. As linguist Carsten Levisen puts it,

> Words carry in them small stories. Small stories about big things: emotion, sociality, personhood, values, and worldviews. Words portray the world from naïve perspectives, from speakers' conventional wisdoms, not the sophisticated view of experts. And this is precisely why the study of words has much to offer. Words can give us a unique insight into the ethnotheories of the everyday: ways of thinking, ways of feeling, and ways of living.

Language is meaningless without meaning. Meaning, however, isn't fixed. The meanings of words can shift or evolve over time. Sometimes, a word broadens to encompass more than it originally did. Take the word *dog* for example, which originally referred to a specific type of dog, a powerful breed that originated in England. Over time, its meaning expanded to include all breeds, from chihuahuas to a Saint Bernard. Then again, words can also narrow in meaning, coming to refer to less than they once did. In the Middle Ages, *girl* referred to any young child, regardless of gender. Over time, its meaning shifted, and today it refers specifically to a young or adolescent woman. Some words undergo a negative shift in meaning, a process known as pejoration. In medieval times, for example, *silly* (then spelled *sely*) meant "happy," "blissful," or "blessed." Across time, some words take on increasingly negative meanings. *Silly* gradually shifted from these positive meanings to less favorable senses such as "weak, feeble, insignificant," to its modern-day meaning of "lacking good sense, empty-headed, foolish." The opposite process is called amelioration, where words with negative meanings develop more positive ones. Though less common, a classic example is *nice*. When it first appeared in Middle English, it described someone who was "foolish" or "ignorant." Over the centuries, however, it came to mean "kind," "considerate," and "friendly." Interestingly, some words like *bad* and *wicked* developed both negative and positive slang meanings, depending on context.

Over the course of the history of English, many words have died out too. They're just no longer in the language. For instance, the Old English word *ymbsittend* meant "around-sitter," a person who sits near you. Today, we just call them *neighbors*.

Cookies and Biscuits

These definitions of language are not restricted to any single one of them. They apply not only to English, but also to unrelated languages around the world, such as Arabic, Chinese, and Spanish, as well as to Indigenous tongues like Pitjantjatjara, traditionally spoken in Central Australia. But our task in defining language isn't complete. The word *language* can also refer to a specific system of communication used by a particular country or community, such as English or Swahili. Today, there are an estimated 7,000 languages in use across the globe.

The boundaries between languages aren't always clear-cut, though. For instance, Serbian and Croatian are nearly identical in vocabulary and grammar. They're so similar, in fact, that they were once officially merged as "Serbo-Croatian" when Yugoslavia was formed after World War I, a state that also included Bosnia and Herzegovina, Macedonia, Montenegro, and Slovenia. This linguistic union was controversial. Many Croatians objected to the name, asking why it wasn't called Croato-Serbian instead. Following ongoing conflict, the country fractured, and the language was split into national varieties, renamed according to their respective regions. As this shows, naming a language isn't just a linguistic matter, it's also deeply shaped by history, politics, and culture.

There are thousands of languages in the world today, but countless more dialects. So, what's the difference between a language and a dialect? In everyday usage, "dialect" is often used pejoratively to describe speech considered slangy or associated with marginal, uneducated, or unsophisticated ways of speaking. From a linguistic perspective, every language consists of dialects, and everyone speaks one. A dialect is simply a form or variety of a language used in a particular geographic region, such as Canadian English, South African English, or New Zealand English. These are called *regional dialects* because they reflect the language of a specific area. A language gives rise to dialects when it begins to diverge in different places. Although dialects may use different words, grammar, and pronunciation, they are typically *mutually intelligible*, meaning speakers can understand one another. They are still considered part of the same language. To complicate matters further, each of us has an *idiolect*, our own individual and evolving way of using language that changes throughout our lives.

Let's explore some of the quirks that make regional dialects so distinctive. One of the main differences lies in vocabulary: Different dialects often have their own words for the same thing. Take food, for example: Americans say *cookie* for the sweet round treat that Australians would call a *biscuit*. Confusingly, Americans use *biscuit* for a soft, bread-like roll that Aussies would know as a *scone*. Australian English is a lively regional variety known for its love of abbreviations. You'll hear *footy* for football, *sunnies* for sunglasses, and *mozzy* for mosquito. The classic greeting *G'day* (short for "good day") has become iconic, though it's less common among younger Australians today. And while *Crocodile Dundee*'s Paul Hogan might've invited you to "Throw a shrimp on the barbie," most Australians would raise an eyebrow – they say *prawn* not *shrimp*. That famous line actually came from a 1980s tourist campaign called "Come say G'day!" aimed at charming American visitors.

Regional dialects don't just vary from country to country, they pop up within countries too. Take the United States: Southern American English is spoken in states like Georgia, Mississippi, and Tennessee, and it comes with some signature expressions. For example, *y'all* is the go-to second-person plural pronoun, and *fixin' to* means you're about to do something (as in, "I'm fixin' to go to the store"). Then there's the trademark *bless your heart,* an idiom that sounds sweet but is often southern sarcasm for "you poor fool."

Within a single country, different regions can have their own unique words for everyday things. In the US, what you call a carbonated beverage depends on where you're from. In Pennsylvania, it's *pop*. In California, it's *soda*. In parts of Texas and Louisiana it's *soft drink*. But across most of the South, it's all just *coke* (even if it's actually a Sprite). Thanks to globalization, many of these colorful local dialects are slowly fading. Still, they add flavor (and sometimes confusion) to the way we speak.

Dialects don't just differ in vocabulary, they also have their own twists on grammar. In British English, for instance, people might use *shall* to make a suggestion: "Shall we meet at the coffee shop?" Meanwhile, American English speakers are more likely to say, "Do you want to meet at the coffee shop?" Scottish English has its own grammatical character too. "Would not" becomes *wouldnae* and "not" is often shortened to *no* as in "He's surely no going to be there." Across dialects, these grammatical and vocabulary nuances may vary, but there are usually enough similarities to keep things mutually intelligible.

That said, some varieties of English have taken quite a different path from the original. Consider Singaporean English, for example. A speaker might say, "I go bus stop wait for you," meaning they'll wait at the bus stop. It might sound ungrammatical to speakers of other dialects, but in Singaporean English, it's perfectly correct. In fact, that sentence could be translated word-for-word into Malay or Chinese without changing its structure, which reflects the multilingual environment in which this dialect developed.

Indian English stands out in colorful and conspicuous ways. English speakers around the world have borrowed a few of its gems, *karma*, *khaki*, and *curry* have made themselves quite at home. (It's less known that *avatar*, *jungle*, and *shampoo* come from Hindi too.) But other expressions might leave outsiders scratching their heads. In Indian English, *flick* doesn't mean to give something a quick tap, it means to steal it. And if someone's *chewing your brains*, they're not zombies, just seriously pestering you. Some verbs are used without an object. In Indian English, you might hear someone say, "We enjoyed very much." One of its hallmarks is the tag question *isn't it?*, which does a lot of heavy lifting. You might hear, "You can come tomorrow, isn't it?" where others might expect "can't you?" To some ears, these differences might sound "wrong" or "ungrammatical," but that's just linguistic bias talking. Dialects like Indian English show how regional shades of English can evolve so much over time they start becoming distinct languages in their own right.

"Bad" English

Dialects can be regional, or social. A *social dialect* refers to the vocabulary and grammar used by a particular community or social group. This might include people from a specific socioeconomic class, profession, age bracket, or ethnic background. A well-known example is African American English (AAE), also popularly known as Ebonics or Black English. It's famous for its use of double negatives in phrases like *I don't know nothing* or *ain't no*, which might make a grammar teacher squirm, but are perfectly grammatical within the dialect. Contractions like *wanna* (for "want to") and *imma* (for "I'm going to") are also common, giving it a punchy, rhythmic style.

African American English is also a major source of modern slang. Words like *lit* (meaning "exciting," "excellent," or "fun"), *slay* (to do something exceptionally well), and *ghost* (to suddenly cut off contact, especially in dating) have crossed into mainstream English, often through pop culture, music, and the Internet. What starts in one community often ends up shaping how the rest of us talk. And then there's *aks*, a pronunciation of *ask* that gets a lot of attention, though it's got deeper roots than most people realize. Believe it or not, the verb goes all the way back to Old English, where it appeared in two forms: *ascian* and *acsian*. By Middle English the latter had become *axsian*, eventually shortening to *ax* or *axe*. Over time, these forms gave rise to the two versions we know today: *ask*, which became the standard, and *aks*, a nonstandard form that still thrives in many dialects.

Some social dialects hit the linguistic jackpot, they're chosen as the "standard," meaning they become the official go-to in government documents, business meetings, news broadcasts, and school textbooks. This standard dialect is often seen as the "correct" version of the language, the one that supposedly does everything right. But here's the twist: it's really just a social dialect with better PR. Other dialects that differ from the mainstream version, like Cockney English or African American English, are classified as "nonstandard." These varieties are often unfairly dismissed as incorrect, corrupt, sloppy, inferior, bad, or even broken versions of English. (As noted, Singaporean and Indian English face the same kind of judgment.) But let's dispel that misconception: Nonstandard dialects have a comprehensive set of rules. Their grammar is every bit as structured and systematic as so-called "proper" English, it's just a different system.

Back in the 1970s, a landmark court case even recognized Ebonics as a legitimate dialect of English, contributing to a broader recognition of linguistic diversity and equality. No dialect is inherently superior or correct; each simply offers a different way of expressing the same ideas. So why does one dialect become "standard" while another doesn't? It comes down to social forces of power, politics, and prestige. As linguist Max Weinreich famously put it, "A language is a dialect with an army and navy." On the flip side, some nonstandard dialects carry covert prestige, a kind of hidden respect or social value. Among people who strongly identify with Black culture, for example, African American English is rich with identity, pride, and belonging.

Language variation isn't just about where you come from or the social group you belong to, it also depends on how and why you're speaking. This brings us to registers. These are different styles or levels of language tailored to particular situations, audiences, or purposes. Think of the dense, often indecipherable legalese in contracts or courtrooms that's packed with formal words like *hereinafter* and Latin phrases such as *habeas corpus* or *prima facie*, which sound worlds apart from everyday conversation. Or consider medical jargon, replete with Latin and Greek roots like *hypertension* and *idiopathic*, that doctors use to describe conditions and treatments in ways that can baffle patients. Switching registers is like changing the gear of your language: You might shift from casual slang with friends to a polished tone in a job interview or an academic paper. Registers reveal just how flexible language is, adapting not only to who we are and where we're from but also to what we're doing and who we're talking to.

Every language has its own set of dialects, which differ in vocabulary, grammar, and also in accent, that is, the way words are pronounced using specific sounds or phonemes (as we discussed earlier). But even when the vocabulary and grammar stay the same, it's often accent that people notice first, and judge most quickly. Accents carry powerful social meaning, signaling not just where someone comes from but often how they're perceived. Some people insist, "I don't have an accent," believing that only others do. But that's a common misconception. Everyone has an accent, shaped by their regional and social background.

Perhaps the most widely recognized English accent is Received Pronunciation, or RP. Often dubbed the King's English (or Queen's, depending on the reigning monarch) and also known as "BBC English," it gained prominence in the 1920s as the standard voice of the BBC's newsreaders and presenters. RP is closely linked with wealth, education, and social privilege, and to many ears, it still represents what is considered "proper" or "correct" English. But accents vary wildly across countries, cultures, and communities – and they often come loaded with stereotypes. These perceptions can be flattering or unflattering. For example, RP is typically tied to social status and influence, while the Yorkshire accent, with its working-class roots, is sometimes unfairly labeled as rustic or unsophisticated.

Just like nonstandard grammar, nonstandard accents can carry covert prestige. In a Yorkshire pub, for instance, a local accent might be admired, with speakers seen as down-to-earth, honest, and part of the community. By contrast, an outsider speaking the King's English could come across as pompous, pretentious, or out of touch. One deeply rooted and harmful stereotype is that speakers of African American English are lazy, uneducated, or even criminal, reflecting broader racist assumptions imposed on the Black community throughout US history. This accent is often stigmatized because of its association with poverty and systemic inequality, driven by discriminatory attitudes. Yet within the Black community, the accent fosters pride, identity, and group solidarity. African American English also carries covert prestige beyond the community. It has profoundly influenced popular culture, especially in jazz, R&B, and hip hop, shaping the sound and style of modern music and language.

One theory suggests that African American English shares features with nonstandard English dialects spoken in the Caribbean, such as Jamaican English and Puerto Rican English. These varieties emerged from a blend of British English and West African languages. When groups of people who don't share a common language (or *lingua franca*) need to communicate, they often develop a simplified, makeshift language to bridge the gap. These are known as *contact languages*, typically born out of trade, colonization, enslavement, or other situations where people from different language backgrounds are forced to interact.

Caribbean English varieties, for example, arose from the encounter between British colonizers and the enslaved Africans brought to the islands to work on sugar plantations. In such contexts, a *pidgin* often develops, a stripped-down language with a limited vocabulary and simplified grammar, borrowing elements from the different languages in contact. A pidgin serves as a practical means of communication, though it isn't anyone's native language. Regrettably, "pidgin" is frequently mischaracterized as "broken English" or gibberish, but that view overlooks the complexity and value of these languages.

A pidgin can take several different paths. In some cases, it fades from use, like Hawaiian Pidgin, which has been largely replaced by English. Other pidgins, such as those in parts of West Africa, may persist for decades or even centuries. But sometimes, a pidgin takes on a new life when children grow up hearing and speaking it as their first language, and it transforms into a fully developed native tongue. This process is known as creolization. As the language adapts to meet the everyday needs of its new generation of speakers, its grammar becomes more complex and its vocabulary expands. The result is a *creole*, a natural language that has grown from a once-simplified system. Importantly, no language is inherently lacking or inferior. Every language, whether a global giant or a local creole, is fully equipped to meet the needs of its speakers and can grow and evolve over time.

One example of a creole language is Bislama, spoken in Vanuatu, a group of islands in the South Pacific. In the nineteenth century, hundreds of thousands of Pacific Islanders were taken, often by force, as indentured laborers to work on plantations, mainly in Australia and Fiji. With so many different languages spoken among the workers, a localized pidgin emerged, combining English vocabulary with Melanesian grammar. When laborers returned home, they brought this pidgin with them, and it gradually spread throughout Vanuatu. As children began learning and using it as their first language, it developed into a fully-fledged creole. For much of its history, Bislama was primarily a spoken language. But in recent decades, linguists have worked to codify it, establishing standardized rules for writing and spelling.

ABCs

Of course, language isn't just spoken, it's written too. No definition of language is complete without considering writing. Yet historically, written language has often been treated as a second-class citizen. In Plato's *Phaedrus*, Socrates reflects on the invention of writing and argues that it is inherently inferior to speech. In his view, writing was a poor substitute for the spoken word; it couldn't respond, clarify, or defend itself. A written text, he claimed, is silent and static.

Even early linguists downplayed its role. Ferdinand de Saussure, for instance, remarked in a lecture: "Language and writing are two distinct systems of signs; the second exists for the sole purpose of representing the first." Leonard Bloomfield went so far as to reject writing as language, stating, "Writing is not language, but merely a way of recording language by visible marks." More recently, however, French philosopher Jacques Derrida pushed back against this idea. He argued that written symbols are valid signifiers in their own right and should not be dismissed as simply secondary to speech.

Most of the world's languages have a writing system, though a few, like Pirahã in the Amazon, remain unwritten. As mentioned earlier, Bislama was only recently codified using the Latin alphabet. English, too, is written with the Latin (or Roman) alphabet, which originally belonged to the ancient Romans for writing Latin. They adapted it from the Etruscan alphabet, itself evolved from the Greek alphabet, around since the time of Socrates. The Greek alphabet traces back to the Phoenician script, which ultimately derived from Egyptian hieroglyphs.

The earliest recorded Old English was written using Anglo-Saxon runes, but by the Middle Ages, the Latin alphabet began to be used for

English, introduced by Catholic missionaries from Rome. However, the ancient Romans wouldn't recognize our modern alphabet, since they didn't use lowercase letters or diacritics, the accent marks found in words like *café*, *jalapeño*, and *Motörhead*. They also lacked some letters we now use, namely U and W, because the letter V stood for both the /u/ and /w/ sounds. The Anglo-Saxons added a few symbols of their own – for example, 'þ' (thorn), which represented the 'th' sound in words like *three*, though this letter eventually fell out of use.

For the most part, alphabets assign a symbol or letter to represent each phoneme. There are many alphabets in use worldwide, for example, Cyrillic, which writes Russian and Serbian, and the Arabic alphabet, used for Arabic and various languages across Asia and Africa. (Arabic is also classified as an *abjad*, a system that primarily records consonants, leaving vowels to be inferred from context, though diacritics sometimes mark them.) Braille, the tactile writing system used by people with visual impairments, is an alphabet as well. (Technically, Braille is a code, not a language.)

The Latin alphabet has become the dominant writing system, used by about 70 percent of the world's population. Yet, it's far from the only kind of system out there. Syllabaries assign a symbol to each syllable, as seen in Cherokee and Japanese kana. Logographic systems use symbols to represent entire words or morphemes. Chinese characters, for instance, are made up of radicals that convey meaning and hints about pronunciation. Meanwhile, ideographic systems use symbols to represent ideas or concepts, such as Egyptian hieroglyphs, which can stand for things like "sun" or "pharaoh." Hieroglyphs are especially complex, combining over a thousand characters that blend alphabetic, syllabic, logographic, and ideographic elements. Some languages even use more than one writing system; for example, Serbian is written in both Cyrillic and Latin scripts.

The writing system, or orthography, of a language only approximates how it is spoken. English spelling has evolved over more than a thousand years, and the connection between letters and sounds has become anything but straightforward, making English notorious for its spelling inconsistencies, frustrating both learners and native speakers alike. For example, the letter 'c' is pronounced /s/ in *ice* but /k/ in *cream*. The /k/ sound can be spelled with 'c' as in *cand*y or 'k' as in *ketchup*. Sometimes a letter is not pronounced at all, like the 'k' in *knight*, and sometimes a single sound requires multiple letters, like the 'th' in *three* (making that old thorn symbol seem pretty handy).

To highlight English spelling's absurdities, it's been jokingly suggested that "fish" could be spelled as 'ghoti', using 'gh' as in *laugh*, 'o' as in *women*, and 'ti' as in *nation*. These quirks or irregularities have inspired countless humorous memes and spelling poems, like this playful piece known as "The Chaos".

> I take it you already know,
> of tough and bough and cough and dough?
> Others may stumble, but not you,
> on hiccough, thorough, lough and through.
> Well done! And now you wish, perhaps,
> To learn of less familiar traps?
> Beware of heard, a dreadful word
> That looks like beard and sounds like bird,
> And dead: it's said like bed, not bead –
> For goodness sake don't call it deed!
> Watch out for meat and great and threat
> (They rhyme with suite and straight and debt).
>
> A moth is not a moth in mother,
> Nor both in bother, broth in brother,
> And here is not a match for there
> Nor dear and fear for bear and pear,
> And then there's dose and rose and lose –
> Just look them up – and goose and choose,
> And cork and work and card and ward,
> And font and front and word and sword,
> And do and go and thwart and cart –
> Come, come, I've hardly made a start!
> A dreadful language? Man alive!
> I'd mastered it when I was five!

Earlier, we explored grammatical rules, but, as it turns out, some rules are made to be broken. English is full of irregular verbs: for example, the past tense of *eat* is *ate*, not *eated*. In some rare cases, a verb doesn't just bend the rules, it throws them out entirely. This is known as suppletion, when a form is replaced by an entirely different word. The classic example is *go* and its past tense *went*. That's because *go* comes from Old English *gān*, while *went* actually originated from a different verb altogether: *wend*.

Grammar humor even makes its way into memes, like the one that laments: "Sadly, the days of people using proper English are went."

English spelling, too, has suffered from rule-breaking, largely thanks to pronunciation changes over time. One of the biggest shake-ups was the Great Vowel Shift, which took place between Geoffrey Chaucer's and William Shakespeare's eras. During this period, long vowel sounds shifted dramatically: Words like *bite*, *to*, *good*, and *mouse* would have sounded more like *beet*, *toe*, *goad*, and *moose*.

And it wasn't just vowels, some consonants changed too. The *k* in *knife*, *know*, and *knight*, for instance, was once pronounced. There's a playful nod to this in *Monty Python and the Holy Grail*, where the French guard mocks King Arthur and his knight by calling them "kanigits."

Spelling often did not keep up with these major changes in pronunciation. In fact, much of our modern orthography hasn't changed significantly since Chaucer's time in the 1300s, which helps explain why English spelling can feel like such a puzzle today.

English spelling has also been shaped by contact with other languages. Around 1440, the German goldsmith Johannes Gutenberg invented the movable-type printing press, inspired by Chinese woodblock printing (and the screw press used for winemaking). In 1476, William Caxton introduced the printing press to England, helping to solidify the form of written English. Caxton's printer began to standardize certain spellings, much like how the Bislama dictionary later helped codify its written form.

However, Caxton also introduced new irregularities. Some of his typesetters were European and brought their own native spelling habits with them. For instance, the word *ghost* was spelled *gost* or *goost* in English, but Caxton's Flemish printers inserted an 'h' based on their word *gheest*, and the 'h' stuck. To justify lines of text, compositors often altered the length of words by adding or changing letters rather than adjusting spacing. That's why you sometimes see an extra *e* at the end of words like *name*, *love*, and *write.* This created the appearance of a longer word, especially in a setting where they were paid by the line. Later on, classic language enthusiasts modified spellings even further. The word *dette*, borrowed from French, became *debt* to reflect Latin *debitus.* While most English words follow regular patterns, about 4 percent are so irregular and unpredictable that their spelling must be memorized outright, words like *said, are,* and *yacht.*

English spelling and punctuation remained inconsistent for quite some time, and the much-maligned *aks* is a perfect case in point. Though it's criticized today, as we know, its roots trace back to Old English, where it was actually the formal written form of the word. Caxton even used it in his edition of Geoffrey Chaucer's *Canterbury Tales*, the first book ever printed in England. In "The Parson's Tale," we read of a "man that ... cometh for to axe him of mercy." (This was written in Middle English, the vernacular of the day, when Latin or French were still the standard for formal writing.)

The spelling also appears in the first complete English Bible, translated by Miles Coverdale, where Matthew 7:7 reads, "Axe and it shal be giuen you." Today, *ask* has become the standard – but *aks* still survives in African American English and several British dialects. In the animated sitcom *Futurama*, set a thousand years in the future, characters consistently say *aks*, suggesting it may still be around for some time, if not becoming the standard. As mentioned earlier, this swapping of sounds is called metathesis. It's shaped many everyday words and is the reason why Old English *frist* became *first*, *bridd* became *bird*, and *hros* turned into *horse*.

Writing usually reflects the standard variety of a language, but that raises the question: whose standard? Even today, there's plenty of variation in spelling. Consider the differences between American and British English: *color* vs. *colour, analyze* vs. *analyse, jewelry* vs. *jewellery.* The choice often comes down to regional or even personal preference. Interestingly, Irish playwright George Bernard Shaw sometimes advocated for American-style spellings like "honor" and "theater," and he was known to mock the inconsistencies of British spelling. (In fact, Shaw is often credited with the witty quip that *fish* could be spelled as ghoti.)

For centuries, these variants coexisted, until dictionary makers began shaping conventions. Samuel Johnson leaned toward spellings influenced by other languages, especially French and German. Meanwhile, across the

Atlantic, Noah Webster aimed to simplify English spelling to improve literacy and promote a distinct American identity. His reforms emphasized phonetics, spelling words more like they sound.

Spoken and written communication complement each other and have evolved together, often influencing one another. Writing isn't an artificial bolt-on to speech; it has profoundly shaped the way we use language. It's helped standardize pronunciation, introduced new words and grammar, and encouraged speakers to consciously reflect on their language choices. Crucially, it has also preserved older forms of language that might otherwise have been lost.

Just as speech varies in dialect, pitch, and accent, writing has developed its own conventions: vocabularies, syntax, styles, typefaces, fonts, and even color. For example, Caxton's original edition of *The Canterbury Tales* looks nothing like today's Penguin Classics version. His book was lavishly decorated with elaborate floral borders, gold illumination, and hand-drawn red and blue initials. Clearly, the written word has undergone significant transformation. Today, writing is recognized as an integral part of language itself, a prestigious and powerful visual form that allows us to express and preserve ideas, information, and knowledge across time and space.

Sign of the Times

Language isn't just spoken or written; it's also signed. Sign language shares many of the same core features as spoken language, including structure, how it's learned, and how it's processed in the brain, clearly showing that it *is* language in every sense. So, when we talk about what language is, we must include signed languages, too. One of the earliest mentions of sign language appears in Plato's *Cratylus*, where Socrates asks Hermogenes, "If we hadn't a voice or a tongue, and wanted to express things to one another, wouldn't we try to make signs by moving our hands, head, and the rest of our body, just as dumb people do at present?"

A common misconception is that sign language is merely a visual version of spoken language, a direct translation of words into gestures. But sign language is far more than that. It blends hand shapes, body movement, and facial expressions into a rich, fully formed linguistic system with its own rules for pronunciation, grammar, and word order. In Deaf communities, many people even have distinctive "name signs" assigned by peers or respected members. This is just one of the many ways sign languages reflect a unique and vibrant cultural identity.

Another common misconception is that there's just one "universal" sign language that everyone understands. In reality, there are over 300 distinct sign languages worldwide, used by more than 70 million people as their first language. Among these, American Sign Language (ASL) is the most widely used globally. With around half a million native speakers in the United States alone, ASL ranks as the third most common language in the country after English and Spanish. Just like spoken languages, different countries have their own unique sign languages. Even within a single country, regional varieties can introduce subtle differences in how signs are used and understood.

Sign languages have largely developed independently from spoken languages. For example, English is the dominant spoken language in the United States, Canada, the United Kingdom, Australia, and New Zealand, but their sign languages are all different. ASL is used primarily in North America, although it is actually based on French Sign Language. This means it is almost unintelligible to users of British Sign Language (BSL), Australian Sign Language (Auslan), or New Zealand Sign Language (NZSL). Just like spoken languages, no two sign languages are exactly the same – they vary according to community and culture. And we'll revisit this topic throughout the book, uncovering deeper insights as we go.

Where Does Oral Language Happen?

Our definition of language must also include how we physically produce spoken language. Speech is like an orchestra, requiring the precise coordination of many parts of the body. This topic bridges phonology and anatomy, specifically the workings of our vocal apparatus. More than one hundred muscles are involved in speech, all influencing the flow of air from our lungs to create the distinct patterns we recognize as language. Among these muscles are the vocal folds, often called "cords," though that's a bit misleading. "Cord" suggests a string-like structure that vibrates when plucked, but vocal folds are actually muscular flaps on either side of the larynx, or voice box, capable of vibrating rapidly to generate sound. The pharynx, or throat, which serves both digestive and respiratory roles, also functions as an articulator in speech production. It helps resonate and modify the sounds created by the vocal folds. Other articulators include parts of the mouth: the lips, tongue, teeth, hard and soft palates, and the glottis, all working together to shape sound. In short, when we speak, air is exhaled from the lungs, the vocal folds vibrate to produce voice, and the articulators sculpt those vibrations into recognizable speech.

There are two main categories of sounds we produce: consonants and vowels. These can be further classified according to their specific features. Consonants, for instance, are described in terms of place of articulation, that is, where in the mouth the sound is formed. This refers to the point where parts of the vocal tract, such as the tongue or lips, come together to create a constriction and shape the sound. (You can test some of these out as you read.) Bilabial sounds are made when both lips touch each other, as in /b/, /p/, and /m/. When the lower lip touches the upper teeth, we produce labiodental sounds, like /f/ and /v/. If you press your tongue against the ridge just behind your top teeth, the bumpy area on the roof of your mouth, you're making an alveolar sound. This includes familiar consonants like /t/, /d/, /n/, /l/, /s/, and /z/.

Glottal sounds are produced in a different way, by briefly closing the vocal folds to block the airflow. This creates what's known as a glottal stop. The clearest example in everyday speech is the little catch in the middle of *uh-oh*. In accents like Cockney English, the glottal stop sometimes replaces the /t/ sound in words like *bottle* and *butter*. In *My Fair Lady*, Eliza Doolittle's speech is peppered with glottal stops, like in her famous line, "I ain' done no'in' wrong by speakin' to the gen'leman." Glottal stops are even more common in other languages, such as German and Arabic.

Consonants are also described in terms of their manner of articulation, that is, how the tongue and lips move to shape the airflow when producing a sound. Stops (or plosives) involve a complete block of airflow, like the

/p/ in *pig*. Fricatives partially block the air, creating friction, as in /f/ in *fan* or /v/ in *van*. Affricates blend a stop and a fricative, such as /ʤ/ in *jam*. Nasals let air flow through the nose while the mouth stays closed, think /n/ in *nut*. Liquids involve a partial closure by the tongue, like /l/ in *lip* and /r/ in *red*. Finally, glides (or approximants) are smooth, vowel-like sounds, /j/ in *yet* and /w/ in *win*, that typically glide right into a following vowel.

One more important feature of consonants is whether they're voiced or voiceless. Voiced sounds are produced when the vocal folds vibrate, like /b/, /d/, and /m/. Voiceless sounds, such as /p/, /t/, and /k/, are made without any vibration at all. You can test this yourself: Place your hand on your throat and say a sound, if you feel a buzz, it's voiced. Many consonants come in pairs that are identical except for voicing. These are called minimal pairs. For example, /f/ and /v/ are both labiodental fricatives, but /v/ is voiced, while /f/ is voiceless.

As a fun side note, /h/ doesn't have a partner in English. It stands alone, voiceless, with no voiced equivalent. As we know, it's also famously "dropped" in some dialects. In Cockney English, as spoken by characters like Eliza Doolittle, /h/ disappears from words like *hardly* and *happen*. And in American English, the /h/ is skipped in *herb*. More generally, English speakers don't pronounce the /h/ in *hour*, *honest*, and *honor*, thanks to their French roots, where the sound doesn't exist. Because it lacks a voiced counterpart and is already disappearing in places, some linguists have speculated that /h/ might one day vanish from English altogether. So maybe Eliza Doolittle wasn't just bending the rules ... she might've been ahead of the curve!

Consonants are produced when the airflow is blocked by the lips, tongue, or throat. Vowels, on the other hand, are made when air flows freely, without obstruction. While there are only five basic vowel letters – 'a', 'e', 'i', 'o', and 'u' – English actually has around twenty different vowel sounds. Vowels are classified based on the position of the tongue and lips when the sound is made. High vowels are produced with the tongue close to the roof of the mouth, like the vowel in *hit*. Low vowels are made with the tongue low and flat, as in *cat*.

Vowels can also be rounded or unrounded, depending on the shape of the lips. For example, your lips round to say *boot*, but stay unrounded for *beet*. When a vowel is produced as a single, steady sound, it's called a monophthong, like the vowel in *bed*. When two vowel sounds glide together in a single syllable, that's a diphthong, as in *sky* or *boy*. Vowels also vary in length: short vowels, like the one in *cup*, are brief, while long vowels, like in *feet*, are held a bit longer.

This is just a basic overview to set the stage for other topics. Phonology can get surprisingly complex. For a deeper dive into the fascinating science of speech sounds in languages, see the references for suggested reading.

Another key player in the vocal apparatus is the hyoid bone, a small, horseshoe-shaped bone located in the front of the neck, just below the mandible (lower jaw) and above the thyroid. Unlike other bones in the body, the hyoid doesn't connect to any other bone. Instead, it "floats," suspended by muscles and ligaments. The hyoid supports the tongue and helps raise the larynx when we breathe, eat, swallow, and speak. It provides a stable base for the muscles that control the tongue and larynx, making it crucial for the kinds of fine, coordinated movements needed to produce speech sounds.

Interestingly, other animals have hyoid bones too: mammals, birds, reptiles, horses, even big cats. But in humans, it's uniquely positioned to work in tandem with our larynx and tongue, enabling the wide range of sounds used in language. In recent decades, the hyoid has become a focus of growing interest. Fossilized hyoid bones are offering new clues about the evolution of speech, and the emergence of language itself. (Stay tuned, there's more on this coming up in the next chapter.)

But language doesn't just happen in the vocal tract, it also happens in the brain. In fact, language is primarily processed in the left hemisphere. Interestingly, there's evidence that many other animals, including monkeys, mice, birds, and frogs, also use the left side of the brain to process or produce their species-specific vocalizations. This phenomenon is known as lateralization, where one hemisphere of the brain takes the lead in managing a particular function. Several key regions of the brain are involved in language. As noted in the Introduction, Broca's area, located in the left frontal lobe, plays a major role in forming words and producing speech. Wernicke's area, found in the temporal lobe, helps us understand language and interpret meaning. Other areas, like the angular gyrus, also contribute to language processing.

In recent years, researchers have uncovered even more clues about how language works in the brain, including the discovery of a gene called FOXP2, which is active in several brain regions, such as the basal ganglia and inferior frontal cortex. This gene is now believed to play a crucial role in the development of language abilities.

We'll dive further into the brain, cognition, and language in the chapters ahead, because the story of how we learn, use, and even lose language is just getting started.

The Last Word

As we've seen, the question "what is language?" can't be answered with a single tidy definition. Language is a system of communication, yes, but it's much more than that. It's multifaceted, involving signs and symbols, sound and meaning segments large and small, dialects and accents, and even writing and signing. Language is both cognitive and social. And it has physiological and neurobiological underpinnings. This chapter has served as a primer on the foundational principles of language, so now we can talk the talk. (If these themes whet your appetite for language science, check out the references in Further Reading for deeper dives.)

Now that we've defined what language is, let's explore who has it, and ask the bigger questions: *where*, *when*, and *how* did language emerge?

2

· · · · · · ·

Where Did Language Come From?

What's the greatest invention of all time? It's a hotly debated question. Some say fire or the wheel. Others argue for paper, the printing press, penicillin, the telephone, or the Internet. And of course, there's sliced bread, the gold standard against which all other inventions are jokingly measured. But many would agree that the greatest invention of all is language. Without it, we wouldn't have any of those other innovations. We also wouldn't have culture, art, history, religion, or science.

So, who invented language? Unlike Gutenberg with the printing press, Alexander Graham Bell with the telephone, or Otto Rohwedder, who built the first bread-slicing machine in Chillicothe, Missouri, on July 7, 1928, we can't credit language to any single individual. Its origins are murky, lost to prehistory. Unlike the neat story of sliced bread, the question of where and when language began remains one of the world's greatest unsolved mysteries.

This naturally raises even more intriguing questions: How did language emerge in the first place? Some theories suggest it began with humans mimicking the sounds of nature or animals. Others propose that speech evolved from grunts and groans, or from gestures, dance, or even music. There are also those who believe language has divine origins. Some scientists argue that language appeared suddenly in our species, while others believe it developed gradually over the course of evolutionary history. And what was the very first language, anyway? No wonder the question of how language began has been called "the hardest problem in science."

Adding to the complexity, researchers don't always agree on what exactly counts as language. Most agree that communication becomes language when it involves symbols and syntax, that is, rules for combining those symbols in meaningful ways. For this reason, many argue that language is uniquely human. Still, some suggest our early hominin relatives might have had a form of speech too. And animals certainly have their own ways of communicating. We've all heard stories about talking parrots, signing chimpanzees, and even monkeys that seem to use grammar. Of course, popular culture has long delighted in the idea of talking animals, from Mickey Mouse to the witty horse Mr. Ed, blurring the line between imagination and reality in our understanding of animal communication.

So, what should we make of all these claims? Let's explore who truly has language, and how it might have come to be.

Handy Men and Wise Humans

Who spoke the very first word? We'll never know. Language can't be traced to a single person, moment, or place, only to a genus and species within a broad window of human history. Even then, the when and where of its emergence are still the subject of ongoing debate. Estimates vary widely, but many researchers believe that language, as we know it, first appeared in sub-Saharan Africa during the Middle Stone Age. Somewhere between 200,000 and 50,000 years ago, early *Homo sapiens* likely developed the capacity for complex speech. To understand how language evolved, scientists look back along our hominin family tree in search of a proto-language, the hypothetical common ancestor of all human tongues. Some suggest that speech emerged suddenly in our species, sparked by a chance genetic mutation. Others argue that language evolved gradually, perhaps even beginning in species before *Homo sapiens*.

The development of speech has been tied to a range of biological changes: walking upright (bipedalism), increases in brain size, and the anatomical refinements of our vocal tract. But language isn't only biological. It's deeply social. It may have been shaped by tool use, the creation of art, cooking, communal living, and the rise of travel and trade. One often-overlooked factor? Human babies are altricial, they're helpless at birth and must rely on caregivers for a long time. This extended dependency creates a unique environment for social bonding and learning, including the acquisition of language. Still, the evidence we have is fragmentary and open to interpretation. Bones and artifacts offer clues, but unlike stone tools, teeth, or pottery, language leaves no physical trace. We'll never excavate the first word or unearth a fossilized sentence. The origins of language remain one of the greatest mysteries of our species.

Some scientists contend that language is unique to our species. Others believe it evolved slowly over millions of years and wasn't exclusive to *Homo sapiens*. According to this view, a proto-language may have existed as far back as *Homo habilis*, a species that lived between 2.3 and 1.6 million years ago. Nicknamed "handy men," *Homo habilis* were the first known makers of stone tools. These early tools, discovered alongside their fossils in Kenya and Tanzania, were crafted by chipping volcanic rock to create sharp, jagged edges for cutting and chopping food. Compared to their ancestors, *Australopithecus*, these hominins walked more upright, a key shift that freed their hands for other tasks, such as gesturing.

Even more significantly, *Homo habilis* had a larger, more human-like brain. Endocranial casts, internal molds of the skull, reveal that regions associated with speech in modern humans were already developing. Notably, they had a bulge in Broca's area, a part of the brain known to be involved in producing language. For these reasons, some researchers propose that *Homo habilis* may have been capable of rudimentary speech. What it might have sounded like, though, remains a mystery.

Some scientists speculate that language may stretch as far back as *Homo erectus*, a species that lived between 1.8 and 0.3 million years ago. Often nicknamed the "upright man" for their bipedalism, the name is a bit misleading as other hominins had been walking on two legs for millions of years before them. What *Homo erectus* did do, however, was light the way forward in other remarkable ways. They were the first known hominins to use fire deliberately, perhaps for warmth, cooking, and protection from predators. They ventured far beyond Africa, with fossils discovered across Europe and Asia, from France and Greece to China and Indonesia, where the famous "Java Man" was unearthed, a key piece of evidence supporting Darwin's theory of evolution.

There's no direct proof that *Homo erectus* had language, but some clues suggest they might have had the cognitive toolkit for it. Their brain was twice the size of earlier hominins', they crafted sophisticated tools, were skilled hunters, and even managed to cross open seas to reach distant islands. Intriguingly, zigzag engravings on ancient shells in Indonesia hint at a capacity for symbolic thought, and possibly even art. If *Homo erectus* did have some form of speech, we don't know what it sounded like. But their achievements suggest a mind capable of abstract thinking, planning, and perhaps even the roots of language as we know it.

Homo sapiens neanderthalensis are our closest relatives. Neanderthals lived from around 250,000 to 30,000 years ago, roaming the earth alongside *Homo sapiens*, and even interbreeding with us. Though long extinct, their genes live on in modern human DNA. Today, the name "Neanderthal" is often wielded as an insult, conjuring images of brutish, unintelligent, and uncivilized beings, with heavy brows, large noses, and protruding jaws. But the fossil record tells a different story, one of intellect and empathy. Evidence suggests they cared for their seniors, buried their dead, and may have included symbolic objects in their burials.

In recent decades, discoveries have added weight to the idea that Neanderthals may have had the capacity for speech. In a cave in Israel, scientists found a Neanderthal hyoid bone. As explained in the previous chapter, this small "floating" bone anchors the larynx at the top of the vocal tract. While many animals have this bone (a remnant of ancient fish gills), only in humans is it positioned to support complex vocalization. The reconstructed Neanderthal vocal tract suggests they could likely produce consonant-like distinctions and a range of sounds similar to our own.

Their ear anatomy also indicates they may have relied on spoken communication in daily life. It's possible they supplemented speech with gestures during social interactions. Adding to the evidence, Neanderthals possessed the FOXP2 gene, as discussed previously, which is associated with language in humans, and found in birds and mammals, where it plays a role in developing vocalizations. For all these reasons, many researchers think Neanderthals likely communicated vocally, though exactly how their language sounded remains unknown.

In the ultimate game of survival of the fittest, modern humans outlasted the Neanderthals and have been around from about 300,000 years ago to the present day. (Based on fossils from Jebel Irhoud, Morocco.) *Homo sapiens*, literally "wise humans," stand out from other hominins thanks to our large brains, high foreheads, smaller brow ridges, and prominent chins. Our bodies also evolved to talk: the voice box (larynx) dropped lower in the throat, and the space above the vocal folds lengthened, giving us the ability to produce a vast range of sounds.

Forget the image of the club-wielding, wild-haired caveman, that's pure myth. Early *Homo sapiens* were nomadic hunter-gatherers who crafted sophisticated tools and held elaborate burial rituals. And the anatomically modern human beings, our early modern ancestors, left behind plenty of evidence for creativity and culture. They made clothes, carved sculptures, created fine artwork, jewelry, clay figurines, musical instruments, and cave paintings, all of which probably required some form of communication.

Somewhere along the way, *Homo sapiens* developed full-fledged speech. And this turned out to be one of our greatest evolutionary advantages. Language helped early humans coordinate hunts, farm more effectively, and protect themselves from the dangers of the natural world. It's also the bedrock of culture and civilization. Without language, there'd be no wheel, no printing press, no telephone, no Internet, and certainly no sliced bread.

Bow-Wow, Ding-Dong, Pooh-Pooh

Now that we have a general sense of *when* language emerged, and *with whom*, the next big question is: *How* did it happen? It's a captivating mystery, one that even Plato puzzled over. But it's also maddeningly elusive. We may never arrive at a definitive answer. The topic is so speculative (and so contentious) that in 1866, shortly after the Paris Linguistic Society was founded, they banned all discussion of language origins to avoid academic brawls. The London Philological Society followed suit a few years later in 1872.

Nevertheless, that hasn't stopped curious minds from trying. Scholars from philosophy, anthropology, psychology, linguistics, and cognitive science have all taken a stab at explaining how language began. The theories are as varied as they are imaginative. Some suggest language grew out of grooming, gestures, dance, or even music. In the nineteenth century, early theorists like philologist Max Müller proposed lively origin stories and gave them witty (if slightly tongue-in-cheek) names, like the *Bow-Wow Theory*, which claimed language started by mimicking sounds found in nature.

The Bow-Wow Theory suggests that the very first human languages sprang to life by imitating sounds from the world around us. This is called onomatopoeia, or echoism. Think of words like *splash*, *crash*, and *bang*; they sound just like what they mean. These words mimic noises found in nature: human burps and hiccups, a duck's quack, a snake's hiss, or even the classic *bow-wow* of a dog. Onomatopoeia isn't limited to nature, either. Take the *tick-tock* of a clock or the *Biff! Pow! Zap!* bursts in superhero comics.

The idea behind the Bow-Wow Theory is that copying sounds from our surroundings may have helped jump-start language. But there's a catch: Different languages hear animal sounds in their own unique way. While English speakers say a dog goes *bow-wow* or *woof-woof*, Indonesians hear *guk-guk*, Turkish people say *hev-hev*, and the Irish swear the dog's cry is *amh-amh*. So, even though animals worldwide make the same sounds, humans interpret them very differently. James Joyce even plays with this idea in *Ulysses*, where a particularly annoying cat doesn't *mew* or *meow*, it cries out something more like "mrkgnao!" Plus, if language really started with onomatopoeia, we'd expect many more words that actually sound like what they mean. But since those words make up just a tiny fraction of any language, it seems the Bow-Wow Theory only tells part of the story.

The related *Ding-Dong Theory* suggests there's a mysterious, maybe even instinctive, link between sounds and meanings. Think about it: Words like *itsy-bitsy*, *teeny-weeny*, *mini*, and *wee* just *sound* small. Meanwhile, *lump, bump, rump,* and *plump* all sound big, round, and squishy. Then there's *glide, glow, glimmer,* and *glitter,* which all shimmer with smooth, shiny vibes. This idea, known as *sound symbolism,* was behind the name Kodak, created in 1888 by film photography inventor George Eastman. He liked the hard 'k' sound, calling it "a strong, incisive sort of letter."

The belief that sounds can carry meaning goes all the way back to Plato's dialogue *Cratylus,* where two philosophers argue about whether words are just arbitrary labels (as Hermogenes thinks) or if they actually reflect something deeper (as Cratylus insists). And maybe Cratylus had a point. In the 1920s, researchers ran a quirky experiment: Participants were shown two shapes, one curvy, one spiky, and asked which was called *takete* and which was *maluma.* Most people picked *takete* for the spiky shape and *maluma* for the round one. Decades later, the same experiment was repeated using the made-up words *bouba* and *kiki.* The result? A whopping 95 percent of people thought *bouba* matched the soft, round shape, and *kiki* went with the sharp one. Other than these few curious examples of sound symbolism, there's no strong reason to think that the sounds of words are naturally tied to what they mean.

The *Pooh-Pooh Theory* is an early, and pretty charming, idea that speech got its start from interjections: those spontaneous, emotional outbursts like "oh!" for surprise or "ouch!" when something hurts. These little bursts of sound are our instinctive vocal reactions to feelings like shock, pain, excitement, or frustration. Modern interjections even include colorful expletives, from the tame "fiddlesticks!" to the much more expressive "fuck!", perfect for when you stub your toe. Some folks think these interjections are the ancient roots of speech, dating back to our ancestors' earliest vocal expressions. Just think of Fred Flintstone's iconic Stone Age shout "Yabba dabba doo!" But like onomatopoeia, interjections are only a tiny slice of language. Similarly, they vary a lot across languages: English speakers say "ouch!" for pain, while Greeks say "aou!" Surprise is "oh!" in English but "ach!" in Czech.

Then there's the *Yo-He-Ho Theory,* which suggests language evolved from the grunts, groans, and snorts people made during heavy manual labor. Think of sailors chanting "yo-heave-ho" to keep in rhythm while hauling ropes or rowing. It's an appealing idea that the sounds of teamwork and effort might have influenced how early speech developed, even if it's not exactly how things happened.

We don't usually think of language as anything like sucking, chewing, or licking, but just like speaking, all these actions involve moving the mouth, tongue, and lips. The *Ta-Ta Theory* playfully suggests that our first words came from tongue and mouth gestures that mimicked body and hand movements. Saying "ta ta" was basically like waving goodbye, with your tongue. This idea even had a fan in Charles Darwin himself. He also imagined a musical stage in human communication, asking, "Did our language commence with singing? Is this the origin of our pleasure in music? Do monkeys howl in harmony?" Darwin pictured early humans using their voices like male gibbons, creating musical calls for courtship and competition. Building on this, the *Sing-Song* or *La-La Theory* proposes that language evolved from rhythm and melody. Early humans might have started out humming, whistling, and singing before their sounds turned into fully-fledged speech.

A modern twist on the musical origins theory is the "putting the baby down" hypothesis. This suggests that once our early human ancestors started walking upright, mothers had to set their babies down while foraging for food. This meant finding new ways to comfort them from a distance, prompting parents to use soothing, melodic coos to calm their little ones, along with sing-song baby talk. (We'll return to this in the next chapter.) Music has often been called the universal language, and the *Ho-Hiss Theory* builds on that notion. It proposes that early human sounds, like grunts, huffs, and squawks, gradually evolved into song. A lighthearted version of this plays out in the movie *Iceman*, where a thawed-out Neanderthal, nicknamed Charlie, is befriended by a scientist. In a heartwarming moment, he sings Neil Young's "Heart of Gold," and Charlie joins in with his own rendition, grunting along to the melody and tapping out a beat with a pair of bones.

Finally, there's the *Eureka! Theory*, the notion that language was an ingenious invention, like sliced bread or the wheel. According to this view, our ancestors had a lightbulb moment and decided to assign random sounds to specific things. Over time, those sounds snowballed into full-blown language. Maybe this only happened once, sparked by a group of early humans who had just the right mix of genes and vocal anatomy to string complex sounds together. That's the idea behind *monogenesis*: that all languages trace back to a single origin. *Polygenesis*, on the other hand, suggests that language was invented multiple times, independently, in different parts of the world.

Unfortunately, we don't have the evidence to say for sure. What we do have is plenty of speculation. Each theory about the origin of language explains a tiny piece of the puzzle, but none tell the whole story. It's likely that language evolved through a mix of sounds, facial expressions, and gestures before becoming the symbolic system we know today. Unless someone invents a time machine, the birth of language will remain one of the great unsolved mysteries of our species.

The Original Language

Theories about the origins of language appear in religious traditions too. Many creation myths tell us that language was a divine gift bestowed upon humanity. In Greek mythology, Hermes, the god of language, introduced linguistic diversity and, with it, the division of people into different nations. Hinduism teaches that the goddess Sarasvati, who created the universe, also gave birth to Sanskrit. According to Judeo-Christian tradition, language was a gift from God to Adam and Eve in the Garden of Eden. In the Book of Genesis, God creates all living creatures and brings them to Adam, who then names them: "And whatsoever Adam called every living creature, that was the name thereof." Other scriptures suggest that it was God, not humans, who named everything first. In the Qur'an, Allah teaches Adam the names of His creations: "And He taught Adam all the names of everything." This divine tongue is known as the Adamic, or original, language.

So, exactly *which* language did God give to humans? Some theologians have tried to trace the Adamic language supposedly spoken in the Garden of Eden, or Paradise, if we're talking about Islam. Popular theories claim it was Hebrew, Aramaic, Arabic, or some other ancient Semitic language. The idea of an Adamic tongue supports the theory of monogenesis: that there was once a single, original language. The Book of Genesis even says, "And the whole earth was of one language, and of one speech."

Admitting to multiple original languages, however, would mean questioning whether Adam was truly the ancestor of all humankind. The Bible tackles this linguistic puzzle with the story of the Tower of Babel. According to the tale, Adam's descendants all spoke the same language. But in a rebellious, post-flood moment of hubris, they began building a tower in the land of Shinar, a "Gate of God" so tall it would pierce the heavens. Who needs God when human hands can reach the heavens? God, unimpressed and probably a little offended, saw this as blasphemy. As punishment, he scrambled their speech, creating a "confusion of tongues" so they could no longer understand one another, much less finish their celestial construction project. And so, they scattered, taking their new languages with them. As the story goes, we may never know what language Adam and Eve spoke, because whatever it was, it got lost in translation at Babel.

Across the globe, anthropologists have documented remarkably similar creation myths that attempt to explain the origins of linguistic diversity. These stories often center on themes of natural disaster, disease, and even cannibalism, dramatic ruptures that broke humanity's original unity. The Kaska people of Canada speak of a great flood that dispersed the population and fractured a once-unified language. "Before the flood, there was but one centre," they say, "for all the people lived together in one country, and spoke one language."

In East Africa, the Wa-Sania, a Bantu-speaking people, tell of a time when all humans shared a common tongue, until a mysterious illness swept through the population. The sickness garbled their speech, which fragmented over time into the world's many languages. And among the Aboriginal people of Encounter Bay in South Australia, there is a story of Wurruri, a reviled woman whose death drew many tribes. They did not come to mourn her but to consume her remains. Each group ate a different part of her body, and in the aftermath, they each began to speak a different language, unable to understand one another from that moment on. In each of these myths, humanity begins with a single language. But that shared tongue is lost through catastrophe and consequence, replaced by the linguistic diversity we see today.

So, what was humanity's original language? According to science, we don't know, and we may never know for certain. What we do have are clues. Linguists believe that today's languages evolved from ancient, undocumented tongues known as proto-languages. These prehistoric ancestors left no written records, but their traces can be found in the patterns that link modern languages across continents and centuries. One of the earliest insights came from an unlikely source: an eighteenth-century British judge named William Jones. In a landmark 1786 paper, Jones observed striking similarities between Sanskrit, Greek, and Latin. These languages, he argued, must have "sprung from some common source." This insight laid the groundwork for the idea of a long-lost proto-language that gave rise to many others.

Although proto-languages are not directly attested in any surviving texts, linguists have painstakingly reconstructed them using the comparative method. By analyzing shared features in vocabulary, sound systems, and grammar across related languages, scholars can infer the structure of these ancestral tongues. Take Proto-Indo-European, for example. Thought to have been spoken during the Neolithic or early Bronze Age, it's the reconstructed common ancestor of the Indo-European language family, which includes English, German, and French, as well as Sanskrit, Greek, and Latin, just as Jones surmised. Though not everything he claimed holds up. He mistakenly grouped Egyptian and Japanese into the same family. Still, his core insight endures. Many of the world's languages may trace back to a common source, now lost to time but not entirely beyond our grasp.

Since the nineteenth century, linguists have been assembling a kind of genealogical map of human speech: the language family tree. This model, popularized by German linguist August Schleicher, imagines languages as branches diverging from a common trunk, each one tracing back to a shared ancestor. But not all languages fit neatly into this structure. Contact languages, for instance, evolve through borrowing from multiple sources, making them hybrids rather than direct descendants of a single proto-language. And then there are the real mysteries: languages that appear to have no relatives at all. These linguistic orphans, known as language isolates, include Basque, spoken in parts of Spain and France; Tiwi, an Aboriginal language of northern Australia; and Sumerian, the ancient language of Mesopotamia. Each developed in isolation, with no proven ties to any known language family. Their very existence supports the theory of polygenesis, the idea that language didn't emerge from a single source but independently in multiple regions.

While many proto-languages have been reconstructed, one of the oldest may be Proto-Afroasiatic, the ancestor of languages like Arabic, Akkadian, and Classical Hebrew. Thought to have originated among nomadic hunter-gatherers in the Mesolithic era, it likely dates back to around 15,000 to 10,000 BCE. Beyond that, the linguistic record fades. The further back we go, the harder it becomes to trace the roots of human speech. Eventually, the trail vanishes into prehistory, leaving behind more questions than answers.

A more approachable question than *what was the first language?* is *What's the world's oldest living language?* Even this, however, sparks fierce debate, with several languages vying for the title. Despite religious traditions that point to Hebrew, Aramaic, or Arabic as the oldest tongues, the linguistic record tells a more complex story. While undeniably ancient, these are not the oldest continuously spoken languages. That distinction may belong to Tamil, a Dravidian language spoken in southern India and Sri Lanka, with written records dating back roughly 5,000 years. Chinese is another strong contender, with inscriptions dating back at least 4,500 years. Some argue for Sanskrit, which emerged around 1500 BCE, though it has largely become a liturgical language in modern times.

What these languages share is longevity and continued use, albeit in forms quite different from their ancient origins. Like all living languages, they have evolved significantly. The classical versions of Tamil, Chinese, and Sanskrit would be almost unrecognizable to modern speakers, just as Shakespearean English can sound foreign to contemporary ears. Still, the survival of these languages, adapted, reinterpreted, and reimagined across millennia, is a testament to the endurance and flexibility of human communication.

From its mysterious origins, human language has diversified into more than 7,000 living languages spoken around the world today. In addition to these, there are hundreds of extinct languages, those with no surviving native speakers, and dead languages, such as Latin or Akkadian, which are no longer evolving but live on in ancient texts, religious rituals, and scholarly study. There are likely many more languages we've yet to discover, lost to time or spoken in isolated communities. Language, like any living system, follows a natural life cycle: it emerges, changes, and eventually fades. Over time, countless languages have disappeared, and we continue to lose them at an alarming rate, around nine per year.

Sanskrit, for instance, is considered a dead language, no longer evolving or used in everyday conversation, though still preserved in liturgical contexts and revived in academic and cultural circles. A handful of other ancient languages are still in use today, Hebrew, Aramaic, Farsi, Egyptian Coptic, Arabic, and Greek among them. But these, too, have changed significantly from their classical forms. Just as Modern English bears only partial resemblance to Old or Middle English, these languages have transformed over centuries, shaped by time, culture, and contact with other tongues. It's worth noting that all of this knowledge is provisional. Our understanding of linguistic history continues to evolve, subject to new discoveries, emerging evidence, and the unearthing of languages that history may have quietly buried.

The Original Writing System

But the story doesn't end with spoken language, there's also writing. Speech likely predates writing by tens of thousands of years, if not more. In comparison, the invention of written language is a relatively recent innovation, but a transformative one. Writing allowed humans to preserve stories, transmit knowledge, and record history in a durable, visual form. Unlike spoken language, which leaves no direct trace, written language offers tangible evidence. We may not have fossilized verbs or preserved syntax, but we do have ancient inscriptions etched in stone and clay.

Based on the available evidence, writing first emerged in Mesopotamia. Most scholars agree that the earliest known writing system is Sumerian. The oldest attested written document is the Kish Tablet, discovered in present-day Iraq and dating to around 3500 BCE. Inscribed on a limestone tablet, it recounts the legend of Etana, the King of Kish, who rides an eagle to the heavens to seek out the sky-god Anu. Etana's goal is to find the mythical "plant of birth," which will grant him the ability to father a son. There are multiple versions of the tale. Some end with Etana's success, others with his tragic fall back to earth. Interestingly, the Sumerian King List names his successor as "Balih, son of Etana," though both are said to have ruled for hundreds of years. Interpret that as you will.

The Kish Tablet was inscribed using pictographs, visual symbols that represented words or phrases. The early Sumerian pictographic inventory included depictions of humans, animals like fish and oxen, body parts such as the heart and hand, and elements of the natural world, including the sun and sky. Over time, these images evolved into cuneiform, widely regarded as the world's first true writing system.

The term *cuneiform* comes from the Latin *cuneus*, meaning "wedge," a reference to the stylus used to press wedge-shaped marks into soft clay tablets, which were then baked to preserve the text. The Sumerians found it far easier to impress straight lines into clay than to carve rounded shapes, and as a result, the original pictographs became increasingly abstract and stylized. What began as representations of tangible objects gradually shifted toward phonemic symbols, characters that represented sounds. These sounds could then be combined to construct words, allowing for more complex expression. As centuries passed and empires rose and fell across the Fertile Crescent, cuneiform spread. It was adapted by numerous cultures, including the Akkadians, Babylonians, Assyrians, and Hittites, each modifying the system to suit their own languages and needs. Despite its humble origins in simple pictographs, cuneiform laid the foundation for written communication in the ancient world.

Early writing was often carved into stone or pressed into clay tablets, materials durable enough to survive the millennia. Yet it's likely that other civilizations also recorded information on more ephemeral, organic materials, such as bamboo, bark, or leather, that haven't withstood the passage of time. In ancient China, for example, it's believed that people once tied knots in cords as a rudimentary system for accounting and recording significant events, a practice that predates formal writing.

Elsewhere, forms of proto-writing took unique and culturally rich shapes. In Australia, message sticks, carved wooden objects used by Aboriginal peoples, were only recognized by Western scholars as recently as the nineteenth century. These hand-sized sticks were carried across long distances by messengers to accompany verbal communications: an invitation to ceremony, a warning of conflict, or news of a death. The sticks featured engraved or painted markings, lines, dots, symbols, or patterns, each encoding specific meanings understood within the cultural context. Crucially, the messenger played a vital role, not only delivering the physical object but also ensuring its correct interpretation. The spoken message brought the symbols to life, anchoring meaning in performance as much as in inscription. Some of these message sticks are believed to be thousands of years old, offering a powerful reminder that writing, broadly conceived, has taken many forms beyond ink and parchment.

Around the same time that cuneiform emerged in Mesopotamia, Egyptian hieroglyphs were taking shape. The word *hieroglyph* means "sacred carving," an apt name for these intricate symbols that functioned not only as representations of objects and ideas but also as phonemic components encoding sounds and syllables. Hieroglyphs adorned the walls of temples, tombs, and pyramids, as well as coffins, statues, and scrolls of papyrus, lending grandeur and permanence to religious and political texts. Despite their similar timing, cuneiform and hieroglyphs evolved independently, each reflecting the unique cultural and linguistic needs of its society.

Meanwhile, across the world in ancient China, another writing system was being born. Chinese pictographs were incised onto tortoise shells and ox bones, objects known as oracle bones, used in divination rituals to communicate with ancestors and deities. Like many early scripts, these were deeply tied to spiritual and ceremonial practices, often employed to venerate gods or immortalize kings.

Writing systems, like spoken languages, have their own origin stories. According to Sumerian myth, writing was the invention of Enmerkar, a semi-divine king and son of the sun god Utu. The Egyptians credited Thoth, god of wisdom and writing, with the creation of hieroglyphs. In Chinese legend, it was Cang Jie, a four-eyed scribe of the Yellow Emperor, who invented writing after observing the tracks of animals and the patterns of nature. His invention was so momentous that it caused ghosts to wail and millet to rain from the heavens. While Sumerian cuneiform and Egyptian hieroglyphs eventually fell out of use, the Chinese writing system has endured for millennia. It has evolved from ancient pictographs to modern simplified characters, introduced in the twentieth century to increase literacy. Unlike its extinct cousins, the Chinese script continues to connect the present to a deep and storied past.

Signing Apes and Talking Horses

After revolutionizing our understanding of biology in *On the Origin of Species*, Charles Darwin turned his keen intellect to another great mystery: the origins of language. Drawing elegant parallels between biological evolution and linguistic development, Darwin argued that language, like species, emerged through slow, naturalistic processes rather than sudden invention. In *The Descent of Man*, he wrote, "No philologist now supposes that any language has been deliberately invented; each has been slowly and unconsciously developed by many steps." Darwin built on Victorian theories about the birth of speech, noting the role of onomatopoeia and sound symbolism, those words whose sounds mirror their meanings, like *splash*, *buzz*, or *crash*. He believed these sonic echoes of the physical world might have served as early building blocks of human language.

Crucially, Darwin saw language as evolving in a manner strikingly similar to biological species. Just as mammals like elephants, kangaroos, and chimpanzees trace their lineage back to a common ancestor, so too do languages diverge from shared roots. The Germanic language family, for example, branched out into distinct tongues like German, Dutch, and English. Dialects split and morph over time, sometimes developing into entirely new languages, mirroring the speciation seen in nature.

He even extended the principle of natural selection to vocabulary itself, observing that language evolves through "the survival of certain favoured words in the struggle for existence." Over generations, countless words, languages, and writing systems have disappeared, just as species go extinct, while others have endured and flourished. Darwin's linguistic insights, while less famous than his biological research, laid the groundwork for understanding language as a living, adaptive, and ever-changing phenomenon.

Darwin recognized striking parallels between the ways humans and nonhuman primates communicate without words. "The movements of the features and gestures of monkeys are understood by us," he observed, "and they partly understand ours." He also noted that animals and humans produce similar vocalizations in moments of intense emotion, fear, joy, surprise, suggesting a shared evolutionary basis. From this, Darwin hypothesized that language evolved from the vocal mimicry of such instinctive sounds. "I cannot doubt," he wrote, "that language owes its origin to the imitation and modification of various natural sounds, the voices of other animals, and man's own instinctive cries, aided by signs and gestures."

According to Darwin, these primal expressions gradually transformed into a symbolic system, driven by the "pressure of social wants." For him, language, alongside fire, was among humanity's greatest discoveries. And while he acknowledged in *The Descent of Man* that language had "justly been considered as one of the chief distinctions between man and the lower animals," he emphasized that the roots of human speech lay deep in our animal past.

Others took a very different view, arguing that language was not a product of nature but a mark of humanity's higher faculties, an expression of reason, even divinity. Some likened its emergence to the development of art rather than the outcome of evolutionary forces. Among the most vocal proponents of this perspective was Max Müller of Bow-Wow Theory fame. He proposed that language began through the imitation of natural sounds, animal cries, environmental noises, and instinctive vocalizations. Yet Müller also insisted that language marked a fundamental divide between humans and other animals. He famously called it "the one great barrier between the brute and man," and dismissed the idea that natural selection could account for its emergence: "No process of natural selection will ever distil significant words out of the notes of birds and the cries of beasts."

The debate continues today. Many modern scholars maintain that language is uniquely human. Noam Chomsky, for example, rejected the notion that language evolved from animal communication. Instead, he argued that it arose suddenly through a genetic mutation, as an innate and universal feature of the human mind. (And more on this matter in the next chapter.) Steven Pinker, a cognitive psychologist whose views were influenced by Chomsky's theories, also saw language as biologically rooted, but considered it a product of evolution. Both agreed that while animals do communicate, only humans use language in the full sense, a richly structured, grammatical system capable of infinite expression.

Over the years, numerous researchers have attempted to test the hypothesis that language is a uniquely human trait by teaching simplified forms of language to our closest evolutionary relatives: great apes. Chimpanzees, bonobos, and gorillas, who share the vast majority of their DNA with humans, have been the primary subjects of these studies. One of the earliest such efforts took place in 1892, when Richard Lynch Garner tried to teach a chimpanzee named Moses to say a handful of words, including *mamma, feu* (French for "fire"), and *wie* (German for "how"). Despite generous bribes of corned beef, Moses never managed to articulate any of them.

In the 1930s, psychologists Luella and Winthrop Kellogg undertook a more immersive experiment. They raised a young female chimpanzee named Gua alongside their infant son, Donald, treating them as siblings. After nine months, both could respond to simple verbal commands. But while Donald soon began speaking recognizable words, Gua made no such progress. The experiment came to an abrupt end when Donald began mimicking Gua's grunts, hoots, and screeches with alarming enthusiasm.

In the 1940s, yet another husband-and-wife research team, Keith and Catherine Hayes, took a similar approach: They adopted a baby chimpanzee named Viki and raised her in their home as though she were a human child. They eagerly reported that Viki babbled like an infant and eventually learned to articulate four words: *mama, papa, cup,* and *up.* To the Hayeses, this seemed to suggest that chimpanzees might possess the capacity for human speech.

However, later analysis of Viki's vocalizations painted a less optimistic picture. What had been interpreted as babbling was more likely playful grunting, and while Viki could approximate certain human-like sounds, her vocal abilities were biologically constrained. Unlike humans, non-human primates lack the vocal anatomy required for speech. The human larynx sits lower in the throat, and our tongue is significantly more flexible, an anatomical configuration that allows us to produce a far greater range of distinct, nuanced sounds than our primate cousins.

In the 1960s, researchers Allen and Beatrix Gardner challenged earlier attempts to teach spoken language to apes, arguing that these projects were limited not by cognitive shortcomings but by physiological constraints. Rather than focusing on speech, they turned to gesture, an important component of natural chimpanzee communication in the wild. Their innovative approach involved raising a young female chimpanzee named Washoe in a human-like environment and teaching her American Sign Language (ASL).

Washoe was treated much like a human child. She had her own bedroom filled with books and toys, hosted pretend tea parties, wore clothes, ate meals at the family dinner table, and even brushed her teeth before bed. Under this immersive care, Washoe became the first nonhuman to learn a human language in the form of ASL. Researchers reported that she acquired a vocabulary of around 350 signs, some of which she passed on to her adopted son, Loulis, by guiding his hands into the correct shapes and motions. Perhaps most intriguingly, Washoe appeared to use language creatively. Upon seeing a swan for the first time, she reportedly signed "water" and "bird," a spontaneous combination that suggested symbolic reasoning. Her caregivers believed that she was not only capable of communication but also demonstrated signs of self-awareness, emotional depth, and the ability to form meaningful relationships with humans.

In the 1970s, Francine "Penny" Patterson began a groundbreaking experiment in interspecies communication with a young gorilla named Hanabiko, nicknamed "Koko," whom she met at the San Francisco Zoo. Patterson set out to teach Koko a modified form of ASL, which she dubbed "Gorilla Sign Language." After years of dedicated training, she reported that Koko had developed an active vocabulary of more than 1,000 signs, placing her linguistic ability roughly on par with that of a human toddler.

Patterson also immersed Koko in spoken English from an early age and claimed that the gorilla could recognize over 2,000 spoken words.

According to Patterson, Koko was capable of understanding not only basic vocabulary but also grammatical categories such as nouns, verbs, adjectives, and even abstract concepts. She asserted that Koko could combine signs in novel ways to convey original and meaningful thoughts. Beyond language, Koko was presented as a complex emotional being, an artist who painted still lifes, a nurturing figure who cared for kittens, and a creature capable of forming deep social bonds. Her extraordinary story captured the public imagination. She appeared on the cover of *National Geographic* and met a parade of celebrities, including Mister Rogers, Robin Williams, Betty White, Flea, and Sting.

In another ambitious experiment of the 1970s, psychologist Herbert S. Terrace set out to replicate, and critically evaluate, the earlier successes of Project Washoe. His goal was to test the provocative claim that nonhuman primates could acquire language. The subject of his study was a chimpanzee cheekily named Nim Chimpsky, a playful jab at linguist Noam Chomsky, who famously argued that language is a uniquely human trait. Nim was raised in a human household, treated like a child, and immersed in ASL from infancy. He cuddled with his human siblings, slept in a bed, and even suckled from his adoptive mother's breast.

But as Nim grew older, the illusion of domestication fell apart. He became increasingly aggressive, lashing out by biting, tearing apart furniture, and destroying his surroundings. In short, he began acting like what he was: a wild animal. Despite years of training, Nim acquired only a modest vocabulary, somewhere between 25 and 100 signs, and strung together rudimentary combinations like "Banana me eat" and "Tickle me Nim."

Terrace ultimately concluded that Nim was not using language in the true sense, but merely mimicking signs to elicit rewards such as food or affection. The project was abruptly terminated. Tragically, Nim was sent to a research facility and later sold for medical testing. Though he was eventually rescued and relocated to a sanctuary, his early life among humans left him ill-equipped to reintegrate with other chimpanzees. Raised as a human child, he remained caught between two worlds, but never quite at home in either.

Over the years, numerous studies have attempted to teach great apes to communicate using speech, sign language, keyboards, or touchscreens, often with mixed and controversial results. In the aftermath of these experiments, and amid allegations of abuse and neglect, the scientific community began to scrutinize both the ethics and the validity of such research. Critics argued that apes like Washoe, Koko, Nim, and others, powerful wild animals capable of inflicting serious harm, were excessively anthropomorphized. Researchers often projected human intentions onto their actions, treating them less like nonhuman primates and more like surrogate children: dressing them in clothes, throwing them tea parties, assigning them pets, and feeding them soda and candy.

In retrospect, many now contend that their linguistic abilities were significantly overstated. While these apes could reproduce signs, it's debatable whether they grasped the underlying concepts. Like Nim Chimpsky, their signing may have been a means to an end, a strategy to obtain rewards, rather than genuine expressions of thought, intention, or abstract meaning.

Another major concern was the role of the trainers and researchers. Much of the apes' communication was interpreted through the lens of human handlers, who may have unconsciously projected their own expectations onto ambiguous gestures. Footage from the training sessions suggests that the apes were often mimicking trainers or responding to subtle, perhaps unconscious, cues, raising serious doubts about the objectivity of the results.

Observers have drawn comparisons to a classic cautionary tale in animal intelligence research: the case of the so-called "talking horse." (And no, this isn't about Mr. Ed.) In the early twentieth century, a horse named Clever Hans, a celebrated Orlov trotter, captivated the public with what appeared to be astonishing intellectual feats. Hans could seemingly solve math problems, tell time, read, spell, and even understand spoken and written German. He would answer questions by tapping his hoof, with uncanny accuracy.

However, a formal investigation by psychologist Oskar Pfungst uncovered a less magical truth. Hans wasn't actually performing calculations or decoding language. Instead, he was responding to subtle, unintentional cues from his trainer: changes in posture, facial expression, or body tension that signaled when to stop tapping. This phenomenon became known as the *observer-expectancy effect*: a cognitive bias in which researchers inadvertently influence the behavior of their subjects or interpret ambiguous responses in ways that confirm their expectations.

It has since been argued that similar dynamics may have shaped the results of ape language studies. Washoe, Koko, Nim, and others may not have been expressing complex thoughts or mastering human language but rather mirroring the hopes, gestures, and cues of their human handlers. Though the apes have long since passed, their legacy remains the subject of fierce debate. Today, the field of animal language research continues to provoke controversy, raising difficult questions about interpretation, ethics, and the limits of cross-species communication.

Dolphin Names and Honeybee Dances

Studies of language-trained nonhuman primates offer a glimpse into what these animals can achieve, with intensive training and under highly artificial conditions. Yet, as evolutionary biologists have pointed out, there was never any selective pressure for apes to evolve the ability to communicate with humans. In this sense, these experiments may reveal less about the linguistic potential of apes and more about the extraordinary uniqueness of human language itself.

Perhaps the more compelling insight isn't that animals lack language as we define it, or that a few can be taught to mimic human symbols, but that many species already possess rich and intricate systems of communication, ones that serve their own ecological and social needs. Instead of asking whether animals can communicate *like* us or *with* us on our terms, perhaps we should be asking how they communicate with one another on their own terms. How might apes like Washoe, Koko, or Nim have signaled, socialized, and shared meaning with their kin in the wild?

Nonhuman primates possess complex and nuanced systems of communication, relying on a blend of vocalizations, facial expressions, gestures, and touch, much like our early ancestors likely did. Chimpanzees such as Washoe, for instance, use a range of vocal signals to convey specific meanings. Grunts often refer to food, while "hoos" signal threats, and panted grunts serve as social greetings. Their vocal repertoire is complemented by expressive facial cues and a wide array of gestures. In one study, researchers observed that when a mother extended her foot to her infant, it was an invitation to climb onto her back.

Chimpanzees also use body language in subtle yet purposeful ways. "Leaf clipping," in which a chimp deliberately bites fragments from a leaf in a conspicuous display, appears to function as a courtship behavior – an invitation to flirt. Tactile signals play a key role as well: A tap on the body can mean "stop that," while a hand fling or the slapping of an object conveys "move away." Even seemingly playful acts like blowing raspberries serve communicative purposes: They can express contentment during grooming or signal a desire for attention or food.

Gorillas, like Koko, also employ both verbal and nonverbal means of expression. Their vocalizations, grunts, hoots, and cries, serve various social functions, from locating food and attracting mates to initiating grooming and reinforcing bonds. A low humming sound, for example, often indicates pleasure while eating. Emotional states are likewise communicated through body language: a grimace that resembles a human smile often indicates fear, and direct eye contact, far from affectionate, is considered an aggressive challenge.

Together, these behaviors suggest that while primates may not speak in the linguistic sense, they are far from silent. Their forms of communication are sophisticated, intentional, and deeply embedded in the social fabric of their species.

The communication systems of nonhuman primates have also been extensively studied, revealing remarkable complexity across species, from bonobos and orangutans to a variety of monkey species. Among the most fascinating are vervet monkeys, who possess an impressively nuanced system of alarm calls. These acoustically distinct vocalizations serve to alert the group to specific predators from the ground, the sky, and the underbrush, triggering precise survival strategies tailored to each threat.

As small primates on the menu for numerous predators, vervet monkeys rely on finely tuned signals. A sharp "chirp" signals the presence of a terrestrial predator such as a leopard, lion, or cheetah, prompting the troop to scramble up into the safety of the trees. In contrast, a high-pitched "chutter," typically reserved for snakes, especially pythons, causes individuals to stand upright and scan the ground for slithering creatures. A low-frequency "rraup" warns of aerial predators like martial eagles, triggering evasive behaviors such as ducking under vegetation or glancing skyward.

Researchers estimate that vervets use up to thirty distinct vocalizations, which young monkeys gradually learn by observing the reactions of adults. Intriguingly, some of these calls transcend species boundaries. Diana monkeys, for example, emit specific alarm calls in response to eagles, calls that are understood by yellow-casqued hornbills. United by a mutual enemy, both species respond to the warning, illustrating an extraordinary case of interspecies communication shaped by shared survival pressures.

The animal kingdom boasts an astonishing variety of communication systems, from the familiar to the downright bizarre. Nonhuman primates use vocalizations, gestures, and facial expressions (much like we do) but across the animal world, communication also happens through color displays, dances, scents, and intricate soundscapes.

Sound-based communication is especially diverse. Beyond the calls of monkeys and apes, it includes the clicks, pulses, and whistles of marine mammals like whales and dolphins. Whales, in fact, produce the loudest sounds of any animal: The call of a blue whale can reach a staggering 180 decibels, louder than a jet engine. These underwater giants, along with dolphins and porpoises, rely on echolocation to navigate and interact across vast ocean distances. By emitting low-frequency booms or rapid high-frequency clicks, they listen for returning echoes to hunt prey or locate members of their pod.

Interestingly, whales don't have vocal folds like humans. Instead, they force air through a set of "phonic lips" located in their nasal passages, creating loud clicks by slapping these structures together, not unlike a blown raspberry. Within whale populations, researchers have even documented distinct "dialects" unique to different pods. Dolphins take it a step further: Each one develops a unique signature whistle, essentially a name-call that identifies them to others. (Remarkably, elephants appear to have name-like vocal calls, too.) Echolocation isn't limited to the sea. Bats and certain bird species use it as well, though sound travels more efficiently through water than air, giving marine species an acoustic edge in their vast, dark habitats.

When we think of singing animals, birds are usually the first to come to mind, and for good reason. In the avian world, complex songs are used not only to woo mates but also to defend territory from rivals. But birds don't just sing; like vervet monkeys, they also produce alarm calls, warning their flocks and families of intruders, predators, or other threats. Charles Darwin, in *The Descent of Man*, saw striking parallels between birdsong and human language. "The sounds uttered by birds offer in several respects the nearest analogy to language," he wrote, noting how birds, like humans, use their voices to convey a spectrum of emotions: distress, fear, anger, joy, even triumph. Darwin speculated that human language may have begun as a form of melodic expression. He likened baby birds learning to sing to human infants babbling, both acquiring the rhythms and structures of sound through social learning. In one especially poignant observation, he described a South American parrot that had learned to mimic the speech of an extinct tribe, its voice preserving the only known echoes of a vanished language.

African grey parrots are famous for their vocal abilities, and none more so than Alex, the subject of a groundbreaking thirty-year study by psychologist Irene Pepperberg. Under her guidance, Alex developed a vocabulary of around 150 words. But he didn't just mimic sounds, he could identify colors, shapes, and objects, recognize quantities up to six, and grasp abstract concepts like bigger versus smaller. Some skeptics argued that Alex's performance was due to unconscious cues from his trainer, drawing comparisons to Clever Hans, the horse that seemed to do arithmetic. Others dismissed it as mere mimicry. (Interestingly, seals are also surprisingly skilled vocal mimics, capable of imitating human speech and song.) But Pepperberg maintained that Alex's abilities reflected genuine intelligence. Supporting her view, recent studies have revealed that many of our feathered friends show impressive memory, learning, counting, and reasoning abilities. Furthermore, birds like parrots and crows have brains densely packed with neurons, comparable in cognitive power to those of nonhuman primates.

Like parrots, great apes, and even horses, dogs are well known for their ability to learn and respond to human symbols. With training, they can follow vocal commands and interpret gestures, especially pointing, a skill they share with dolphins. Charles Darwin, a devoted dog lover, believed dogs were not only emotionally intelligent but also cognitively astute. "As everyone knows," he wrote, "dogs understand many words and sentences," comparing their receptive language skills to those of human infants, able to grasp meaning long before they can speak. (And we'll come back to the topic of babies and language in the next chapter.)

Some, however, have pushed that idea into the realm of fantasy. During World War II, Adolf Hitler established the *Tier-Sprechschule*, an "animal talking school," to explore canine communication, including experiments in human–dog telepathy. The Nazis dreamed of creating an army of highly trained dogs that could read, write, and speak, ready to serve alongside German soldiers. Trainers claimed astonishing breakthroughs. One German pointer named Don allegedly barked out, "Hungry! Give me cakes!" (in German, of course). While another, when asked, "Who is Adolf Hitler?" reportedly responded, "*Mein Führer!*" Unsurprisingly, many of these claims were steeped in propaganda and wishful thinking rather than science.

Beyond vocalizations, many animals rely on chemical communication, using scent to mark territory, signal reproductive readiness, or establish social hierarchies. Dogs and cats are known for this, but they're not alone. Within gorilla troops, pheromones convey vital information about an individual's age, health, and fertility. Dominant silverbacks may also release a sharp, musky odor to intimidate rivals or deter predators. Insects take chemical signaling to another level. Ants, moths, wasps, and bees use pheromones to attract mates, coordinate colony defense, and lay down trails for others to follow. Among the most sophisticated are honeybees, whose famous "waggle dance," first described by Aristotle, combines movement and direction to relay the location of food, water, or potential nesting sites. The angle of the dance maps the direction relative to the sun, its tempo indicates distance, and the bee's enthusiasm signals the quality of the find. Some spiders have evolved their own form of choreography. Male peacock spiders, with their vividly colored abdominal fans, perform elaborate courtship dances to impress females. But there's no room for missteps. If the performance fails to convince, or even sometimes if it succeeds, the female may kill and consume her would-be suitor in a grim ritual known as sexual cannibalism.

Color is one of nature's most versatile tools for communication. In the animal kingdom, vivid hues often serve as warnings, like the electric blue skin of the poison dart frog, which boldly advertises its toxicity. Others borrow this tactic, flaunting bright colors to mimic poisonous species and deter predators without actually posing a threat. Color can also signal attraction or aggression. Cephalopods, highly intelligent invertebrates such as octopuses, squid, and cuttlefish, use waves of shifting color to communicate with remarkable nuance. A male octopus might flush deep red when courting a female or responding to a threat, much like a human might blush with excitement or rage. Chameleons, famous for their camouflage, also use color as a kind of visual language. Their skin acts like a dynamic billboard, broadcasting mood, status, and intent. During confrontations, males may turn fiery red and yellow to assert dominance. Females, meanwhile, use color to express sexual availability. A darkened body signals disinterest, while a mated female may display striking turquoise tones with yellow stripes and black spots to advertise her pregnancy, and her refusal to mate again.

From sounds and smells to dances and dazzling colors, some forms of animal communication feel almost alien, like signals from another world. Others, such as vocalizations, facial expressions, and gestures, strike a familiar chord. In these behaviors, we may glimpse not only other species, but also reflections of ourselves and our evolutionary past. Increasingly, researchers suggest that some animal communication systems may be more language-like than once believed.

As Stephen Fry reminded us in the previous chapter, human language is characterized by infinite combinatorial possibilities. Remarkably, studies of Campbell's monkeys suggest a primitive form of syntax at work. Though they have just six distinct calls, these monkeys combine them in structured sequences to create new meanings, governed by apparent rules. They even use a kind of affixation: The call "krak" serves as a specific alarm for leopards, while "krak-oo" signals a more general disturbance. Another call, "boom," is used in non-predatory contexts, often to summon the group for travel. Put together, a sequence like "boom boom krak-oo krak-oo" seems to warn of a falling tree or collapsing branch. Other primates, including capuchins, putty-nosed monkeys, bonobos, gorillas, and chimpanzees, also show evidence of combining calls in syntax-like ways. It's possible these systems echo an early stage in the evolution of human language, when our ancestors began building a rich expressive repertoire from a small set of basic sounds. And who knows? Other species may possess equally complex communicative abilities that we've yet to decode.

Historically, nonhuman animals have been cast as primitive brutes, instinct-driven and intellectually inferior. Even today, scientists often refer to their vocalizations as "calls," reserving the term "language" for humans, as if it were a unique evolutionary gift. But the examples above challenge this bias. They reveal that animal communication systems are far more sophisticated than we've traditionally acknowledged, and that the building blocks of language may not be exclusively human after all.

In the long-standing debate over human language versus animal communication, we've typically approached the question from an anthropocentric perspective, placing ourselves at the top and judging all other species by our standards. This mindset not only reinforces the idea that human language is superior, but edges into speciesism. We forget that we, too, are animals.

Perhaps it's time we stopped asking how animal communication measures up to human language and instead considered how well it serves the animals who use it. These systems are rich, diverse, and well adapted to their communicative needs, just like human languages. They may be different, but they are not deficient.

The study of animal language isn't a matter of black and white. It's gray, spotted, striped, feathered, and furry.

The Last Word

The search for the origins of language has led us down countless rabbit holes. Questions about where, when, and how language emerged, and who truly possesses it, often generate more uncertainty than clarity. But that's the nature of science: Each answer opens the door to new, often more complex, questions. Some may be unanswerable for now, others may remain mysteries indefinitely. Scientific knowledge is always provisional, evolving as new evidence comes to light.

Language may be humanity's greatest invention, but its origins may forever be our greatest enigma.

With that in mind, let's now explore how language can be created from the ground up.

3

How Do We Learn Our Mother Tongue?

Having explored the nature and origins of human language, new and intriguing questions naturally arise: How exactly do we acquire language? How does a tiny baby go from random babbles and burps to mastering their mother tongue, all in just a few short years? Toddlers seem to soak up language like little sponges, picking it up so naturally it almost feels like a kind of magic.

Yet, while a child's language development is undeniably fascinating, it can also be a source of frustration and anxiety for parents and caregivers. Mistakes abound as children navigate this complex journey, prompting the common concern: Is my child progressing as expected or falling behind? Importantly, these early false starts are not setbacks or failures but essential steps in the learning process, offering valuable insights into how language is acquired. Kids teach us a lot about how language works just by stumbling and trying again.

So, let's take a closer look at how children develop language, what their slip-ups can tell us, and what happens when language learning doesn't quite go according to plan.

Plato's Problem

First language acquisition often seems so effortless that it makes people wonder: Is language something we're born with? This question has puzzled thinkers for thousands of years. Back in ancient Greece, Plato asked how we can know so much with so little input. If certain truths aren't learned from experience, he argued, then maybe they come from within. In his dialogue *Meno*, Plato describes Socrates questioning a young boy about geometry. The boy, who had never studied the subject, managed to answer correctly. Plato took this as evidence that the boy wasn't learning something new but remembering something he already knew deep down. In modern times, the mystery has captivated philosophers like Bertrand Russell and Willard Van Orman Quine, and also linguist Noam Chomsky, who dubbed it "Plato's Problem." The idea behind it, known as innatism, suggests that some knowledge – possibly including language – is hardwired into us from birth.

Theologians and philosophers have long wondered whether children might hold the key to discovering the original human language. In the past, some speculated that if babies were raised without hearing any language at all – not even the language of their parents – they might spontaneously begin to speak this so-called "natural" language. They often assumed it would be one of the classical tongues, like Greek, Latin, Arabic, Sanskrit, or Hebrew. As we know, Hebrew in particular was believed by many to be the divine language that God gave to Adam and Eve in the Garden of Eden. Historical records reveal that curious minds once carried out experiments to uncover how children acquire language, and which language would emerge in isolation. Of course, this was long before the days of ethics committees, and some of their methods would raise more than a few eyebrows today.

Nothing but Noise

In *Histories*, the ancient Greek historian Herodotus recounts one such experiment. He writes that in the seventh century BCE, the Egyptian Pharaoh Psamtik I set out to discover the world's original language. To do this, he ordered that two newborns be taken from their mothers and raised in complete isolation, without any exposure to spoken language. His theory was simple: Whatever language the children eventually spoke would be the natural, original language of humanity.

The infants were placed in the care of a shepherd, who was instructed to feed and care for them alongside his herd of goats but was strictly forbidden to speak in their presence. For two years, the shepherd listened intently for their first words. Then one day, the children raised their arms and cried out, "Bekos! Bekos!" This was believed to be the Phrygian word for bread. The discovery was reported back to Psamtik, who concluded not only that the capacity for language is innate, but that the original human language must have been Phrygian, a language once spoken in ancient Anatolia, in what is now modern-day Turkey.

Experiments in which children are raised without human interaction are known as language deprivation studies. And for good reason, they are now considered deeply unethical. Back in the thirteenth century, however, the Holy Roman Emperor Frederick II, known for his fascination with science and his taste for unusual experiments, attempted one of his own. He wanted to uncover the world's very first language.

According to the monk Salimbene di Adam, Frederick instructed caregivers to feed, bathe, and care for a number of infants, but under no circumstances were they to speak to them. The goal was to see whether the children would naturally begin to speak Hebrew, Greek, Latin, Arabic, or perhaps the language of their biological parents. The results were tragic. The babies, deprived of human touch and affection beyond basic care, didn't survive. As Salimbene noted, the emperor's efforts were in vain, because "the children could not live without clappings of the hands, and gestures, and gladness of countenance, and blandishments." Even in the pursuit of language, the need for love and connection came first.

In the fifteenth century, James IV of Scotland reportedly tried to solve the mystery of the original language. He sent two infants to the remote island of Inchkeith in the Firth of Forth, accompanied by a nurse who was unable to speak. The idea was to observe which language the children would naturally acquire if left completely unexposed to human speech. Writing nearly a century later, the Scottish historian Robert Lindsay of Pitscottie described the event: "The king also caused to take one deaf woman, and put her in Inchkeith, and give her two bairns with her, and furnish her in all necessary things pertaining to their nourishment, desiring hereby to know what languages they had when they came to the age of perfect speech." According to Lindsay, when the bairns finally began to talk, they spoke fluent Hebrew. He was understandably doubtful. So was the novelist Sir Walter Scott, who commented a century later that it was far more likely the children would "scream like their dumb nurse, or bleat like the goats and sheep on the island."

When word reached the Mughal Emperor Akbar the Great that Hebrew was being called the "natural language," he decided to put the idea to the test. Unlike others before him, Akbar suspected that language didn't just emerge on its own but required social interaction and exposure. According to the memoirs of Venetian writer Niccolò Manucci, who recorded the story a century later, Akbar arranged for twelve newborns to be raised in total silence. Each child was placed with a nonverbal nurse and a "mute porter," and all were confined to a château whose doors were to remain firmly shut. No one inside was permitted to speak. Twelve years later, Akbar gathered his court and assembled a panel of judges, led by a rabbi, to assess the outcome. The plan was simple: Speak to the children in Hebrew and see what happened. But the children couldn't respond. In fact, they couldn't speak at all. They made "nothing but noise." To Akbar (grandfather of Shah Jahan, who would later build the Taj Mahal), the conclusion was obvious: Language is not something we are born with but something we learn through connection, experience, and education.

This theme continues to echo in modern fiction and pop culture. In an episode of *The Twilight Zone* titled "Mute," twelve-year-old Ilse Nielsen is found after a fire destroys her home and kills her parents. When she's rescued, she doesn't speak a word. At first, people assume she has a disability or that she was neglected. But it turns out her parents were members of a secret society that had rediscovered humanity's lost ability for telepathy, and that's the only way Ilse knows how to communicate. As she gradually learns to speak English, she loses her telepathic abilities, trading one form of communication for another.

A similar idea surfaces in the film *Nell*, in which a young girl is raised in isolation by her mother in a remote cabin. After her mother suffers a stroke, Nell begins to speak in a private language shaped by her mother's altered speech. When authorities eventually find her, Nell is wild and uncommunicative, but by the end of the film, she has learned to speak fluent English. Not all stories like this have happy endings. Take Cassandra Cain, better known as Batgirl, who is raised in total isolation and trained from birth to become the world's greatest assassin. She develops extraordinary skill in reading body language, but remains nonverbal and struggles with basic social interaction. These stories may be fiction, but they reflect a real fascination with what language means, where it comes from, and what happens when it's taken away.

Fortunately for the would-be subjects of these historical experiments, many of the accounts are probably fictional too. There are a few clues that point in that direction. For one, most of the stories don't appear in the historical record until long after the events supposedly took place, and there are no corroborating sources to back them up. Some accounts also carry a strong whiff of bias or political agenda. For example, Salimbene, who documented Frederick II's language experiment, was openly critical of the emperor, and his *Chronicles* reflect that.

The many versions of these tales that continue to circulate are also a hallmark of urban legend. And rightly so. Deliberately withholding language from a child to test how they develop it would be both cruel and unethical. This kind of research has been dubbed the "forbidden experiment" because it would require isolating children from all ordinary human contact. No modern ethics committee would ever approve it. Unfortunately, though, there have been real-life cases of language deprivation. These situations were not born of scientific curiosity, but of mistreatment or extreme isolation.

Wild Children

Children who grow up cut off from human language and culture are often referred to as wild or feral children, though that label sounds more than a little outdated today. These children are typically orphaned, abandoned, or survivors of severe neglect or abuse.

Legends and folklore are full of stories about such children being raised by wild animals. According to Roman myth, the twins Romulus and Remus were nursed by a she-wolf in a cave. They would become the founders of the city of Rome, so things worked out rather well for them. Other tales tell of children brought up by wolves, dogs, bears, goats, and even more improbable creatures like pumas, gazelles, or ostriches.

Many of these stories are now considered exaggerations, hoaxes, or misunderstood cases involving disability. One of the most famous examples emerged in the early twentieth century, when two girls, eight-year-old Kamala and eighteen-month-old Amala, were reportedly found living with a pack of wolves in Bengal, India. The girls were nonverbal and, according to some accounts, howled at the moon like wolves. But today, most experts believe they were likely autistic. Their caretaker, an English missionary, has since been accused of exploiting them for money, turning their tragic story into a kind of traveling sideshow.

In real-life reports, feral children are often described as unsocialized and lacking even the most basic social skills. They're said to refuse clothing, move on all fours, hunt for food, eat raw meat, and behave like untamed animals, snarling, scratching, and biting. And almost without exception, they do not speak.

This stands in sharp contrast to the feral children of literature, who somehow manage to become fluent linguists despite growing up in the wild. Forget the misquoted movie version of "Me Tarzan, you Jane," Edgar Rice Burroughs' original Tarzan is a remarkably cultured character. Raised by great apes, he teaches himself to read English from books left behind in his parents' cabin, and eventually learns to speak English, French, Swahili, Arabic, Latin, and more. Rudyard Kipling's *The Jungle Book* offers a similar fantasy. Mowgli, the "man-cub," is raised by wolves and later taken in by the warm-hearted Messua, who teaches him English. Within days, he's speaking fluently.

Of course, reality tells a different story. Kipling may have drawn inspiration from the case of Dina Sanichar, a six-year-old boy found living in a cave with wolves in Uttar Pradesh, India. He reportedly couldn't speak, but growled, whined, and barked like a wolf, offering a much more sobering picture of what happens when a child grows up without language.

Well-documented cases of wild children are extremely rare, but one of the most famous is that of Victor of Aveyron. In the late eighteenth century, a young boy was found wandering the woods near Saint-Sernin-sur-Rance in southern France. He was about nine years old, nonverbal, and seemingly unaware of social norms. Villagers took him in and gave him the name Victor. At first, he was cared for by a widow named Madame Guerin but, unaccustomed to human society, Victor repeatedly ran back to the forest and had to be recaptured several times. This was the Age of Enlightenment, and Victor quickly became a subject of fascination in the debate over what separated humans from other animals. Some viewed him as a kind of blank slate, while others saw him as primitive, *l'enfant sauvage* ("savage infant"). The philosopher François Dagognet described him as "the wild boy [who] walks on four legs, eats plants, is hairy, deaf and mute." A young physician-in-training, Jean Marc Gaspard Itard, took Victor under his wing, hoping to "civilize" him and teach him to speak. At first, Victor showed promise – he could understand basic language and even read simple words – but he never progressed beyond a rudimentary level. The only two phrases he ever learned to write were *lait* ("milk") and *Oh, Dieu!* ("Oh, God!"). Victor died of pneumonia at the age of forty, never having learned to speak fluently.

Fast-forward to the modern era, and we encounter the most famous case of a so-called "wild child." In 1970, Los Angeles welfare services discovered thirteen-year-old "Genie," the pseudonym of Susan Wiley, a survivor of extreme abuse, neglect, and social isolation. For most of her childhood, Genie had been locked in a small bedroom, where she was strapped naked to a child's potty chair and confined in a makeshift harness for up to thirteen hours a day. At night, she was bound in a crib with her arms and legs immobilized. Genie's father, convinced she was intellectually disabled, subjected her to brutal physical and emotional abuse. He forbade her mother and brother from speaking to her, and she was given virtually no exposure to language. If she made a sound, he would beat her with a wooden plank and growl outside her door like a dog to frighten her into silence. When she was rescued, Genie shuffled with a strange, bunny-like hop and showed signs of deep trauma, including involuntary urination and defecation under stress. Doctors described her as one of the most profoundly damaged children they had ever seen. Because she had been denied meaningful human interaction and linguistic input during the critical years of development, Genie had not acquired language in a typical way. In the early months after her rescue, she could say only her own name and a handful of words, including "blue," "orange," and "mother," alongside the heartbreaking phrases "stop it" and "no more."

Over the next five years, Genie was shuffled between hospitals and foster homes, all the while becoming the focus of intense scientific interest. Linguists and psychologists saw in her an unprecedented, though tragic, opportunity to explore one of the most fundamental questions in language science: What happens if a child grows up without language?

Genie's early progress suggested her father had been wrong, she was not intellectually disabled. She began to play, chew solid food, dress herself, and take delight in music. Linguist Susan Curtiss took a special interest in Genie, forming a close bond with her while working to teach her English. Genie's vocabulary quickly expanded; soon she could correctly name most everyday objects. But pronunciation remained a struggle. She often dropped or swapped sounds, making her speech difficult to understand. Grammar, too, proved elusive. Her utterances were short and stripped down, often resembling the speech of much younger children: "Ball belong hospital," or the hauntingly direct "Father hit Genie big stick" that recalled her traumatic past.

Though her expressive language was limited, Genie understood far more than she could say. And where words failed her, she relied on gestures, facial expressions, and even drawings to get her point across. Despite years of effort and some notable breakthroughs, Genie's language abilities remained far below typical levels. In the end, she never fully acquired fluent speech.

Nature or Nurture?

These extraordinary cases of language deprivation take us full circle, back to the question supposedly posed by Pharaoh Psamtik: Is language something we're born with? Several thousand years later, in the 1950s,

Noam Chomsky shook up the scientific world with a bold answer: Yes. Chomsky, who's nowadays better known for being a social critic and political activist than for his pioneering theories in linguistics, argued that children aren't blank slates but come equipped with a built-in capacity for language. According to his theory, humans are born with an internal blueprint for all possible human languages, what he famously dubbed *Universal Grammar*. This idea became the cornerstone of the "nativist" theory of language acquisition.

Chomsky's theory was a direct challenge to the reigning psychological view of the time, championed by psychologist B. F. Skinner. Skinner, a behaviorist through and through, saw the mind of a newborn as a *tabula rasa* – a blank slate. This was a concept originally proposed by seventeenth-century philosopher John Locke that emphasizes nurture in human development. Skinner believed that children acquire language the same way they learn to tie their shoes or use the potty: by observing, imitating, and being rewarded. When a toddler babbles "mama," mom claps, smiles, and gives them a hug. And just like that, language is learned through reinforcement. This approach, called operant conditioning, was Skinner's bread and butter: behavior shaped not just by praise, but by the strategic use of both rewards and consequences.

Chomsky, however, wasn't convinced. He pointed out that children don't just parrot what they hear. They come up with sentences they've never heard before, sometimes even ones that adults would never think to say. To explain this, he invoked Plato's Problem, arguing "the poverty of the stimulus." This is the idea that the linguistic input children receive is far too limited, messy, and imperfect to explain how quickly and accurately they master their native language. Chomsky's response to the age-old question of how we know so much with so little experience is that we must be born with some built-in knowledge about how language works. Or, to put it another way, we're wired for words.

Building on the idea that humans are born with an innate ability to learn language, Chomsky introduced the concept of the *language acquisition device* (LAD), a theoretical innate cognitive system or module hardwired into our brains from birth. This mental tool is said to kick into gear during infancy, developing rapidly and reaching full maturity around puberty, before gradually fading away. Chomsky's LAD aligns with scientific evidence pointing to specific brain structures dedicated to language learning and processing. (But it's not this simple, and more on this matter soon.)

Interestingly, Chomsky also speculated that language may have emerged as a kind of "hopeful monster," a sudden mutation or cognitive leap, rather than a trait honed through incremental evolutionary pressures. According to him, humans alone possess this remarkable device; while some primates can communicate through signs and symbols, they simply can't master the complexities of grammar. In other words, language is a uniquely human gift. Psychologist Steven Pinker builds on Chomsky's work but otherwise embraces an evolutionary perspective. He views language as an instinct shaped by natural selection, hence his famous term, the "language instinct."

If language really is an instinct, it raises a troubling question: Why didn't Victor or Genie ever fully acquire one? In Genie's case, Susan Curtiss and her fellow researchers concluded that she had missed the "critical period" for language learning, a limited window in early life during which the brain is primed to absorb language. Without exposure during this crucial time, a child may never develop full linguistic ability. In the 1960s, this idea was formalized by linguist Eric Lenneberg as the *Critical Period Hypothesis* (originating from research first put forward by neurologists Wilder Penfield and Lamar Roberts). According to the theory, there's an optimal age range, sometime between early toddlerhood and puberty, when language acquisition happens most naturally. After that, the window narrows dramatically.

The idea of a critical period wasn't new; zoologists had long observed time-sensitive developmental phases in other animals, including dogs, cats, monkeys, horses, and sheep. Ducklings imprint on their mothers within hours of hatching, and songbirds must hear adult songs early on or they may never learn to sing properly. Human language, it seems, may follow a similar pattern. Genie's tragic story appeared to support this hypothesis. Isolated from meaningful human interaction from the age of twenty months to nearly fourteen years old, she was deprived of language during the critical period. Researchers speculated that the brain's language centers had atrophied from disuse, like a muscle left immobile for too long. Even if the capacity for language is hardwired, Genie's case suggests that early and sustained exposure is essential to fully unlock it.

As we touched on in the Introduction, the "nature versus nurture" debate stretches back to ancient Greek philosophers like Plato and Aristotle. Over the centuries, it has captivated thinkers and scientists alike, from John Locke to Francis Galton and Charles Darwin. The fierce and enduring question of whether language is shaped by nature, nurture, or a blend of both continues to spark debate today. Chomsky's theory of Universal Grammar was largely based on research into European languages, yet evidence from many other world languages challenges this neat framework. Some scholars also argue that Chomsky may have underestimated the complexity of animal communication systems. As we've seen, creatures like monkeys and birds use patterns that resemble grammar to convey meaning, and the full extent of animal communication remains a mystery.

Regarding the much-celebrated language acquisition device, no one has ever pinpointed this hardwired "language module" in the brain. In fact, more recent research has moved beyond the idea of isolated language centers to emphasize dynamic language networks spanning the entire brain. (We'll return to this idea in the chapters ahead.) In a broader sense, the whole human brain functions as one vast, intricate language acquisition device.

Today, the idea of a critical period remains influential, though it has evolved into the concept of sensitive periods: windows of time when language learning happens most naturally. However, the exact nature and length of these periods remain hotly debated. (Sensitive periods also play a key role in how children and adults acquire second languages, so we'll swing back to this topic later in the book.) Importantly, nativist theories often overlook the crucial role of social interaction and language exposure in speech development. As Charles Darwin noted back in 1871, "Humans don't speak unless they are taught to do so," adding that language "is certainly not a true instinct, for every language has to be learnt."

Nowadays, many researchers favor an emergentist or usage-based approach. This is the idea that language arises from a child's interaction with their environment, combined with their general cognitive abilities. Simply put, children learn language by doing, using the same learning processes that underlie all human learning.

Me Want Cookie!

Now that we've explored atypical language development in children deprived of social interaction and language exposure, let's turn to the typical path. Chomsky was right: Children can learn any language at all. More precisely, they can acquire any language they're exposed to, whether it's English, Arabic, Japanese, Basque, or even a contact language like a pidgin. (And remember, a pidgin becomes a creole when it's learned as a first language by children.) But what does first language acquisition actually look, and sound, like? For parents, a child's first word is an unforgettable moment, full of excitement and pride. Whether the toddler says "mama," "dada," or something more idiosyncratic (like "train," in the case of my son), it marks a major developmental milestone.

Children make it look easy, but the journey to native fluency is anything but straightforward. It's not instantaneous, as in *The Jungle Book*, where Mowgli supposedly picks up language in a matter of days. Nor does it happen in isolation, like Tarzan growing up without exposure to human speech. And despite what Hollywood might suggest with chatty babies in *Look Who's Talking* or *The Boss Baby*, infants don't emerge from the womb with witty one-liners. In reality, most children pass through fairly well-defined stages of language development. First, they listen to the sounds around them. Then they begin to imitate. Eventually, they produce words, phrases, and sentences that grow in complexity. It's a remarkable process, slow, steady, and shaped by the social world.

Language development begins remarkably early, in the womb. Even before birth, babies are tuning in to the soothing sounds, gentle rhythms, and melodic cadences of language, especially from their mother's voice and the voices of those around her. Recent research suggests that the human brain is astonishingly attuned to language from the earliest stages of prenatal development. The auditory system matures between twenty-six and thirty weeks of gestation, enough for the fetus to hear at this point. This revelation won't surprise many mothers, especially those who've felt their baby suddenly jump at a loud noise like a slammed door. In a striking parallel from the animal kingdom, a study of superb fairy-wrens found that chicks learn vocal "passwords" from their mothers while still inside the egg, suggesting that the ability to recognize and respond to sound begins even before birth.

Just days after birth, infants already respond differently to speech than to non-speech sounds. Newborns show a strong preference for listening to language over other noises and can distinguish speech from non-linguistic sound. They respond most strongly to the familiar rhythm and tone of their mother tongue when compared to unfamiliar languages. They also show a clear preference for their mother's voice, an early and deeply emotional sign of bonding. That voice, after all, has been a constant comforting presence in the womb, along with the rhythm of her heartbeat. It's common for expectant mothers to talk, read, and sing sweetly to their unborn babies, and there's good reason for this. Studies show that newborns can remember sounds they heard in utero, even recognizing specific stories and poems introduced during the final weeks of pregnancy. It's evident that both language and human connection start taking shape long before we enter the world.

This stage is followed by the pre-talking phase, spanning from birth to around six months of age. Often dubbed the "silent period," it's anything but silent (anyone who's spent time with a newborn can confirm that). Babies cry, cough, whimper, breathe, burp, snort, suckle, sigh, swallow, giggle, groan, click, and emit all sorts of charming (and sometimes less-than-charming) sounds. What they *can't* do just yet is produce the full range of speech sounds. That's because their vocal tract is still developing. At birth, a baby's vocal anatomy closely resembles that of a chimpanzee, with a shorter vocal tract and a larynx positioned much higher in the throat than in adults. In fact, newborns can breathe and swallow at the same time, a handy adaptation, but not one suited for speech. For language to emerge, the vocal tract must undergo key changes: The larynx gradually descends, reshaping the vocal tract and paving the way for more complex sounds. Around the three-month mark, babies begin to coo, making soft, melodic "comfort sounds" that often feature pure vowel tones like "ooo," "eee," and "aaa." These early vocalizations mark the first musical notes in the symphony of speech to come.

These early noises are more than just cute, they're essential practice. By experimenting with sound, babies learn how to control the airflow from their lungs and coordinate their vocal folds. These vocalizations, paired with expressive faces, also serve a communicative purpose: They let care-givers know when the baby is hungry, angry, tired, uncomfortable, or content. Still, this isn't language. Not yet. This stage is primarily receptive. The baby isn't speaking, but they're soaking up the language around them, tuning in to its sounds, rhythms, and patterns. And they're learning a great deal by doing so. Even as they babble and experiment with sounds, infants are actively trying to make sense of what they hear. Remarkably, they begin to recognize short words and simple phrases long before they can speak them. Research shows that babies suck more rapidly on pacifiers when something captures their interest, like hearing a recording of their mother's voice. (Baby Maggie from *The Simpsons*, famous for her orange pacifier, does the same – her signature sucking speeds up when she's excited.)

Next comes the babbling stage, typically emerging between six and nine months of age. This marks the beginning of the expressive phase, when babies start to play with sound in earnest. They babble, producing strings of nonsensical syllables, not yet forming real words, but laying crucial groundwork for speech. Maggie Simpson, ever the pop culture reference, sometimes pops out her pacifier to babble or squeal with glee. During this stage, babies experiment with pitch and tone, trying out shrieks, yells, growls, and even early whispers. Physically, they're developing too – their teeth are coming in, and the muscles involved in articulation are gaining strength and coordination. They begin to produce consonants that are easier to articulate, often starting with sounds like *b, p, m, n, d, t, k,* and *g,* in roughly that order. These are combined with vowels to form rhythmic, repetitive syllables like "na-na-na" or "ga-ga-ga."

What's remarkable is how universal this stage is. Across cultures and languages, babies babble in surprisingly similar ways. They even produce sounds not found in their native language. English-learning babies might click like they're speaking Zulu or Khoisan, while Japanese infants often produce a crisp /r/ sound that many adults struggle with. But as babies grow, their babbling becomes increasingly shaped by the sounds of the language, or languages, they hear every day.

In the nineteenth century, Charles Darwin documented the early development of his first-born son, William, in a diary-style account titled *A Biographical Sketch of an Infant* – affectionately dubbed "the Daddy Diaries." This was one of the earliest serious studies of child development. In it, Darwin observed his son producing speechlike syllables during the babbling stage: "When five and a half months old, he uttered an articulate sound 'da,' but without any meaning attached to it." At first glance, this baby jargon seems meaningless, but babbling is, in fact, a form of communication. It lays the foundational blocks of language while also helping babies get attention and express emotion. Infants imitate what they see and hear, and over time, their vocal play becomes more structured and social. They begin to babble with sentence-like intonation, pause as if expecting a reply, and take turns in a rudimentary form of conversation.

Some of these sounds start to resemble actual words, repeating patterns like "da-da-da" or "ba-ba-ba" that often charm adults and hint at emerging language. Commentators have speculated that if Pharaoh Psamtik really did conduct his infamous language deprivation experiment, the reported word *bekos* was likely a fanciful interpretation of typical baby babble. Others have joked that the babies were simply mimicking the bleating of the goats they were raised among.

After babbling comes the holophrastic, or one-word, stage, typically between nine and eighteen months, when babies begin producing single, isolated words like "yes" and "no." These early words often revolve around basic needs and interests, like "milk," "ball," and "teddy," as well as familiar names like "mama" and "dada." In a famously delayed debut, Maggie Simpson finally says her first word: "Daddy," but only when no one is around to hear it. The long-awaited moment came in Season 4, Episode 10, with none other than Elizabeth Taylor lending her legendary voice to the one-word cameo.

We don't remember our first words, first steps, or anything else from our earliest years, a mystery known as "infantile amnesia." But even at this early stage, babies' one-word utterances often pack the meaning of full sentences. "Up" might mean "pick me up," "carry me," or "hold me." "Juice" translates to "I'm thirsty." And "cookie" is clearly a demand – immediate and non-negotiable. Some children even invent their own vocabulary. Charles Darwin, in observing his infant son William, recorded one such case of linguistic creativity: "At exactly the age of a year, he made the great step of inventing a word for food, namely *mum*, but what led him to it I did not discover." Instead of crying when hungry, William would use *mum* as a demonstrative word or a verb, meaning "Give me food." Over time, he expanded its use, calling sugar *shu-mum*, and later, after learning the word "black," labeling licorice *black-shu-mum* – "black-sugar-food."

By this age, many children have built a modest but growing vocabulary, often around twenty words. But there's a noticeable gap between what they can say and what they can understand. A child might not be able to pronounce "vacuum cleaner," but if you ask them to point to one, they'll likely get it right. Language comprehension typically outpaces speech production in early development. To bridge this gap, children rely heavily on gestures. They wave, clap, nod, shake their heads, and blow kisses. Their body language becomes part of their communication toolkit: pulling on a parent's sleeve, grabbing objects, stamping their feet, or emphatically pointing to make a request or share interest. Darwin, observing his son, noted one such moment: "When a little over a year old, he used gestures to explain his wishes; to give a simple instance, he picked up a bit of paper and giving it to me pointed to the fire, as he had often seen and liked to see paper burnt."

Pointing, in particular, is a key milestone. It signals the emergence of *joint attention*, the ability to coordinate focus with another person. This shared attention is crucial for language development, helping children connect words to their corresponding objects, actions, or ideas. Interestingly, many of these gestures are not uniquely human. Young children share a repertoire of expressive behaviors with our closest relatives: chimpanzees, bonobos, gorillas, and orangutans. In captivity, mother chimps even teach their young how to blow raspberries, smack their lips, and blow kisses, gestures that echo the playful, preverbal communication of human toddlers.

Next comes the two-word stage, typically emerging between eighteen and twenty-four months. At this point, toddlers begin pairing words to form mini-sentences, simple but meaningful combinations like "cuddle teddy," "my cake," "Daddy sleep," and "Mommy busy." These early phrases are surprisingly expressive and can carry a range of meanings depending on context, intonation, and gesture. This stage marks a major leap in linguistic development, as children move from isolated words to more structured communication. Their two-word phrases are packed with content, mostly nouns and verbs, which are the core building blocks of meaning. What's missing are function words: articles like "a" and "the," and auxiliary verbs like "have," "do," and "be." So instead of saying "I want a cookie," a toddler might simply announce, "want cookie."

Yet even in this stripped-down form, toddlers tend to string their words together in a grammatically correct order: "read book," not "book read"; "eat cookie," not "cookie eat." This suggests that, even at this early stage, they're already picking up on the patterns and rules of the language they hear around them. Children typically enter the two-word stage with a vocabulary of around fifty words, but by the end of it, they may know more than six hundred. This is a staggering rate of growth, and a sign that their language learning is accelerating rapidly.

The telegraphic stage typically emerges between two and three years of age, when toddlers move beyond simple two-word phrases and begin forming longer, more expressive sentences – often three, four, or even five words long. These early sentences still leave out many grammatical words, but they pack in meaning. Think of Cookie Monster's iconic line "Me want cookie!" – a perfect example of the kind of speech that resonates with his young audience. This stage gets its name from the now-obsolete telegram, where messages were intentionally clipped to save on word costs: "Arrived London Monday," for instance. Similarly, toddlers might say "cat drink milk" instead of "the cat is drinking milk." While function words like "is," "the," and "a" are often dropped, the message still comes through loud and clear.

During this phase, toddlers begin mastering key elements of grammar as plurals, possessives, and verb tenses start to appear in their speech. Their sentences grow more sophisticated as their cognitive and linguistic abilities take off. This is also a time of dramatic vocabulary growth, often referred to as a *word explosion*. Children may learn ten or more new words each day, absorbing language at an astonishing pace. Their comprehension leaps ahead too. They can now understand and respond to multi-step instructions, like "Go to your room and get your books," even if, as any parent knows, their willingness to follow directions doesn't always match their ability to understand them.

The multiword stage begins around age three and continues well beyond. This is the final major phase of early language acquisition, when children start producing longer, more complex sentences and make significant strides in grammar. By now, they've begun to incorporate articles, prepositions, conjunctions, and inflections, the small but essential building blocks of fluent speech. One of the most famous experiments demonstrating children's grasp of grammar is the "wug test." This involves a made-up creature called a "wug," a small, bird-like figure with a bulbous body and a pair of antennae. Children are shown a single wug and then asked what two of them would be called. Most naturally respond "wugs," revealing they've internalized the rule for plural formation, even for words they've never heard before. This clever test highlights how children actively apply linguistic rules rather than just mimicking adult speech.

Still, exposure has long been recognized as influencing how children speak, right down to their accent and choice of words. Take the so-called "Peppa Pig Syndrome," for example, a term coined somewhat playfully to describe how young children, especially outside the UK, sometimes started adopting British accents or expressions after watching a lot of the cartoon *Peppa Pig*. Parents have reported toddlers in the US suddenly saying things like "telly," "give it a go," "on holiday," or calling the gas station the "petrol station." While there's no scientific evidence supporting it being a syndrome, it's a charming example of how children pick up not just vocabulary but also the rhythms and cultural flavor of language from their surroundings.

Beyond mastering grammatical rules, children's vocabulary also undergoes dramatic growth. By age three, most children know around a thousand words. By five, that number can balloon to 10,000 or more, as they rapidly absorb new words from conversations, books, and their environment. Alongside this lexical leap, they begin to grasp the subtleties of language: indirect requests, humor, sarcasm, irony, and other forms of abstract or nonliteral expression. The linguistic toolkit is expanding rapidly, and so is the sophistication with which it's used. This is fueled in part by growing social awareness and the development of what's called *Theory of Mind*, the ability to understand that others have different thoughts, feelings, and intentions.

This stage also marks the bridge from spoken to written language. Children begin to identify the letters in their own names, write them, and spot familiar words in books or on signs. They learn that print carries meaning and follow the conventions of reading: left to right, top to bottom (at least in English). This period of "reading readiness" can begin as early as four, though for some children it starts closer to seven. Either way, the foundations for literacy are taking root, and fast. Between the ages of four and six, children typically develop *phonological awareness*, the ability to recognize, isolate, and manipulate the individual sounds (or phonemes) within spoken words. This involves *categorical perception*, which is our tendency to perceive speech sounds as distinct categories, like /b/ and /p/. In other words, our brains sharpen the boundaries between sounds that matter in our language and blur those that don't. This foundational skill allows them to hear and play with the smallest units of sound: to blend them together into words, pull them apart, and recognize patterns like rhymes. It's an essential stepping stone to learning how to read.

Phonological awareness helps children connect sounds to letters, unlocking the alphabetic principle: the understanding that written letters represent spoken sounds. Reading and writing begin with recognizing the letters of the alphabet and the sounds they make, then blending those sounds to form words, sentences, and eventually meaning. It's a gradual process, one that mirrors spoken language development but with an added layer of symbolic complexity. Just like speech, literacy depends on rich exposure: to printed words, to stories read aloud, and to active, guided practice with caregivers and teachers. The more language children hear and see, the more fluent and confident they become. (In the coming chapters, we'll explore the mechanics of reading and writing in greater depth, including challenges such as dyslexia that can affect these abilities.)

By the end of these early stages, children typically achieve native proficiency in their mother tongue. But language acquisition doesn't stop there. In fact, it never really does. Throughout childhood and well into adulthood, our linguistic abilities continue to evolve. Language learning is cumulative. New knowledge builds on what we already know, layer by layer. In that sense, learning a language is never truly finished. It's a lifelong process for all of us.

Baby Talk

As we can see, language development is a natural, ongoing process. From the prenatal period onward, learning happens continuously, often behind the scenes, through everyday exposure to language during play, routines, and interactions at home and in the community. Still, parents and caregivers play a pivotal role in shaping a child's early speech. They help children learn how to form sounds, then words, and eventually sentences.

One powerful way to support language development is through what linguists call *motherese* or *parentese*. This is the sing-song, exaggerated tones adults instinctively use when speaking to babies. Commonly known as "baby talk," parentese goes far beyond phrases like "goo goo ga ga" or "coochie coochie coo." It's an expressive and affectionate speech style marked by real words, grammatically correct sentences, heightened pitch, stretched-out vowels, and a slower, more deliberate rhythm, all delivered with enthusiasm and warmth. This style of communication grabs a baby's attention, invites them to listen, and encourages them to respond.

Well-meaning friends or relatives may advise speaking to babies as if they're adults to promote "correct" language, but research shows that baby talk, done right, actually supports brain and speech development. It also helps build a strong emotional bond between child and caregiver. (Fun fact: studies have shown that cats respond positively to baby talk too.

They can even tell the difference between their owner's everyday voice and the special voice used just for them.)

As we've seen, while children are busy mastering the complex rules of language, they make plenty of mistakes along the way. And just like the stages of language development, many of these errors follow predictable patterns. Some of the most common missteps involve semantics, the meanings of words. One type of semantic error is *underextension*, which often appears in toddlers between the ages of two and three. In these cases, children grasp that a word refers to a particular object but fail to generalize it beyond a specific instance. For example, a child might learn the word "dog" but use it only to refer to Fido, the family pet, not to other dogs they encounter.

At the opposite extreme is *overextension*, when children use a single word to label a broader range of objects than it actually refers to. A child might call every four-legged animal a "dog," every round toy a "ball," all vehicles "cars," or every man "Daddy." These errors aren't random; they reflect a developing mind trying to make sense of the world by drawing connections and mapping language onto experience. It's all part of the process of learning to speak with nuance and precision.

When it comes to syntax, one of the most common developmental missteps is *overgeneralization*, when toddlers apply a grammatical rule too broadly and in surprisingly creative ways. For instance, in forming plurals, they might say "foots" instead of *feet*, or "mouses" for *mice*. The same happens with irregular verbs: "eated" instead of *ate*, "comed" for *came*, or "goed" in place of *went*. These aren't slip-ups from copying adult speech; rather, they reflect a child's active attempt to decode the patterns of language.

And there's logic at play here. These errors make sense. They follow the rules of regular grammar, just applied in the wrong places. They're a sign that the child is learning not by rote but by trying to make the system work. Such mistakes act as temporary placeholders until the correct forms are learned through repeated exposure, everyday use, and, eventually, memorization. Over time, children internalize the irregularities and refine their grasp of grammar, one exception at a time.

Pronouns are another linguistic hurdle that often trip up young children. One of the most common challenges is confusing "me" and "you," a mix-up that makes perfect sense when you consider how context-dependent these words are. Toddlers are still learning that pronouns shift depending on who's speaking, and that "me" for one person is "you" to someone else. It's a subtle but crucial distinction. This confusion is humorously illustrated in the film *Tarzan the Ape Man*, in a scene that plays like a linguistic version of Abbott and Costello's "Who's on First?" routine. After rescuing Jane from a leopard, Tarzan struggles with the slippery nature of pronouns:

> JANE: "Thank you for protecting me."
> TARZAN: "Me?"
> JANE: "I said, thank you for protecting *me*."
> TARZAN (pointing at her): "Me?"
> JANE: "No. I'm only 'me' for *me*."
> TARZAN (pointing at her again): "Me."
> JANE: "No. To *you*, I'm 'you'."
> TARZAN (pointing at himself): "You."

It's a brilliant dramatization of a very real developmental stage. One that every child must navigate as they come to grips with perspective-taking in language.

Most toddlers get the hang of basic pronouns like *I*, *my*, and *mine* by the age of three or four. But even beloved TV characters don't always follow the rules. Take Cookie Monster, for example. He's estimated to be between four and six years old, yet still mixes up first-person pronouns with phrases like "Me want cookie." (According to *Sesame Street* puppeteer Frank Oz, one diligent typist used to correct Cookie Monster's grammar in the scripts.) In response to a viewer complaint about the character's syntax, the show's creator replied dryly, "I don't think somebody's going to grow up a lawyer and say, 'Me want to represent you.'"

Elmo, the high-pitched, red-furred monster, makes a different but equally familiar error: *illeism*, the act of referring to oneself in the third person. "Elmo wants this," he might say, instead of "I want this," echoing the speech patterns of real toddlers. Of course, parents do this too when they say things like "Mommy is going to work now." A classic literary example of illeism comes from Julius Caesar's writings, particularly *The Gallic*

Wars, in which he narrates his military campaigns using his own name rather than "I." For instance, "Caesar defeated the Helvetii" (*Caesar vicit Helvetios*). This rhetorical choice lends his writing a tone of objectivity and authority, as if he were being written about rather than writing it himself. Another well-known example appears in *The Lord of the Rings* by J. R. R. Tolkien, where Gollum frequently refers to himself in the third person like this: "Gollum won't hurt nice hobbitses. No, no!"

Sesame Street characters like Cookie Monster and Elmo speak in simplified, childlike ways not just to sound friendly, but because they mirror the actual speech of young children. They model the kinds of creative linguistic workarounds that kids invent when they don't yet have all the pieces of language figured out. And despite some adults' concerns, research shows that watching these shows doesn't harm children's speech development. On the contrary, errors are a vital part of learning. Children don't acquire language by avoiding mistakes; they learn by making them, over and over, until the patterns click into place.

It's completely normal, and undeniably charming, for children to also make errors in pronunciation as they learn to speak. These sound mistakes are known as phonological processes, through which children simplify complex speech sounds to make them easier to produce. Common substitutions include saying "fink" instead of *think*, "lellow" for *yellow*, "pasghetti" for *spaghetti*, and "wabbit" for *rabbit*. *Sesame Street*'s Baby Bear humorously exemplifies this by replacing his r's with w's, calling himself "Baby Beaw."

Children also sometimes add sounds, turning *blue* into "bu-lue," (we might remember this is called epenthesis). Or they might omit sounds entirely, saying "pay" instead of *play* (which is a good example of elision). The most challenging sounds to master – such as j, l, r, th, sh, ch, s, and z – tend to be acquired last. When sibilants (or hissing sounds) like *s* and *sh* are consistently misarticulated, a child may have a speech impediment known as a lisp. A classic pop culture example is pig-tailed Cindy Brady from *The Brady Bunch*, whose genuine lisp was featured in several episodes. In one memorable scene, she is teased by a bully who chants, "Baby talk, baby talk. It's a wonder you can walk." The lisp wasn't just skillful acting by Susan Olsen, it reflected her own authentic speech pattern.

Stuttering, or stammering (e.g. "b-b-b-ball" or "I-I-I want a cookie"), is also relatively common in young children. It involves disruptions to the natural flow of speech, such as repetitions, hesitations, or the prolonged stretching of sounds, syllables, or words. Most of these phonological patterns fade as children grow and their speech matures. However, persistent issues may signal a speech disorder. In Susan Olsen's case, her pronounced lisp was severe enough to require speech therapy into her late teens. Eventually, she opted for surgery to help correct it.

Some speech disorders are congenital and may result from structural issues like a cleft palate, dental problems, hearing loss, or impaired control of the mouth's muscles. These are classified as speech disorders, not delays. In cases of language disorders, children are often aware that they're struggling to communicate properly. By contrast, children with language delays may have trouble both using and understanding language. Some kids outgrow these challenges, but many require speech therapy or additional support. Early intervention is key, especially during the sensitive periods of language development when the brain is most primed for learning.

The stages of first language acquisition follow a systematic and predictable path, though children don't all move through them at the same speed, and that's entirely normal. Interestingly, research shows that, on average, girls tend to reach language milestones slightly earlier than boys. Studies have found that girls often produce their first words and sentences sooner, build larger vocabularies more quickly, and may outperform boys in areas like eye contact, gesture use, and joint attention. Boys are also more likely to be late talkers and are overrepresented in diagnoses of language disorders. These sex-based differences appear across a range of languages and cultures. Some researchers suggest that biological factors, such as neurological development or hormonal influences, might play a role, though these theories remain controversial. It's difficult to tease apart the effects of nature and nurture in shaping early language skills.

That said, the differences between boys and girls tend to be small and usually even out over time. As with all aspects of development, there's a wide range of individual variation. Some children speak early, others later; some skip stages or develop particular strengths. Ultimately, each child charts their own course through the remarkable process of learning language.

Kmart Sucks

These stages offer a useful framework for tracking how a child's language is developing or where it might not be progressing as expected. Language milestones serve as signposts along the path of typical development. When a child doesn't meet these markers for their age, it may indicate a delay, disorder, difficulty, or disability. There are many possible reasons for differences in language learning. For instance, infants who have undergone a tracheotomy often don't babble and may continue to struggle with pronunciation if typical breathing isn't restored by age two. Other children may have apraxia of speech, a motor planning disorder that affects their ability to produce sounds. These infants might not coo or babble at all, instead relying on gestures or grunts to communicate. Their first words may be delayed or reduced to a single syllable, for example, "ma" might stand in for *mommy*, *milk*, and more.

As noted earlier in this book, one key discovery in understanding language disorders is the FOXP2 gene, which plays a vital role in speech and language development. Mutations in this gene can lead to conditions like childhood apraxia of speech, in which the brain struggles to plan and coordinate the movements needed for speaking. Many types of speech, language, and communication disorders can affect a child's ability to speak, listen, read, and write. These conditions can impact both expression and comprehension, shaping how a child interacts with the world. While they vary in severity and cause, such challenges are surprisingly common, affecting an estimated 10 percent of children.

Language delays are common among neurodivergent children, particularly those with Autism Spectrum Disorder (ASD), a developmental condition that affects social communication. One of the hallmarks of autism is a delay, or even absence, of early language milestones. Some autistic children may not babble at all, and those with more significant forms of the condition may remain nonverbal throughout life. When speech does emerge, it often sounds atypical, marked by an unusually high pitch, a flat or robotic tone, or unusual rhythms. People with autism often find it challenging to grasp the figurative or nuanced aspects of language, such as irony, sarcasm, jokes, and idioms. Nonverbal communication is also affected: They may not use or understand gestures, struggle to interpret facial expressions or body language, and frequently avoid eye contact.

A distinctive feature of autism is echolalia, the repetition of words, phrases, or entire sentences. For example, if asked, "Do you want a cookie?" a child might respond by echoing "cookie" instead of answering "yes." Echolalia can occur in typical development, but persistent or pronounced use may indicate a disorder. Echolalia may also include quoting lines from movies, songs, or previous conversations, a behavior sometimes referred to as "TV talk." These patterns are famously illustrated in the film *Rain Man*, in which the autistic character Raymond Babbitt frequently echoes phrases like "I'm an excellent driver" and "Kmart sucks." (The nickname "Rain Man" comes from a childhood mispronunciation of "Raymond" by his younger brother Charlie.) Raymond's echolalia includes repeating fragments of past conversations and scenes from pop culture. In moments of distress, he soothes himself by reciting Abbott and Costello's classic "Who's on First?" routine. This is a form of vocal stimming, or self-stimulation, which may also take the form of humming, whistling, or even shrieking.

Down syndrome, also known as trisomy 21, is another condition that can delay language development. It's a genetic disorder caused by the presence of an extra chromosome, and it affects both cognitive and physical development. Children with Down syndrome often face challenges with speech due to structural differences in the vocal tract, palate, and tongue, which can delay babbling and make articulation more difficult. They also tend to rely on phonological processes, like simplifying complex sounds, well beyond the age when typically developing children have moved past them.

Interestingly, many children with Down syndrome develop strong nonverbal communication skills early on, such as using gestures or learning sign language, even before they acquire fluent speech. Charles Darwin's tenth and youngest child, Charles Waring, is believed to have had Down syndrome, nearly a decade before the condition was formally identified by physician John Langdon Down. In his personal diary, Darwin observed that his son was "small for his age and backward in walking and talking." At just eighteen months old, Charles Waring died of scarlet fever, only two days before Darwin was scheduled to deliver his first public lecture on the theory of evolution. Instead of presenting his groundbreaking ideas, Darwin attended his son's funeral.

Cerebral palsy is another condition that can significantly affect language development. It's a neurological disorder caused by brain damage that occurs before, during, or shortly after birth, and it impacts muscle coordination and body movement. Because speech relies on precise control of muscles in the tongue, lips, vocal folds, and diaphragm, children with cerebral palsy often experience difficulty speaking. While some may develop typical speech, around 75 percent have notable language impairments. These can include ataxic or "scanning" speech, characterized by a breathy, monotone, slurred, and slow delivery.

Public awareness of cerebral palsy remains limited, and the condition is frequently misunderstood. People often misinterpret its visible symptoms, such as an unsteady gait or slurred speech, as signs of intoxication. In response, the phrase "I'm not drunk, I have cerebral palsy" has become a slogan of advocacy and awareness. The speech of Genie, the so-called "wild child" who was subjected to extreme social isolation, was similarly slow, slurred, and halting. Upon meeting her, people often assumed she had cerebral palsy or was deaf, highlighting how speech patterns alone can lead to mistaken assumptions about a person's condition or background.

Sign Language Acquisition

An essential part of learning to speak is being able to hear, but, of course, not all children have that ability. Roughly four in every thousand children are born with some degree of hearing loss. In the earliest stages, however, deaf and hearing-impaired infants develop much like their hearing peers. They cry, coo, and begin to babble vocally right on schedule, and at first, their sounds are indistinguishable from those of hearing babies. But as development continues, a key difference emerges: While hearing infants begin to produce more structured consonant-vowel combinations, deaf infants typically do not, and their vocal activity tends to diminish around this stage.

For children born into Deaf families who use sign language, a different but equally rich developmental path unfolds. These babies begin to *manual babble* – a kind of gestural babbling in which they experiment with hand shapes, movements, and patterns drawn from the signs they see around them. While all babies use their hands to gesture, deaf and hearing-impaired infants exposed to sign language engage in more complex and structured hand movements that mirror the rhythm and flow of language. Just as vocal babbling evolves into speech, manual babbling gradually takes on the form of signed words and sentences, demonstrating that the underlying processes of language acquisition are remarkably adaptable, regardless of modality.

As we've seen, sign language is simply another modality of language, and like spoken languages, it follows a set of predictable developmental stages. In terms of age, these phases largely mirror the milestones observed in hearing children. Around three months of age, deaf infants who are exposed to sign language begin to visually attend to signing and show sensitivity to facial expressions. Not long after, they start to manual babble, moving their hands in repetitive, language-like patterns, and imitate facial expressions and gestures. Soon they begin to point, wave, and explore objects, building the foundation for early communication.

By around one year of age, deaf babies typically begin to produce their first meaningful signs – words like *eat*, *drink*, *mommy*, and *daddy*. These early signs are often approximations, as infants haven't yet developed the fine motor control to fully replicate adult-level precision. Like any language, sign languages have grammatical rules, and children must learn how to use them. Just as hearing children "mispronounce" words or overgeneralize grammar rules, deaf children make analogous errors in sign. For example, they may omit inflectional markers or use simplified hand shapes. These mistakes are a normal part of language development and reflect a child's growing grasp of the structure and rules of their native sign language.

Just as certain sounds are easier for children to pronounce, some hand shapes are easier for them to form, especially shapes like 5, B, L, C, and

O. Others, such as K, R, X, and 7, are more difficult or "marked," meaning they're more complex and demand finer motor control. By the age of two or three, toddlers begin to sign using grammar, complete with "facial grammar" like raised eyebrows to indicate yes–no questions, an expressive equivalent of a question mark. As they grow, their signing becomes increasingly sophisticated. They begin telling stories through role-play, fingerspelling, and using eye gaze and facial expressions to add nuance and emotion. In recent years, social media influencers have helped popularize "baby signing" among hearing families, capitalizing on the fact that little hands can communicate long before little mouths can speak.

Earlier, we explored the tale of Emperor Akbar and his infamous language deprivation experiment, which reportedly resulted in children who remained nonverbal. In one alternate telling, however, the children – though never exposed to spoken language – do acquire a form of communication. Not Arabic, Latin, or Hebrew, but a self-invented sign language. According to the account, they "express their thoughts only by gestures, which they use in place of words." As we've seen, early humans likely relied on gesture long before the emergence of speech.

Similarly, Genie, the so-called "wild child" who was deprived of spoken language for most of her early life, developed her own system of gestures to express herself and physically acted out experiences she couldn't yet put into words. Later, when her spoken language plateaued, she began learning American Sign Language. But sign language, like spoken language, is shaped by timing: The sensitive period matters here too. Deaf children who aren't exposed to a signed language until after puberty typically struggle to achieve native-like fluency. The evidence is compelling: The earlier the exposure, the better the outcome.

The many roots of delayed language development bring us back to the haunting stories of so-called wild children. These cases raise a profound question: Were their language deficits the result of missing the sensitive period for language acquisition, or were other factors, such as cognitive or neurological conditions, at play? The sisters Amala and Kamala, once thought to have been raised by wolves, are now believed to have had autism, which would explain their delayed language development. Similarly, modern researchers speculate that Victor of Aveyron may also have been autistic. He often rocked back and forth, another example of self-stimulatory behavior, or stimming, and he never fully acquired speech.

In other cases, emotional and social deprivation appear to be the primary culprits. Genie, for instance, was not cognitively impaired as her father insisted; rather, she was a survivor of extreme isolation, trauma, and abuse. As we know, he beat her or barked at her if she made a sound, likely extinguishing her desire to speak. She was also severely malnourished, fed only a liquid and semi-solid diet, like baby food, cereal, and milk, which likely affected her physical development. Proper nutrition matters. The same muscles used for chewing and swallowing are also used for speaking.

Genie's case leaves us with more questions than answers. Did she miss the critical window for learning language? Or were her cognitive and linguistic limitations the tragic result of prolonged neglect and cruelty? Her story forces us to confront the complex interplay between biology, environment, and human potential.

The Last Word

At first glance, acquiring a mother tongue can seem almost magical. Babies go from cries to conversation in what feels like the blink of an eye. But beneath this everyday miracle lies a complex, step-by-step process. We aren't born knowing language, nor do we emerge fully fluent in the grammar of our native tongue. Instead, language emerges through a powerful interplay of brain-based learning mechanisms and rich social interaction. With every gesture seen, every word heard, every pattern repeated, children begin to piece together the rules of language, intuiting structure, meaning, and grammar from the ground up. Bit by bit, children learn to transform noise into speech sounds, and over time, speech becomes the vehicle for complex thought.

While much about first language acquisition remains a mystery, what we do know reveals an astonishing feat of human learning.

Now that we've explored how children come to master language, let's turn to the ways adults use, shape, and understand it.

4

How Do We Use and Understand Language?

What does it mean to know a language? Language is our most powerful tool for communication, shaping how we perceive, connect, and express ourselves. Speaking, listening, reading, and writing are woven into the fabric of daily life, yet we rarely pause to consider the complex processes that make these acts possible. In this chapter, we explore how adults use and understand language, from spontaneous speech to carefully crafted text. We unpack what happens when speakers speak and listeners listen, when readers read and writers write.

Along the way, we delve into groundbreaking, and sometimes controversial, research that sheds light on how we produce and comprehend language. But language isn't always smooth or flawless. In fact, a large part of using language is *misusing* it. We investigate the common errors that pepper everyday speech: mondegreens, malapropisms, spoonerisms, and slips of the tongue, and ask what these mistakes can teach us about the hidden architecture of language in the mind.

How Do We Speak?

Speech production is the astonishingly complex process through which our thoughts are transformed into spoken language. Far from being a simple, mechanical act, speaking involves a series of finely orchestrated mental operations. Language scientists have developed models to map these internal processes, beginning with *conceptualization*, or message planning. This is a preverbal stage, where we generate ideas, decide what we want to express, and shape the intention behind our words, all before a single syllable is spoken.

Next comes *formulation*, also known as grammatical encoding. Here, the abstract message is converted into language. We retrieve the appropriate words, arrange them into grammatically sound sentences, and prepare them for articulation. Central to this phase is *word retrieval*, the mental search engine that pulls the right words from memory, often with lightning speed and uncanny accuracy. Consider the word *cat*. On the surface, it's just a three-letter word. But behind the scenes, a wealth of associations are being rapidly activated. We may access sensory details: the sound of a purr or meow, the sight of flicking whiskers, the feel of soft fur or scratchy claws. Our minds might conjure up idioms and cultural lore, cats landing on their feet, or having nine lives. We might think of a childhood pet, a viral meme, or a cartoon feline like Garfield or Hello Kitty. And depending on our personal history, the word *cat* might even stir emotions: affection, fear, nostalgia, or annoyance.

In short, speaking isn't merely about saying words; it's about navigating a rich tapestry of memory, emotion, and meaning. Every time we open our mouths to speak, we're performing an extraordinary mental feat, one that reveals just how deeply language is embedded in the architecture of the human mind.

Once we've planned what we want to say, we begin retrieving the actual words from our *mental lexicon*, our internal dictionary that's stored in our long-term memory. But this mental lexicon is far more than a list of definitions. It's a richly interconnected network that stores not just a word's meaning, but also its sound, spelling, grammatical properties, and associations with other words. It functions a bit like a hybrid between a dictionary and a thesaurus, allowing us to link words based on similarities and differences in form and meaning, whether we're choosing between *cat* and *kitten*, or navigating the subtleties between *angry, irritated,* and *enraged.*

This lexicon reflects our *personal vocabulary*, the sum total of all the words we know and understand. It evolves with us, expanding through education, work, hobbies, reading, conversations, and cultural exposure. Everyone's mental dictionary is unique, shaped by individual experiences, interests, and environments. While two people might speak the same language, they often draw from very different lexical reservoirs. On average, an adult's mental word bank contains around 50,000 words, though not all are used equally. Our active vocabulary, the words we speak and write regularly, is much smaller than our passive vocabulary, which includes words we may not use often but can recognize and understand when we read or hear them. Vocabulary size and accessibility also shift across the lifespan. Children, older adults, and individuals with language disorders such as aphasia or dementia typically have smaller, less accessible mental dictionaries, and may struggle more with word retrieval or summoning the right word at the right time. But for most of us, the process is so automatic we hardly notice the extraordinary feat our minds perform every time we open our mouths.

For most adults, retrieving words from our mental lexicon during conversation happens with astonishing speed. So fast, in fact, that we're barely aware it's happening at all. This effortless fluency masks the intricate mental choreography unfolding behind the scenes. As noted in the Introduction, the nineteenth-century physiologist Franz Donders pioneered *mental chronometry*, a method for measuring the timing of internal cognitive processes. His work laid the foundation for modern techniques that allow researchers to explore just how swiftly the mind operates during language production.

In one contemporary study of word recall, participants were shown images of everyday objects – a tree, a snake, a bus – while researchers monitored their brain activity to see how long it took them to name the pictures. Remarkably, the participants were able to select the correct word to match the image in just 200 milliseconds. But even after the word was chosen, the brain continued its work: filtering out related but incorrect terms, assembling the right sequence of sounds, and preparing for articulation. This step is known as phonological encoding, the process by which the sounds and syllables of a word are retrieved and stitched together into a pronounceable form. It's yet another layer of complexity in the act of speaking, reminding us that language is not only rapid but also remarkably efficient.

The final stage of speech production is *articulation*, when our speech motor system springs into action and transforms abstract thought into audible language. As also noted in the Introduction, the eighteenth-century inventor Wolfgang von Kempelen made an early attempt to synthesize this process with his curious "speaking machine." Though likely created to lend credibility to his fraudulent automaton, the "Chess Turk," Kempelen's invention was a fascinating precursor to today's voice-enabled technologies like Siri, Alexa, and Google Assistant. It demonstrated, centuries ahead of its time, that speech could be both modeled and mechanized.

As we explored in Chapter 1, the production of speech involves a sophisticated coordination of the vocal tract. As a recap, when we speak, air is expelled from the lungs and passes through the vocal folds, causing them to vibrate and generate sound. That sound is then shaped by the articulators – our tongue, teeth, lips, and other muscles in the throat and mouth – to produce the distinct phonemes of speech. It's a marvel of biology and engineering.

Phew! While the process might seem labor intensive when broken down step by step, it happens so seamlessly that we hardly notice. In a matter of milliseconds, thought becomes sound. And just like that, the machinery of language delivers our minds to the world.

Tips of the Slung

Speech production is impressively fast, but it's far from foolproof. Even the most fluent speakers sometimes experience a breakdown in word retrieval, leading to what linguists call *lapsus linguae*, the fancy Latin term for slips of the tongue. To manage this, we engage in continuous self-monitoring, both before and after we speak. Much like an internal editor, our brain catches many of these errors before they ever reach our lips. But occasionally, a slip sneaks through. When this happens, we might pause, correct ourselves mid-sentence, and then carry on with the revised version.

Hesitations can also serve other important functions. We pause not only to fix mistakes but to gather our thoughts, mentally search for the right word, or plan our next phrase. These pauses often come with familiar fillers – *um, uh, er* – or discourse markers like *like, well,* and *you know.* Some speakers might even mask their hesitation with a nervous laugh, a clearing of the throat, or a brief stammer. Pop culture occasionally exaggerates these moments for comedic effect. In the British sitcom *The Vicar of Dibley*, the character Jim Trott famously stammers, "No, no, no, no … yes," using repetition as a form of linguistic stalling. In a humorous twist, his ex-wife Doris is later revealed to do the reverse: "Yes, yes, yes, yes … no." These moments highlight the real-world function of hesitation: It buys us time to formulate what we really mean to say.

Despite the stigma often attached to such fillers and pauses, they are not signs of poor speech. In fact, they're ubiquitous, occurring two to three times per minute in casual conversation across languages. Far from being meaningless noise, these moments can convey nuance, signal uncertainty, or subtly manage the flow of interaction. Research even suggests that hesitation can aid word recall. In short, hesitation and repair aren't flaws in our speech, they're features of a system that is flexible, adaptive, and deeply human.

To better understand how we produce speech, language scientists often turn to our mistakes, the spontaneous, often humorous, slips of the tongue that reveal what's happening behind the scenes of fluent speech. These verbal misfires offer valuable insight into the cognitive machinery of speech production. One of the most well-known types is the *spoonerism*, a mix-up in which sounds are accidentally swapped between words. A classic case occurred when radio announcer Harry von Zell, live on air, introduced US President Herbert Hoover as "Hoobert Heaver."

The phenomenon is named after the delightfully absent-minded Reverend William Archibald Spooner, a nineteenth-century British clergyman and Oxford academic whose name became synonymous with these sound-switching blunders. Spooner was known for unintentionally transforming otherwise sober remarks into comic gems, especially when flustered. He once scolded a student for having "hissed my mystery lecture," adding that the young man had "tasted the whole werm." At a formal occasion, he is said to have raised a glass to Queen Victoria with the unfortunate toast: "Three cheers for our queer old dean!" Naturally, he meant to say, "dear old queen." Spoonerisms typically involve the transposition of sounds, syllables, or letters between closely positioned words: "a lack of pies" for "a pack of lies," for instance. Though often accidental, these errors expose the layered and lightning-fast processes that underlie our everyday speech, reminding us that even the most practiced speaker is vulnerable to the brain's occasional misfire.

Spoonerisms most commonly involve switching the beginnings of words, rather than other syllables. At a wedding, for example, Spooner is said to have fumbled a traditional phrase, declaring, "I believe it is kisstomary to cuss the bride." (Of course, he wouldn't have made the reverse error, like "it is *custoss to kimary the bride*," which wouldn't follow the typical pattern.) Dozens of verbal gaffes have been attributed to Spooner over the years, including: "Excuse me, madam, but you are occupewing my pie," and the time he announced from the pulpit, "The Lord is a shoving leopard" instead of "a loving shepherd." As entertaining as they are, many of these quotations were likely apocryphal, dreamed up by humorists, newspaper columnists, or mischievous students rather than Reverend Spooner himself. Still, the legend stuck, and so did the name. Linguists refer to these kinds of errors as metathesis, a transposition of sounds within a word or phrase. We've seen this in earlier examples like "aks" for *ask*, and in the way young children often say "pasghetti" instead of *spaghetti*.

Spoonerisms are not unique to English. They occur in languages around the world and offer fascinating clues about how our minds prepare speech. What makes spoonerisms especially revealing is that they show we often plan entire phrases ahead of time. Otherwise, such coordinated swaps across words wouldn't occur. These errors are more likely when we're tired, rushed, anxious, or distracted, when the brain, like any finely tuned instrument, falters just a little. But not all spoonerisms are accidents. They're also a playful tool, used intentionally in humor, literature, and music. Poet Shel Silverstein embraced the form in his children's book *Runny Babbit: A Billy Sook*, the tale of a bunny with "a sother and two bristers," whose parents "Dummy and Mad" give him chores like "dashing the wishes." Whether by mistake or design, spoonerisms show just how flexible, and fallible, our language system really is.

In psychology, the study of speech errors has a long and storied tradition. These verbal missteps are sometimes referred to as *parapraxes*, a term introduced by the English translator of Sigmund Freud's work. Freud himself never called them *Freudian slips*. That label came later. In his original writings, he described such phenomena as *Fehlleistungen*, a German word meaning "faulty actions" or "misperformances." Freud famously interpreted these slips as glimpses into the unconscious mind. He believed that when we fumble our words, we reveal more than just a momentary lapse, we expose hidden thoughts, repressed memories, and unspoken desires.

Freud developed psychoanalysis as a therapeutic method grounded in the idea that free, uncensored speech could unlock the deeper causes of psychological distress. In this framework, speech errors were not random accidents but meaningful clues. For instance, if someone mistakenly calls their current partner by an ex's name, Freud might have argued that the slip betrays lingering emotional attachment. If a parent repeatedly confuses their children's names, favoring one over the other, he might have read that as evidence of unconscious bias. Even accidental word substitutions, especially those with sexual connotations, were, in Freud's view, windows into the inner psyche. A tongue-in-cheek internet meme sums it up neatly: "A Freudian slip is when you say one thing – but you mean your mother."

Modern language scientists refer to these as *wrong name errors*, and while they're often amusing, they can also be painfully awkward, especially for those in the spotlight. These slips frequently occur when a speaker is nervous, flustered or simply talking too fast for their brain to keep pace. Public figures, in particular, are no strangers to such linguistic landmines. During a speech, former US President George H. W. Bush famously misspoke, saying, "For seven and a half years I've worked alongside President Reagan. We've had triumphs. Made some mistakes. We've had some sex."

After a brief pause, and likely a moment of internal panic, he corrected himself: "Uh ... setbacks." More recently, in 2024, British Prime Minister Keir Starmer intended to call for a ceasefire in the Middle East and the release of hostages. Instead, his tongue betrayed him, and he inadvertently urged for the return of "the sausages."

These gaffes happen to everyone, but when they're delivered on live television or in political speeches, the embarrassment is amplified. Years ago, New York news anchor Ernie Anastos shocked viewers when he appeared to say to the weatherman, "Keep fucking that chicken." The clip quickly went viral, sparking debate about whether he actually dropped the f-bomb or if he had meant to say something more innocent, perhaps "plucking" or "clucking." Then there was the time BBC presenter Jim Naughtie made headlines when he accidentally introduced UK Culture Secretary Jeremy Hunt with an unfortunate spoonerism that swapped the opening sounds of his last name and title. Regardless of intent, these slip-ups remind us just how complex and delicate the process of speech production really is, and how even a momentary lapse can have lasting, and often hilarious, consequences.

In the 1970s, a group of researchers set out to test the theory behind Freudian slips, though it's safe to say their methods wouldn't pass an ethics review today. The study involved a group of self-identified "heterosexual men" divided into three experimental conditions. In the first group, participants were greeted by a middle-aged male professor and asked to repeat word pairs engineered to tempt spoonerisms, such as saying "mack bud" instead of "back mud." In the second group, participants encountered a young, flirtatious woman lab assistant dressed provocatively in what the researchers described as "a very short skirt and sort of translucent blouse." These men were significantly more likely to produce spoonerisms with sexual overtones, such as "fast passion" for "past fashion."

The third group also met with the professor, but with an added twist, they were told they might receive an electric shock during the study (though, in reality, no shocks were given). These participants tended to produce slips reflecting their anxiety, such as "cursed wattage" in place of "worst cottage." Interestingly, all groups made roughly the same number of speech errors, regardless of the experimental manipulation. What differed was the *content* of those errors. The researchers concluded that when a particular idea, whether it's sex or stress, is salient in the mind, it may subtly influence language production. Still, most speech slips don't require a psychoanalytic microscope. When someone says "a blushing crow" instead of "a crushing blow," or "a well-boiled icicle" in place of "a well-oiled bicycle," both phrases often (wrongly) credited to Reverend Spooner, it's unlikely to be the result of deep-seated unconscious urges. More often, it's just the brain momentarily tripping over its own wiring.

You *Are* Effluent, Kim

Spoonerisms belong to a broader category of speech glitches that also includes the *tip-of-the-tongue* phenomenon, sometimes referred to by the lesser-known term *lethologica*. This occurs when a speaker can't retrieve a word that they know they know. It's lodged somewhere in memory, maddeningly out of reach. The French call this feeling *presque vu*, meaning "almost seen," a phrase that perfectly captures the sense of grasping for a word just beyond one's mental fingertips. Most people are intimately familiar with this frustrating experience: You know what you want to say, you can describe the concept, maybe even remember how the word begins or what it rhymes with, but the exact term won't come. In that moment, speakers often reach for placeholders like "whatchamacallit," "thingama-bob," "you know," or "what's the word I'm looking for?", linguistic life preservers tossed into the sea of forgetfulness. The word often resurfaces later, unbidden and annoyingly late.

These lapses typically involve low-frequency words rather than the everyday vocabulary we use fluently. Interestingly, people in the grip of a tip-of-the-tongue moment can often recall partial features of the missing word: its first letter, syllable count, meaning, or near-synonyms, suggesting that retrieval fails at the last moment, not from a lack of knowledge but from a temporary bottleneck in access. A pop culture illustration of this comes from an iconic *Seinfeld* episode, in which Jerry finds himself unable to recall his girlfriend's name. All he knows is that it rhymes with a part of the female anatomy. Desperate, he tries to coax it out by indirect means: snooping in her purse and engineering moments where she might reintroduce herself, without success. Jerry enlists George to brainstorm possibilities, yielding a hilarious series of guesses: Bovary (ovary), Hest (breast), Gipple (nipple), and the infamous Mulva (vulva). When his girlfriend realizes he's forgotten her name, she storms out. Only then does it finally come to him. Jerry races to the window and calls out, "Dolores!" (rhyming with "clitoris"). The elusive word no longer on the tip of his tongue, but it's too late to save the relationship.

When a word is on the tip of the tongue, the speaker knows it exists in memory and trusts that, with a little effort, it can be retrieved. But not all word errors stem from this kind of near-retrieval. In some cases, the speaker confidently uses the *wrong* word without realizing it. This is the case with malapropisms – verbal misfires where an incorrect word is substituted for a similar-sounding one, often with unintentionally comic results. A common example is the mistaken reference to Alzheimer's disease as "old timers," a slip that ironically reflects the memory loss associated with the condition. These kinds of errors are more than just amusing, they reveal how the brain relies on phonological similarity when retrieving words, sometimes prioritizing sound over meaning.

The term *malapropism* comes from a character in Richard Brinsley Sheridan's 1775 comedy *The Rivals*. Mrs. Malaprop is a pompous and pretentious grande dame who fancies herself a linguistic sophisticate but habitually misuses highbrow vocabulary. Her word-mangling is legendary. In one oft-quoted line, she praises a gentleman as "the very pineapple of politeness," when she clearly meant *pinnacle*. Sheridan based her name on the French phrase *mal à propos*, meaning "ill-suited" or "inappropriate," a fitting label for her linguistic missteps. Malapropisms may be accidental, but they often expose just how fragile and fallible language retrieval can be, even among those who consider themselves articulate.

Language scientists refer to malapropisms as *acyrology*, the incorrect or improper use of words. Another term sometimes used is *Dogberryism*, named after the bumbling constable in Shakespeare's *Much Ado about Nothing*, whose earnest misuse of language rivals that of Mrs. Malaprop. Centuries later, malapropisms remain a reliable comedic device, often used to highlight a character's pretensions or linguistic insecurity. A modern example comes from the Australian sitcom *Kath & Kim*, which delights in language blunders. In one episode, Kim declares, "I want to be *effluent*, Mum. Effluent!" to which Kath warmly replies, "You *are* effluent, Kim." Of course, Kim meant *affluent*, but the slip is telling. Malapropisms typically occur when a speaker gropes for a word and retrieves one from the same phonological neighborhood. These substitutes often share key features with the intended word – number of syllables, stress pattern, and grammatical role – but differ drastically in meaning.

English, with its abundance of sound-alike words, is especially prone to these kinds of errors. Malapropisms are particularly common in situations that call for legal, bureaucratic, or otherwise elevated vocabulary. They're also linked to a phenomenon known as *hypercorrection*, when people over-apply language rules or reach for elevated diction to sound educated, only to miss the mark (just like Mrs. Malaprop). These kinds of slips often reflect more than simple confusion. They frequently arise in contexts where people are navigating class, status, or identity. Dogberry is a social climber, hopelessly out of his depth but desperate to appear learned. Mrs. Malaprop is similarly pretentious, using fancy language as armor against her own insecurities. In *Kath & Kim*, the titular characters are self-styled suburban sophisticates who aspire to the cultural elite. In reality, they are "bogans," unrefined and unsophisticated, with a taste for the finer things but little grasp of what those things actually are. Whether in eighteenth-century drama or modern sitcoms, malapropisms continue to reveal the deep connections between language, aspiration, and identity.

Despite the many types of slips of the tongue, human speech remains an astonishingly rapid and seemingly effortless process. On average, we speak at a rate of about 150 words per minute, yet fluent speakers typically make only one error per thousand words. When mistakes do occur, they are usually the result of understandable factors: multitasking, stress, fatigue, distraction, or simply speaking too quickly. The unconscious mind does play a role in these errors, though not quite as Freud envisioned. Slips of the tongue point to the pre-planning involved in speech: We tend to construct a mental blueprint of an utterance before we even begin to speak. What Freud interpreted as repressed thoughts might instead be explained by interference from recently heard, read, or thought words, which can inadvertently intrude into our speech.

Similar errors can surface in writing or typing, where they're known as slips of the pen, or *lapsus calami*. These include classic typos like "form" for *from* or "teh" for *the*, often the result of automaticity overtaking attention. One notable example occurred in 2012, when the University of Texas at Austin's Lyndon B. Johnson School of Public Affairs mistakenly printed "pubic" instead of *public* in its graduation program, a blunder that led to a formal apology and an urgent reprint. These kinds of errors are especially common in the spelling of technical or Latinate words (including, fittingly, *lapsus calami* itself). And just as slips occur in spoken and written language, signers can experience analogous "slips of the hand" in sign language, further evidence that even our most practiced communication systems are prone to momentary glitches.

Understandably, people may worry that verbal slips indicate poor memory or early signs of dementia or Alzheimer's disease, but such concerns are usually unfounded. These are routine cognitive hiccups, essentially human "syntax errors," and they occur across the lifespan. While they may become more frequent with age due to natural language attrition, they are rarely cause for alarm. In contrast, as we'll explore in the next chapter, atypical speech errors can signal language disorders and present serious challenges for communication.

'Scuse Me While I Kiss This Guy

Now that we understand how speech is produced, how do we make sense of it when we hear it? Speech perception is the process of comprehending a speaker's message, whether we're watching TV, listening to the radio, chatting on the phone, or speaking face-to-face. In every case, we rely on our ability to extract meaning from sound. At the heart of this process is the recovery of speech from the acoustic signal, the sound waves produced by the human voice. Like other natural sounds or music, these waves are picked up by the ears and transmitted to the brain for interpretation. This approach, known as the *general auditory theory*, views speech as one type of sound among many that our auditory system is equipped to process.

But speech isn't just a series of neatly enunciated words. We don't speak the way we might read a shopping list, word by word. Instead, everyday speech is fluid and continuous, a phenomenon known as *connected speech*, where words blend into one another. Understanding what someone is saying means rapidly identifying and decoding this stream of sounds in real time, often with remarkable speed and accuracy. However, this task isn't always easy. One of the main challenges is *coarticulation*, the overlap of speech sounds, where the pronunciation of one sound is influenced by its neighbors. This can lead to misperceptions or mishearings. A well-known example of this is the *mondegreen*, where a listener misinterprets a phrase, often giving it a humorous or surreal twist. Perhaps the most famous mondegreen comes from Jimi Hendrix's "Purple Haze," where many hear "'Scuse me while I kiss this guy," instead of the actual lyric, "'Scuse me while I *kiss the sky*."

To understand speech, we need to distinguish between sounds that carry different meanings, like *this guy* versus *the sky*. This ability is known as *categorical perception*: the capacity to hear subtle differences in speech sounds as distinct categories, even when they're acoustically similar. It's a crucial skill because altering just one sound can completely change the meaning of a word. As we discussed in the previous chapter, categorical perception is part of a broader skill set known as phonological awareness, our ability to identify, isolate, and manipulate the sounds of language. Remarkably, we begin to develop this awareness as toddlers, often before we're even able to produce the sounds ourselves. During the first year of life, babies start to become perceptually "tuned" to the sound patterns of their native language. As adults, we can usually tell instantly when someone is speaking a different language.

Once we've perceived a stream of speech sounds, we mentally map them onto stored representations of words, a process called *word recognition*. This happens automatically and with astonishing speed. In fact, it takes the average person just one-third of a second to recognize and understand a spoken word. Interestingly, research shows that speech presented to the right ear is processed slightly faster and more accurately than speech heard through the left. This is known as the *right ear advantage*, and it's tied to how the brain is wired for language. Because the left hemisphere is dominant for language processing in most people, and the right ear has a more direct connection to it via the contralateral pathway, language input to the right ear gets a head start.

Word recognition begins the moment we hear the first sounds of a word. For instance, when a listener hears the initial syllable *ro-* in *rocket*, the brain immediately activates a set of possible matches: *rock, rocker, rocket*, and so on. As more of the word is heard, these candidates are rapidly narrowed down until only one remains. This dynamic process allows us to understand speech in real time, with remarkable efficiency. However, several factors can interfere with our ability to recognize words. Aging, for example, often brings normal declines in hearing and cognitive processing, which can slow speech recognition. At any age, we may also misinterpret what we hear, sometimes because of our own expectations or assumptions about what a speaker is going to say.

Miscommunication can be a source of confusion or comedy. Humor often thrives on misheard speech, especially when language barriers are involved. In one classic scene from British sitcom *Fawlty Towers*, the well-meaning but linguistically challenged waiter Manuel is told by Basil Fawlty, "There's too much butter on those trays." Manuel, misunderstanding the phrase, replies earnestly, "No, señor. Not *on those trays. Uno, dos, tres!*" The humor lies in Manuel's sincere attempt to "correct" what he thinks is a failed attempt at speaking Spanish. Sometimes, our perceptions are shaped not by what is said, but by what we *expect* to hear. As Simon and Garfunkel poignantly observed in "The Boxer," "A man hears what he wants to hear and disregards the rest."

Ambiguity can slow down or derail our interpretation of spoken language. As we listen, we must navigate potentially confusing categories of words, especially *homophones*, which sound the same but carry different meanings, such as *to, too*, and *two*. (*Homographs* look the same, but have different meanings, such as *bat*, which can mean the flying mammal or a piece of sports equipment.) While context usually helps us resolve these ambiguities, it isn't always clear or reliable. This challenge is playfully illustrated by the children's game Telephone (formerly and less appropriately known as

Chinese Whispers, a term now widely recognized as outdated and culturally insensitive). In the game, a whispered phrase is passed from person to person in a line. By the time it reaches the last player, the original message has often been hilariously distorted, revealing just how easily speech can be misheard, misinterpreted, or reshaped by expectation and noise.

When speech is ambiguous or degraded, we lean more heavily on our *mental lexicon*, our internal store of word knowledge, and draw on past experience to interpret what we hear. And when all else fails, our brains are quick to improvise. We often "fill in the blanks," not necessarily with what was said, but with what we assume was meant. This mental shortcut can be surprisingly effective, but it also reminds us just how interpretive the act of listening really is.

The *Ganong Effect* refers to our tendency to interpret ambiguous speech sounds in a way that forms real words rather than nonsense ones. For instance, when presented with a sound that could be heard as either /g/ or /k/, listeners are more likely to perceive it as /g/ when it precedes /ɪft/, forming the familiar word *gift* rather than the non-word *kift*. Conversely, the same ambiguous sound is heard as /k/ when followed by /ɪs/, resulting in *kiss* instead of the meaningless *giss*. In other words, our brains are biased toward real words, and they'll bend perception to make them fit.

Sometimes, we even "hear" sounds that aren't there at all. This is the basis of the *phonemic restoration* illusion, in which listeners perceive a complete word even when certain sounds have been removed or obscured. In a classic experiment, researchers replaced the /s/ in *legislatures* with a cough or a tone, yet participants reported hearing the full word, as if nothing were missing. Our brains simply fill in the gap. This illusion can also be played for laughs. In a notorious NSFW parody of Sesame Street's "Song of the Count," every instance of the word *count* is bleeped. This creates the illusion of explicit lyrics in lines like "I really love to …" and "When I'm alone, I … myself." Even though no actual profanity is spoken, the censored gaps lead listeners to "fill in" the blanks with the words they *expect* to hear, showing just how suggestible and context-dependent speech perception can be.

These auditory illusions reveal that speech perception engages both bottom-up and top-down processing. (This is known as the *Fuzzy Logic Model* of speech perception.) This dual-processing system operates not only at the level of individual words, but also in the comprehension of larger linguistic units like sentences and extended discourse. Top-down processing draws on our schematic knowledge, our broad understanding of the world, topic-specific expertise, and accumulated life experience. It also involves inference-making and the integration of contextual cues, the surrounding information that helps us construct meaning. As we listen, we retrieve words from our mental dictionaries, stored in long-term memory, to make sense of incoming sounds. Top-down processes become especially critical in ambiguous or noisy situations, where the brain must actively resolve uncertainty and fill in informational gaps.

In contrast, bottom-up processes are stimulus-driven and occur as sensory information is received in real time. External inputs, such as sights, sounds, and smells, are captured by our sensory organs and relayed to the brain for further processing. Think of the scent of brewing coffee, a sudden flash of light, the slam of a door, or the unfamiliar sound of a foreign language. These raw sensory cues form the foundation for constructing meaning. For example, if we overhear a conversation in Polish without any prior exposure to the language, our perception is limited to the acoustic patterns of speech, without the ability to anticipate or interpret specific words. Crucially, bottom-up and top-down processes do not operate in isolation. They work in tandem, with incoming data informing our interpretations, and existing knowledge shaping our expectations. Together, they allow us to decode speech, transforming a stream of sounds into meaningful language.

Another fascinating aspect of speech processing is how we make sense of figurative language, those colorful turns of phrase that go beyond the literal. Metaphors, similes, hyperbole, puns, and idioms all fall under this umbrella. Figurative language is essentially when words mean more, or something different, than what they seem to say on the surface. Decoding these expressions taps into complex cognitive processes that researchers are still working to fully unravel.

There are two main theories about how we do this. One proposes a step-by-step approach: We first interpret a phrase literally, and only when that fails do we search for a figurative meaning. The other theory argues that we can entertain both literal and figurative interpretations at once, using context to decide which one fits. Take the phrase "time is money." No one imagines stuffing minutes into a piggy bank. We instantly grasp that the speaker means time is valuable and should be spent wisely. Figurative language makes our communication more vivid and nuanced, and understanding it shows just how agile and imaginative the human mind really is.

Monkey See, Monkey Do

A compelling alternative to traditional models of speech perception is the *motor theory*, which highlights the fact that we're not just passive listeners, we're also speakers. According to this theory, understanding speech is less about decoding sound waves and more about interpreting the speaker's articulatory gestures. In other words, when we hear someone talk, we subconsciously simulate what their mouth must be doing to produce those sounds, and use that information to make sense of what they're saying.

This idea helps explain why dubbed movies can feel so awkward. For instance, think of the English-dubbed version of *The Good, the Bad and the Ugly*, where the mismatched lip movements and dialogue create that unmistakable sense that something's not quite right. When the timing of the voice doesn't sync with the actor's lip movements, our brain notices the mismatch. A classic example of this comes from a famous study that gave rise to the *McGurk Effect*. In the experiment, participants watched a video of a man saying the syllable /ga/, while the audio played /ba/. What most people reported hearing wasn't either of those, but a third sound: /da/. In the study, when participants closed their eyes, they typically heard /ba/. When they watched the video without sound, they clearly saw the man saying /ga/. But combine the two, and their brains blended the conflicting inputs into something entirely different. This striking illusion shows just how much visual information influences what we *hear*, revealing that speech perception is a multisensory experience, not just an auditory one.

This kind of illusion is a perfect example of bottom-up processing, where our perception is shaped by the raw sensory input coming from the environment, in this case, mismatched visual and auditory cues. A more modern twist on this phenomenon came in 2018, when the Internet exploded over the now-infamous *Yanny vs. Laurel* audio clip. Some people were convinced the robotic voice said "yanny," while others were equally sure it said "laurel." So, which answer was right? Surprisingly, neither was wrong. The clip contains elements of *both* words: "yanny" at higher frequencies and "laurel" at lower ones. Depending on your hearing sensitivity, your brain zeroes in on one and filters out the other, locking you into a single interpretation. It was like the auditory cousin of "the dress," that viral photo where people were fiercely divided over whether the dress was white and gold or blue and black. Just as the dress illusion hinges on how we interpret lighting, the Yanny–Laurel debate reveals how perception is not just about what's *out there* but also about what our brains *choose* to hear (or see).

Building on the motor theory, researchers developed the modern concept of *mirror neurons*, a discovery that added a fascinating layer to our understanding of how communication works. For a conversation to succeed, both speaker and listener need to grasp the message. Mirror neurons help bridge that gap. These specialized brain cells fire not only when we perform an action but also when we *observe* someone else performing that same action. This phenomenon was first uncovered in the 1990s, when scientists noticed that a neuron in a macaque monkey lit up both when the monkey picked up a peanut and when it saw another monkey, or a human, do the same. The effect was consistent whether the monkey was watching peanuts, bananas, raisins, or even ice cream cones.

So, what do snacks have to do with speech? Mirror neurons are thought to play a vital role in social interaction, allowing us to mentally simulate the actions and emotions of others. They're part of the reason we wince when we see someone stub their toe or feel tension during an awkward conversation. In the realm of language, these neurons are located in Broca's area. (As noted in Chapter 1, this region is in the left frontal lobe and is key to speech production and processing.) Some researchers believe mirror neurons could be part of a built-in neural mechanism for language, helping us intuitively decode the speaker's intended gestures and meanings. This theory even echoes Noam Chomsky's speculative language acquisition device, proposing that we possess a specialized speech mechanism, or "module," that equips us to acquire language naturally, right from the start. Whether or not this holds true, the idea that our brains are wired to connect through shared experience is both scientifically intriguing and deeply human.

All of this points to a remarkable synergy between speech production and perception, two processes that are deeply intertwined. Some researchers view mirror neurons as the crucial link bridging the two, offering insight into how we both produce language and understand it. But not everyone is convinced. Critics argue that speech perception may not be as uniquely human, or as biologically "special," as some proponents suggest. For instance, studies have shown that we process certain non-speech sounds, like slamming doors, musical chords, and bursts of white noise, in much the same way we process spoken language.

Even more surprisingly, some nonhuman animals exhibit strikingly human-like responses to speech sounds. Chinchillas, for example, those adorably large-eared rodents, have auditory systems not unlike our own. In a 1970s experiment, chinchillas were trained to distinguish between the syllables /da/ and /ta/, running to one side of their cage or staying still to earn a treat. This showed that they, too, could engage in categorical perception, sorting sounds into meaningful categories just as we do. In the 1980s, Japanese quail were trained in similar experiments, learning to peck only when they heard certain syllables.

These findings remind us that while human language is extraordinary, it's not built entirely from scratch. Elements of it, such as sound categorization and learning through reinforcement, are shared across species. Learning, it turns out, is central to speech perception not just in infants and adults, but even in some nonhuman animals. And while they may never learn to read *War and Peace*, these animals offer a humbling reminder: The roots of our linguistic abilities run deep, extending beyond our species, and are firmly grounded in the brain's capacity to recognize, categorize, and respond to sound.

And as we're about to see, speech production and perception aren't just tools for conversation. They're also the foundational skills that make it possible for humans to learn how to read and write.

Leading Us Down the Garden Path

The written word is everywhere, on signs, screens, packaging, and pages. Learning to read is one of the biggest milestones of early childhood education, and for good reason. Reading opens up entire worlds: We can lose ourselves in stories, look up useful facts, or learn something entirely new. And yet, few of us ever stop to think about what an *incredible* skill reading really is. When we glance at a sentence, we're effortlessly transforming a string of symbols into meaningful language, words we can say, think, and understand. It feels automatic, but reading is actually a highly complex process that draws on motor, visual, and cognitive abilities all at once.

As we read, our eyes don't move smoothly across the page like they do when we follow a moving object, such as a child swinging back and forth on a playground swing. That kind of tracking uses what are called *smooth pursuit* movements, slow and steady. Reading, however, relies on *saccades*: quick, jerky eye movements that jump from one word, or even part of a word, to the next. These saccades happen so fast and so frequently that we're barely aware of them. We also use saccades when we scan a still image looking for something specific, like searching for the red-and-white striped guy in a *Where's Waldo?* book (or *Wally*, as he's known outside North America).

Each time our eyes land on a word, a moment called a *fixation*, the image of that word falls on the *fovea*, a tiny spot in the center of our visual field where our vision is sharpest. Just outside of that is the *parafovea*, where things are a bit blurrier, and beyond that is the *periphery*, where visual information becomes too fuzzy to be useful for reading. While we're reading, our brains are constantly coordinating these rapid movements and blurry previews to piece together meaning, often without us even realizing it. Reading may feel second nature to fluent readers, but under the surface, it's a finely tuned collaboration between our eyes and our brains.

When we look at a line of text, our eyes aren't taking in the whole thing at once. In fact, our word identification span, how far we can recognize actual words, only stretches about eight letters to the right of the word we're fixating. Our *perceptual span*, or the total amount of visual information we can process in a single glance, averages around twenty characters. That means while we're focused on one word, we're also getting a fuzzy preview of what's coming next, just enough to keep our reading smooth and efficient.

In English, and other languages read from left to right, this preview window favors the right-hand side. But in right-to-left scripts like Arabic and Hebrew, the perceptual span shifts to the left instead. The brain adapts to the direction of the writing system, tweaking its strategy to maximize comprehension. Some ancient scripts were even more flexible. Egyptian hieroglyphs, for instance, could flow left to right *or* right to left. The direction wasn't random, though. The orientation of a person or animal in the text would always face the beginning of the line, giving the reader a clever visual cue about where to start.

Not all writing systems run horizontally either. Some East Asian languages, like Japanese, are still commonly written in vertical columns, from top to bottom, especially in novels, newspapers, and manga. A few rare scripts even take an unconventional route: written *bottom-up*. Ancient Berber is one such example, as is the Batak script from the Indonesian island of Sumatra, which today appears mostly in art and decoration. However the text is laid out, left to right, right to left, top to bottom, or bottom to top, the human brain is astonishingly adaptable when it comes to reading. The mechanics may change, but the goal remains the same: turning marks on a page into meaning.

Our fixations happen in rapid fire. Thanks to the pioneering work of nineteenth-century physiologist Franz Donders, modern researchers now use eye-tracking technology to study how we read, moment by moment. These tools reveal that we typically spend about a quarter to half a second fixating on each word, but not all words get equal attention. Shorter words, like *pig* or *foot*, and small grammatical connectors, like *but*, *or*, and *to*, tend to receive shorter fixations. More complex or less familiar words and names, say, *Frankenstein* or *monster*, take longer to process. These heavier words often get a second look, or even a third, before we move on. Sometimes we *regress*, meaning we backtrack in the text to reread something after realizing we've missed or misunderstood a key piece of the sentence. Unsurprisingly, reading slows down when a sentence is confusing or oddly written. (Think of those infamous "worst sentence ever" competitions.)

Interestingly, we don't even fixate on every word. Around 15 to 25 percent of words are skipped altogether, usually short, familiar ones like *a* or *the*. Our brains often fill in the gaps, especially when we can predict what's coming next. It's a reminder that reading isn't just a mechanical task. It's a dynamic process of guessing, checking, and interpreting, all happening at lightning speed.

Font can play a surprisingly big role in readability. Some fonts, along with their size and color, may boost reading speed, while others slow readers down or make the text feel like a visual obstacle course. A few fonts are nearly illegible by design. In fact, the chaotic, tangled logos favored by many death and black metal bands are meant to be difficult to decipher, an aesthetic choice that helps keep them underground and outside the reach of the mainstream music industry.

Research suggests that certain fonts, like the ever-reliable Times New Roman or Arial, may be more readable than others. But overall, the results are mixed. There's no one-size-fits-all solution when it comes to font choice. With over 200,000 fonts in existence, individual preferences and reading differences make a big impact. Some typefaces, particularly serif fonts with decorative strokes, can be more challenging for people with learning disabilities. For readers with dyslexia, who often experience letter reversals, slower reading speeds, and trouble with comprehension, sans serif fonts tend to be more accessible. (We'll return to this topic in more detail in the next chapter.)

So, how fast do we actually read? Eye-tracking studies reveal that children read more slowly than adults, as we'd expect. Seven- to eight-year-olds average around 95 words per minute, while eleven- to twelve-year-olds reach about 200 words per minute. Younger readers tend to fixate on words more often and for longer, but with age and practice, they become faster and more efficient at recognizing words and understanding what they read. For adults, the average reading speed hovers around 200 to 250 words per minute. As we age, though, our reading pace tends to slow down slightly, about 10 percent every decade after our forties. This decline is completely normal and doesn't necessarily affect comprehension.

Speed-reading programs promise to supercharge our reading rates; some even claim you can reach 10,000 words per minute, enough to breeze through this entire book in under ten minutes! But the truth is, these claims are wildly exaggerated. While it's possible to skim or scan a text more quickly, true reading, where we fully process and retain meaning, can't be rushed without sacrificing comprehension. So, while it might be tempting to believe in miracle methods, these programs usually promise more than they deliver.

Just as ambiguity in speech can slow comprehension, ambiguity in writing can trip up our reading. Readers make split-second judgments about whether a sentence makes sense, and when it doesn't, the brain has to slam on the brakes. Consider the sentence "We painted the wall with cracks." At first glance, it sounds like we used cracks as our painting tool. These kinds of sentences are known as *garden path sentences* because they lead the reader down a seemingly straightforward path, only to pull a sharp turn and force a rethinking of the whole thing. The confusion comes from a temporary ambiguity: We expect one structure, but the sentence turns out to mean something else entirely. The previous example makes more sense rewritten as "We painted the wall that had cracks in it," but English often allows us to drop words like *that* while still sounding correct ... at least, until we hit a dead end.

Another famously confounding example is "The old man the boat." (which, let's be honest, sounds like a rejected Hemingway title). At first, it feels like something's missing, maybe a verb? But here's the twist: *old* is a noun meaning "old people," and *man* is the verb, as in "to staff" or "operate." So, in plain terms, the sentence means: *The old people crew the boat.* There are plenty of other notorious examples, like "The horse raced past the barn fell" and "The prime number few," phrases that seem nonsensical until you unravel their grammar. Garden path sentences remind us just how much linguistic heavy lifting our brains do behind the scenes – and how fragile, flexible, and endlessly fascinating language really is.

Talking to Ourselves

Now that we know *how* we read, how do we actually make sense of what we're reading? Just like understanding speech, reading involves recognizing sounds and words. Fluent readers can identify written words quickly and with little effort. As we read, clusters of letters automatically trigger stored sounds and meanings in our short-term memory. This process is partly responsible for that "inner voice" many of us hear as we read silently, a phenomenon known as *subvocalization*, where we mentally pronounce or "hear" each word. Most people subvocalize, regardless of their native language. Interestingly, Deaf readers do this too, though instead of an inner voice, they may make subtle hand movements tied to sign language during silent reading.

Understanding written language, like spoken language, draws on a combination of bottom-up and top-down processes. When we're learning to read, or encountering new material, we rely more on bottom-up processing: starting from individual sounds, building up to syllables, then words, phrases, sentences, and overall meaning. It's like assembling a jigsaw puzzle piece by piece. Our inner voice plays a role here too, helping keep earlier letters in mind as we decode the full word. And when we stumble upon unfamiliar terms, like *quinoa, agave, paradigm*, or *macabre*, our brains often attempt a phonemic approximation, sounding them out based on letter patterns and prior knowledge.

Top-down reading processes rely on our prior knowledge, context, and expectations to interpret meaning, rather than starting with the letters and words themselves. A classic demonstration of this is the *Stroop Effect*. In this well-known task, participants are shown a list of color words, like *blue, yellow*, or *green*, but the ink color doesn't match the word's meaning. For example, the word *blue* might appear in red ink, or *yellow* in green. The challenge? Say the *color* of the ink, not the word. This seemingly simple task becomes surprisingly tricky. People slow down, stumble, and make more mistakes when the word and ink color don't match.

Why? Because top-down processing kicks in automatically. Our brains are so primed to read words that the act of reading interferes with our ability to name the ink color. It's cognitively easier to read the word than to override that instinct and focus on the visual feature. A variation of the Stroop task is used in clinical psychology to explore emotional processing. In these tests, participants are shown emotionally charged words like *pain, grief,* or *kill,* alongside neutral words such as *clock, sky,* or *window.* People tend to be slower to name the ink color of the negative words, suggesting that emotional content grabs our attention and disrupts cognitive control.

Relying on past knowledge can speed up interpretation and decision-making, but it can also lead us astray. One striking example is the *Mandela Effect,* a term coined for instances when large groups of people collectively misremember facts or events. It's named after the widespread false memory that Nelson Mandela died in prison during the 1980s, when in fact he lived until 2013, passing away at the age of 95, decades after his release.

These memory glitches show up in spelling and reading, too. A famous case involves the beloved children's books and cartoon series *The Berenstain Bears.* Many fans, some of them quite adamant, recall the name being spelled *Berenstein,* not *Berenstain.* They insist the name must have changed somewhere along the way. But it didn't. This confusion may stem from the fact that *-stein* is a much more common surname ending (derived from the Yiddish word for "stone," *-stein* was often used to describe someone who lived on rocky land). Our brains, shaped by pattern and familiarity, tend to "correct" what we see into something that fits our expectations, even when it's wrong.

Another common example of the Mandela Effect is the way many people misremember the title of the animated show *Looney Tunes* as *Looney Toons.* The mix-up makes sense. After all, the characters are cartoons, but the original title is actually a play on "tunes," highlighting the show's quirky music and sound effects. Our brains tend to favor the version that feels more familiar or logical, even if it's not correct. The same mental shortcut explains why we often miss typos, especially the ones lurking in emails we've already sent. Our brains don't read every letter; they anticipate what *should* be there and "autocorrect" as we go. This mental efficiency frees up resources for the more demanding task of extracting meaning and making connections. A similar phenomenon explains how we can read jumbled words surprisingly well. This effect, often playfully referred to as Typoglycemia, demonstrates how context and word shape help us process even heavily misspelled text. Just take a look at this now-famous example:

> Aoccdrnig to rscheearch at Cmabrigde Uinervtisy, it deosn't mttaer in waht oredr the ltteers in a wrod are, the olny iprmoetnt tihng is taht the frist and lsat ltteer be at the rghit pclae. The rset can be a toatl mses and you can sitll raed it wouthit porbelm. Tihs is bcuseae the huamn mnid deos not raed ervey lteter by istlef, but the wrod as a wlohe.

If you're having trouble reading this, here is the spoiler.

> According to research at Cambridge University, it doesn't matter in what order the letters in a word are, the only important thing is that the first and last letter be at the right place. The rest can be a total mess and you can still read it without problem. This is because the human mind does not read every letter by itself but the word as a whole.

You've probably come across this classic internet tidbit, it's been circulating for decades: "It doesn't matter in what order the letters in a word are, as long as the first and last letters are correct." At first glance, the claim feels convincing. After all, you can read it, right? But while there's a kernel of truth here, the reality is far more nuanced. The meme may have roots in a piece of doctoral research from the 1970s, which found that scrambling the internal letters of words had surprisingly little impact on the reading performance of skilled readers. Still, the meme's sweeping conclusion, that internal letter order doesn't matter, is misleading. Skilled reading doesn't rely solely on the first and last letters of a word. Nor do readers process each letter in strict sequence. Instead, we recognize patterns by analyzing how letters relate to one another within the word. Word recognition draws on whole-word processing, including the shape of the word itself.

This is why text with irregular casing, like AlTeRnAtInG CaPs, is so hard to read: It disrupts the visual contour of the word, even when the correct letters are present. The same principle explains why "ransom note" fonts, cobbled together from mismatched newspaper clippings, are so visually jarring. (This style wasn't just an aesthetic choice; it was originally used to disguise handwriting and obscure the identity of the author.) Popularized by author William S. Burroughs in the 1950s as a literary cut-up technique, this disjointed typographic style was later adopted by the punk band the Sex Pistols in the 1970s, whose visual anarchy captured the spirit of chaos and rebellion.

Not all scrambled sentences are as readable as the viral meme might suggest. Consider the following example: It technically follows the "rules," with the first and last letters of each word in place, but the result is still a jumble of gibberish.

> Salhal I cmorape tehe to a srmmeus day
> Tohu art mroe llvoey and mroe ttreemape
> Rguoh wdnis do skhae the dlinrag bdus of may
> And sremums lsaee htah all too sroht a dtae

In fact, this is the opening stanza of Shakespeare's famous *Sonnet 18*, one of the most iconic and widely recognized passages in the English language.

> Shall I compare thee to a summer's day?
> Thou art more lovely and more temperate
> Rough winds do shake the darling buds of May,
> And summer's lease hath all too short a date

So why isn't the internet meme as difficult to read as it should be? It turns out the author likely tweaked the text to make it easier to decode. Many of the words are short, which means fewer possible letter combinations and less mental effort. Words like *you* and *can* remain unchanged, and of the sixty-eight words in the passage, nearly half – thirty-one – are still in their original form. When four-letter words are altered, it's usually by swapping the middle two letters: *wrod* for *word*, *raed* for *read*, a minimal disruption that barely slows us down. Function words such as *and* and *but* are typically left untouched, which helps preserve the sentence structure and supports our ability to predict what's coming next. Even when longer words are altered, the transpositions are often adjacent (*porbelm* for *problem*), which is far easier to decipher than non-adjacent swaps like *pborlem*. In some cases, the scrambled versions even retain the original sound: *oredr* for *order*, *toatl* for *total*, which may further support recognition.

Importantly, none of the jumbled words form other real or plausible words, like swapping *salt* for *slat*, which would be more likely to trip us up. And because the passage is highly predictable, readers can lean on context to fill in the gaps, just as we do when processing distorted or noisy speech. Still, jumbled text doesn't go unnoticed. Even with these helpful cues, our reading speed slows when the internal letters of words are rearranged. Today, computer programs can scramble and unscramble text with remarkable ease. This comes as no surprise, given that machines vastly outperform humans when it comes to solving anagrams.

Putting Pen to Paper

As discussed in previous chapters, writing is a relatively recent development in human history. From its origins in clay tablets etched with reed styluses to the invention of the printing press and, more recently, digital communication via silicon chips, writing technologies have transformed dramatically. Today, writing may have surpassed speech as our dominant mode of communication. We increasingly rely on the written word in daily life, in emails, text messages, social media, e-books, and yet literacy remains unevenly distributed across the globe. Hundreds of millions of people are still unable to read or write, and in the United States alone, over 20 percent of adults are illiterate, with an additional forty-five million considered functionally illiterate, reading below a fifth-grade level.

While illiteracy now carries a strong social stigma, this wasn't always the case. Even a century ago, significant portions of the populations in industrialized nations were unable to read or write. Historically, literacy conferred power and privilege, restricted to an elite class of professionals. In ancient Mesopotamia, scribes (almost exclusively men) held a monopoly on written knowledge. During the Middle Ages, literacy remained the domain of the clergy, monks, and educated aristocrats (again, predominantly male). Encouragingly, literacy rates have risen steadily over time, with the most dramatic gains occurring in the twentieth century, a testament to the growing democratization of knowledge.

In many respects, writing is the mirror image of reading. While reading involves decoding written symbols into sounds and meanings, writing requires the conversion of spoken language into visual form. Unlike speaking, which emerges naturally through exposure, both reading and writing demand explicit instruction and sustained practice. As we've seen, they are developmental processes, with proficiency unfolding gradually over time. Writing, in particular, is a slower, more effortful activity than speaking or even reading. It is also less instinctive, acquired only after speech, and dependent on fine motor control that develops later in childhood. Most children don't begin forming recognizable letters until around age four or five. Yet, once mastered, writing becomes nearly as automatic as speaking. Crucially, however, written language is not merely spoken language captured on the page. As we explored in Chapter 2, writing takes on a life of its own, shaping not just how we communicate, but how we think about language itself.

In the previous chapter, we examined how children acquire the ability to write. Now, we turn to the cognitive architecture underlying the act itself. Writing is far from a simple mechanical task, it is a complex and cognitively demanding activity that requires the seamless integration of linguistic knowledge, mental planning, and fine motor control. Writers must coordinate multiple processes simultaneously, even when producing a short piece of text. At its core, writing typically involves three key stages: planning, translating, and reviewing. Planning entails generating ideas and organizing them into a coherent structure. Translating involves converting those ideas into language, choosing words, forming sentences, and applying appropriate punctuation. Reviewing is the stage of refinement, where we revise for grammar and spelling but also evaluate the clarity, tone, and logical flow of the text. These processes unfold recursively rather than linearly, and together they underpin everything from tapping out a quick text message to crafting a novel. Of course, disruptions can occur at any point in this process, whether through momentary lapses like typos and unclear phrasing, or more persistent challenges such as writer's block, or even the literal strain of writer's cramp.

It was once thought that writing was governed by a single, dedicated region of the brain, so-called *Exner's area*. Today, however, we understand that writing, like language more broadly, is the product of a dynamic interplay among multiple brain regions. The act of writing draws on a distributed neural network, integrating cognitive, linguistic, and motor functions. The frontal lobe plays a key role in planning and decision-making, laying the groundwork for what we intend to express. The hippocampus retrieves long-term memories, allowing us to summon past experiences and translate them into narrative. Broca's area contributes to the production of written language, while Wernicke's area supports comprehension and revision, helping us assess the coherence of what we've written. The visual cortex assists by interpreting letter shapes and guiding hand movements, translating visual patterns into motor commands. The motor cortex executes those commands, enabling us to grip a pen, form letters, or tap keys in the correct sequence. Even the caudate nucleus, part of the basal ganglia involved in habit formation and procedural memory, plays a role. Highly active in experienced writers (and in skilled musicians), it facilitates practiced, fluent performance, yet remains largely dormant in novices. This pattern underscores a crucial point: Writing becomes more efficient and automatic with practice, as the brain gradually optimizes the circuitry that supports it.

Writing places significant demands on our working memory, a core component of executive function that manages the mental resources needed for tasks we are actively performing. Working memory acts as a mental workspace, temporarily holding information such as a new phone number, a set of directions, or a shopping list. In the context of writing, it allows us to juggle multiple processes at once: organizing ideas, recalling how to spell a word, and constructing grammatically sound sentences, all while keeping our overarching message in mind.

However, this system has its limits. On average, adults can retain about six or seven pieces of information in working memory for roughly thirty seconds. That is, unless that information is rehearsed and committed into long-term memory. Long-term memory, with its vast and durable capacity, supports writing by supplying stored knowledge, such as vocabulary, grammar rules, and topic-specific content. Writing also plays a central role in learning. As literacy rates have increased, so too has the complexity of our language. Written texts tend to use longer words and more noun-heavy constructions, and this lexical and syntactic complexity often carries over into speech. In this way, writing not only reflects our language but also shapes and enriches it.

Writing is not only a cognitive and linguistic activity, it is also a technical skill shaped by motor coordination and physical practice. Each person's handwriting is distinct, even among genetically identical individuals like twins. This individuality is influenced by a range of factors, including fine motor skills, physical characteristics, and aesthetic preferences such as letter formation, spacing, and slant. In the digital age, typing has introduced its own variation in writing technique. Some people rely on the slow and deliberate "hunt-and-peck" method, while others employ professional touch typing or the thumb-based input common on smartphones. Typing is typically much faster than handwriting: The average person types between 40 and 80 words per minute, whereas handwriting speeds generally range from 5 to 20 words per minute. Handwriting speed also varies with age. Children tend to write slowly, young adults write more quickly and legibly, and older adults often experience a decline in speed and precision. Interestingly, research shows that people write faster when copying existing text than when composing their own, and that writing with a pen tends to be faster than writing with a pencil.

Researchers have found that the relative ease of typing on digital devices may actually accelerate reading and writing development in young children, as it places fewer physical demands on developing motor skills. Handwriting, by contrast, is often viewed as slower and more laborious. Although global literacy continues to rise, handwriting proficiency appears to be in decline in our increasingly digital world. Fewer people today possess strong penmanship, and cursive writing in particular is fast becoming a lost art, used mainly in signatures, though even these are now frequently replaced by digital alternatives. A moment of nostalgia for the handwritten word is captured in an episode of *Seinfeld*, when Uncle Leo fondly recalls Jerry's childhood penmanship: "When he was younger, he had a beautiful penmanship. I used to encourage him to print. I remember your 'V.' It was like a perfect triangle." Despite its waning cultural prominence, handwriting offers cognitive benefits that typing does not. Studies show that writing by hand enhances long-term memory consolidation, improving both recall and word recognition. The act of handwriting engages the brain more deeply, supporting cognitive development, learning, and memory in ways that typing alone may not fully replicate. It's a reminder that even in a digital age, there is enduring value in the written word formed by hand.

The Last Word

In this chapter, we've explored how adults use and understand language in its many forms, from speaking and listening to reading and writing. These skills do not operate in isolation; rather, they interact in dynamic and reciprocal ways, shaping and reinforcing one another.

We've focused primarily on typical language use in adults without language disorders, highlighting the remarkable variability in language processing, from differences in vocabulary size to reading speed and expressive fluency. While these abilities can be honed with practice, they are also subject to change over the lifespan, often declining with age. We've also examined the everyday slips and errors that occur in speech, revealing the complex mental processes that underlie even our most routine acts of communication.

Having considered typical language use, we now turn to its breakdown. What happens when language is impaired, disrupted, or lost?

5

How Do We Lose Language?

In the previous chapter, we explored how language typically works: how we speak, listen, read, and write when everything functions as expected. In this chapter, we turn to the other side of that story: What happens when language breaks down. These are not the everyday slips or typos we've already covered, but deeper disruptions caused by disability, neurological disorder, brain injury, and other factors that interfere with our ability to produce and understand language. In the United States alone, an estimated 5 to 10 percent of the population are affected by communication disorders. These numbers are even higher when we consider learning difficulties such as dyslexia. Altogether, this represents millions of individuals navigating the world with language systems that differ markedly from the norm.

This chapter examines how both developmental and acquired disorders can disrupt language processing and production. These disruptions span a broad spectrum, from the involuntary swearing tics associated with Tourette's Syndrome to the fragmented, incoherent speech patterns seen in Wernicke's aphasia and schizophrenia. We also consider alternative forms of communication, including sign languages and the ingenious methods used by figures like Helen Keller and Stephen Hawking to connect with the world. Along the way, we explore language gone awry in pop culture and historical case studies, from Joe Biden's lifelong experience with stuttering to Winston Churchill's pronounced lisp. We'll uncover why Vladimir Lenin could utter only a single word in the final months of his life, speculate on what may have driven Lewis Carroll to pen over 98,000 letters (some scrawled in complete darkness) and reflect on how Beethoven continued to compose masterpieces even after losing his hearing entirely.

Through clinical cases, historical figures, and alternative communication methods, we consider what happens when language falters, and the remarkable ways people adapt when it does.

Tan tan, vot vot, and Cré nom!

As we've seen, everyone occasionally slips up when speaking: mixing up words, forgetting names, or mispronouncing something mid-sentence. But when these errors become frequent and affect a wide range of language, words, names, numbers, it may signal something more serious: aphasia. Just in the United States, around two million people live with this condition, making it one of the most common language disorders. Aphasia can impair the ability to speak, understand speech, read, or write, depending on which areas of the brain are affected, typically those on the left side that govern language.

The causes of aphasia are varied, including strokes, brain trauma, seizures, tumors, or degenerative neurological conditions. And while the term "aphasia" is modern, descriptions of the condition go back thousands of years. The earliest known reference appears in the Edwin Smith Surgical Papyrus, an ancient Egyptian medical text dating to around 1700 BCE. Acquired by American Egyptologist Edwin Smith in 1862, this remarkable document is the oldest known surgical treatise, and the first to use the word "brain." Among its forty-eight case studies is one that seems to describe aphasia: Case 20 details a man with a severe head injury, "a gaping wound in the temporal bone," likely caused by a spear in battle. He's described as "speechless," with neck stiffness and an inability to respond to commands, symptoms that suggest a severe form of aphasia, possibly global aphasia, which affects both speech production and comprehension. Today, we recognize many different types of aphasia, each linked to specific areas of the brain and resulting in distinct patterns of language disruption. Understanding these patterns not only helps clinicians diagnose and treat patients. It also sheds light on how complex and distributed the language system truly is.

Perhaps the most famous case of aphasia is that of Louis Victor Leborgne, better known by his nickname, "Tan." After a series of epileptic seizures in his twenties, Leborgne spent the last twenty-one years of his life confined to Bicêtre Hospital near Paris. He earned the name "Tan" because that was the only word he could say, typically uttered twice in succession, *tan tan*, often accompanied by a wave of his hand. Some have speculated that this odd remnant of speech may have been influenced by his hometown of Moret-sur-Loing, a region known for its tanneries. On rare occasions, especially when agitated, Tan could blurt out a swear word or two. Otherwise, he communicated entirely through gestures. Despite his severe expressive limitations, Tan's comprehension remained intact. He understood everything said to him; he simply couldn't respond with language. But his health continued to decline. Recurrent seizures left him paralyzed on his right side, and he eventually became bedridden. In his final days, gangrene developed in his leg, and he lost the ability to speak altogether; even his familiar *tan tan* fell silent.

In 1861, during Tan's final days, he was transferred to the surgical ward at Bicêtre Hospital and came under the care of neurologist and surgeon Pierre Paul Broca. Broca conducted a detailed examination and concluded that, despite Tan's profound speech limitations, his intellect was intact and there were no signs of head trauma. When Tan died shortly after, Broca performed an autopsy and made a striking discovery: a large lesion, described as the size of a chicken's egg, in the left frontal lobe, specifically in the inferior frontal gyrus.

Just a few months later, Broca encountered another patient, Lazare Lelong, who exhibited a remarkably similar condition. Lelong could only utter five words: *oui* ("yes"), *non* ("no"), *toujours* ("always"), *Lelo* (a distorted version of his name), and *toi* (his approximation of "trois," or "three," which he used for all numbers). Like Tan, Lelong retained strong comprehension despite his limited expressive language. After Lelong's death, Broca examined his brain and found a lesion in the same region as Tan's. From these two cases, Broca proposed a groundbreaking idea: that this particular area of the left frontal lobe was essential for language production. He initially called the condition *aphemie*, though it would later become known as Broca's aphasia in his honor. Today, Broca's findings are considered foundational in neurolinguistics. In fact, Tan's preserved brain is still on display at Sorbonne University's medical museum, a physical reminder of one of the most influential discoveries in the history of language and the brain.

Several notable historical figures are believed to have experienced Broca's aphasia, including Vladimir Ilyich Ulyanov, better known to the world as Lenin. By 1921, the head of the Soviet state was suffering from chronic headaches, insomnia, and fainting spells, all early warning signs of the ischemic strokes that would soon follow. These strokes, caused by blocked blood flow to the brain, deprive neurons of oxygen and nutrients, often leading to lasting damage. Like Tan before him, Lenin became paralyzed on his right side and exhibited signs of aphasia that worsened with each successive stroke.

Once a fiery orator, revolutionary theorist, and architect of the October Rebellion, Lenin eventually lost the ability to speak coherently. At his worst, he could say little more than *vot vot*. (Depending on the Russian translation, this can mean "That's it!" while a single *vot* might mean "here" or "there," depending on the context.) His wife, Nadezhda Krupskaya, tried to reintroduce language from the ground up, starting with children's ABC books. When this failed, she developed a system of communication cards marked with letters and key vocabulary. Through pointing, Lenin was still able to express basic ideas, words like "congress," "people," and "revolution," suggesting that his comprehension remained largely intact. Meanwhile, Soviet propaganda worked hard to maintain an illusion of stability. Carefully staged photographs showed Lenin at his home in Gorki reading newspapers and meeting with Joseph Stalin. But the truth was quite different: His health was deteriorating rapidly, and he never returned to political life. When he died in 1924 at the age of fifty-three, an autopsy revealed widespread atherosclerosis in his cerebral arteries. The condition was likely hereditary; his father had also died of a stroke at the same age.

Charles Baudelaire, the nineteenth-century French poet, suffered a stroke in his forties that affected the left hemisphere of his brain, leaving him paralyzed and severely aphasic. During his celebrated career, Baudelaire coined the term *modernité* and authored the acclaimed *Les Fleurs du Mal* (*The Flowers of Evil*), a landmark of French literature. But after his stroke, he was reduced to repeating a single phrase: *Cré nom!*, a blasphemous expletive roughly translated as "God damn" or "holy shit." This habit was, understandably, distressing to the nuns caring for him during his final years in a convent.

Researchers have proposed two theories as to why this particular phrase persisted. It may have been the last thing he said before the stroke, or the first thing he was able to say afterward. Though aphasia robbed him of language, it wasn't what killed him. Baudelaire died at forty-six, likely from complications of syphilis contracted in his youth. In his final days, Baudelaire's friend and biographer Charles Asselineau described the poet's condition: "He continued to take an interest in the conversations that went on at the foot of his bed, and took part in them only by making small signs with his head or his eyelids. Whenever you looked his way, you found his eye intelligent and attentive, though darkened by an expression of infinite sadness, which those who glimpsed it will never forget." It was a deeply tragic ending for a man whose life and legacy were built on the power of words.

A unifying thread across the cases of Leborgne, Lenin, and Baudelaire is the presence of speech automatisms or verbal stereotypes, like *tan tan*, *vot vot*, and *Cré nom!* These are involuntary, repetitive utterances that carry little to no contextual meaning. They emerge spontaneously and persistently, often to the speaker's frustration, and are seen in up to 20 percent of individuals with chronic aphasia. Both Broca's aphasia and global aphasia fall under the category of non-fluent or expressive aphasias. In these conditions, speech is effortful, halting, and grammatically simplified, if it is possible at all. People with these forms of aphasia often know exactly what they want to say but cannot access or produce the necessary words or sounds. Their ability to comprehend language, however, is typically preserved, which makes the experience all the more frustrating.

One particularly revealing case is that of "Brother John," a French monk with epilepsy who experienced transient aphasia during his grand mal seizures. During these episodes, lasting from minutes to several hours, he became incapable of speaking coherently and, at times, writing as well. Yet his thinking remained intact. Even while aphasic, Brother John could navigate his surroundings, recognize familiar objects, follow complex instructions, use tools, and perform both simple and advanced mathematical calculations. What he lost, however, was his inner speech; his internal monologue seemed to go silent. Still, once the episode passed, he could recall and describe what had happened with clarity. His case powerfully illustrates the distinction between language and thought: While language may falter, the mind can remain fully active beneath the surface.

Seizures, strokes, neurological conditions, and other forms of brain trauma can sometimes lead to a rare and curious phenomenon known as *foreign accent syndrome*. This speech disorder causes a sudden and involuntary shift in pronunciation, rhythm, and intonation, so much so that a person is perceived to be speaking with a "foreign" accent, even though they haven't acquired a new language or dialect. One striking example involved British pop star George Michael. After surviving a severe case of pneumonia and spending three weeks in a coma, he awoke to discover that his familiar North London accent had been replaced by a pronounced West Country twang. No matter how hard he tried, he couldn't shake the new accent, until, to his relief, it vanished three days later. Michael jokingly attributed the shift to *Nighty Night*, a dark British comedy he'd been watching with a friend just before falling ill.

The condition's most famous case is that of "Astrid," a Norwegian woman injured during World War II when bomb shrapnel struck her head. After recovering, she was left speaking with what sounded like a strong German accent. In the context of the war, this made her a target of suspicion and social exclusion from her own community. While foreign accent syndrome remains extremely rare, over a hundred cases have been documented in medical literature. Reported changes include shifts from British English to "French," American English to "British," Spanish to "Hungarian," and Japanese to "Korean." In some instances, the condition resolves on its own. In others, the altered accent persists, depending on the location and extent of the brain damage. (We'll revisit this phenomenon in the next chapter when we explore what happens when people learn entirely new languages.)

Fully under the jimjam

Aphasia isn't limited to Broca's area, it can arise in other regions of the brain as well. Broca's area is connected by a neural pathway to another key language center known as Wernicke's area. Damage to this region results in Wernicke's aphasia, also called receptive or fluent aphasia. Unlike Broca's aphasia, individuals with Wernicke's aphasia can speak fluently and with normal grammar and intonation, but their speech often lacks meaning or coherence, making it difficult for others to understand.

This less common form of aphasia was first identified in 1874 by German neurologist Carl Wernicke. He observed a stroke patient who could hear and speak yet was unable to understand spoken language or read written words. After the patient's death, Wernicke examined his brain and found a lesion in the posterior superior temporal gyrus of the left hemisphere, near the auditory cortex. He concluded that this area must be essential for language comprehension, a hypothesis that would later be validated and honored by naming the region after him.

In most people, Wernicke's area is located in the left hemisphere, particularly in those with left-hemisphere language dominance. However, in rare cases, often among left-handed individuals, it can appear on the right side of the brain. As we've seen, language processing is now understood to rely on distributed networks across both hemispheres, not just one localized spot. (As a side note of interest, researchers of Genie, the so-called "wild child," theorized that she was using her right hemisphere to acquire language, since the language center in her left hemisphere appeared underdeveloped, possibly due to extreme early deprivation.)

People with Wernicke's aphasia typically speak with ease, their speech flows smoothly, with normal intonation, rhythm, and grammar. But while it *sounds* fluent, it's often incomprehensible. They may produce long, grammatically correct sentences that make little or no sense, what clinicians often describe as jargon or "word salad." In one study, a clinician asked a patient, "Tell me where you live." The patient replied, "Well, it's a meender place and it has two … two of them. For dreaming and pinding after supper. And up and down. Four of down and three of up." When asked, "What's the weather like today?" the patient answered, "Fully under the jimjam and on the altigrabber." As these surreal examples show, people with Wernicke's aphasia often create neologisms, made-up words like *pinding, jimjam,* or *altigrabber.*

They also struggle with word retrieval and may substitute one word for another. For example, someone might say "table" when they mean "chair," or swap one sound for another, saying "fox" instead of "box." In more extreme cases, the substituted word may have no apparent connection at all, like saying "apple" instead of "house." These errors, known as *paraphasias*, can also occur in Broca's aphasia. Vladimir Lenin, for example, once attempted to say "lemon" but could only produce the word "rose," to his great frustration.

A key difference is that people with Broca's aphasia are usually aware of their errors, whereas those with Wernicke's aphasia often aren't. They may be completely unaware that their speech doesn't make sense, which can create distress when others struggle to understand them. On top of that, their ability to comprehend spoken language is also impaired. Living with Wernicke's aphasia has been compared to attending a party where everyone else is speaking a foreign language, except it's happening every day.

Wernicke's aphasia is sometimes mistaken for other conditions that also affect language. While aphasia is a neurological disorder and schizophrenia a psychiatric one, they can share strikingly similar speech patterns. In both, individuals may produce word salad, disorganized, incoherent speech, because they struggle to express their thoughts clearly. Difficulties with word retrieval, along with sound or word substitutions, can occur in both disorders, which sometimes complicates diagnosis.

Aphasia is also a common symptom of Alzheimer's disease and other forms of dementia. In these cases, patients may have trouble finding the right words, speaking in full sentences, or understanding what others are saying. One specific type, *primary progressive aphasia* (PPA), involves a gradual breakdown of language skills over time and is often associated with neuro-degenerative diseases like Alzheimer's. Primary progressive aphasia is linked to the shrinking of brain tissue in the frontal or temporal lobes and presents with symptoms such as misnaming familiar objects, mispronouncing words, slowed speech, and difficulty following conversations. Monty Python's Terry Jones is one well-known figure who suffered from PPA. He first suspected something was wrong when he began forgetting his lines, an early sign of a deeper language impairment. More recently, actor Bruce Willis also retired from public life after being diagnosed with aphasia, which eventually progressed into frontotemporal dementia. At first, it affected his ability to memorize scripts; later, it severely compromised his ability to speak at all.

The scribe of the Edwin Smith Surgical Papyrus concluded that aphasia was an incurable condition, "not to be treated," they wrote. Still, they recommended what we might call comfort care: applying "grease" (likely an ointment or animal fat) and pouring milk into both ears. Today, although there is still no cure for aphasia, treatment options have come a long way. Speech therapy remains the most effective intervention, helping to restore or rebuild language skills through targeted exercises. Repetition can aid word retrieval and fluency, while word association tasks help reconnect meanings to the words themselves. Some people, particularly young children and adolescents, may recover language abilities spontaneously, even after severe brain injury.

But for most, recovery is gradual and requires therapy, especially in the first few months after onset. Actor Kirk Douglas was eighty when he had a stroke that left him speaking only gibberish. With the help of speech therapy, he relearned how to communicate and eventually returned to acting, continuing his career well into old age. He passed away at 103, having regained not only his voice, but his audience.

The Cursing Marquise

Charles Baudelaire's accidental exclamation of *Cré nom!* is reminiscent of coprolalia, the involuntary outburst of obscene or taboo language. While it's often exaggerated in pop culture portrayals of Tourette's Syndrome, coprolalia is rare, affecting only about 10 percent of people with the condition. The disorder was first described in 1885 by French neurologist Georges Gilles de la Tourette, who gave his name to the syndrome and famously documented the case of Ernestine Émilie Prondre de Guermantes, the Marquise de Dampierre. The Marquise, an aristocrat of impeccable breeding but unpredictable tongue, became known as "the cursing Marquise" for her habit of erupting into shocking verbal tirades. Her tics included sudden jarring cries of *merde!* ("shit!") and *foutu cochon!* ("fucking pig!"), all delivered without warning in the refined salons of Paris. She had been married off young, a conventional (and futile) treatment for what was then labeled "hysteria." Her symptoms persisted, culminating in a notorious episode at an imperial ceremony. As the Marquise was about to receive a medal before Napoleon himself (she was a royalist), she launched into a thunderous string of insults and barking noises so memorable that witnesses were said to recall them vividly decades later.

Coprolalia isn't simply swearing, it's a form of verbal tic, often targeting taboo topics like sex, excrement, or body parts, and it's usually just as distressing to the person saying the words as to those hearing them. By all accounts, the Marquise was a respectable and educated woman, deeply ashamed of her outbursts. As the pressure to conform to social decorum became unbearable, she eventually withdrew from public life, living out her final years in solitude and dying in her eighties.

Coprolalia is often misunderstood as a deliberate attempt to shock or seek attention. In reality, these swearing tics are involuntary and uncontrollable. They occur automatically, driven by neurological signals in the brain that cannot be consciously suppressed. The buildup to a tic has been likened to the sensation of an oncoming sneeze, trying to hold it back only increases the tension until release is unavoidable. Tics may vanish for weeks or months, or they may intensify when a person is excited, anxious, tired, or angry, much like the Marquise de Dampierre, who, when confronted by Napoleon, erupted into swearing, screaming, and barking like a hound. People with Tourette's who don't experience coprolalia often exhibit similar, though less profane, vocal tics such as throat-clearing, coughing, grunting, gurgling, squeaking, screeching, or making animal noises.

Dr. Samuel Johnson, the author of one of the earliest English dictionaries, is now believed to have had Tourette's Syndrome, though not coprolalia, which is just as well, given his strong disapproval of foul language. Johnson experienced nearly constant compulsions, such as touching posts and carefully measuring his footsteps, along with a range of verbal tics. These unexpected behaviors often startled those meeting the revered writer for the first time. He was known to suddenly whistle, sigh, moan, and groan, and he frequently talked to himself in elaborate monologues, quoting poetry and scripture. He would repeat lines from the Lord's Prayer or fragments of Shakespeare, sometimes obsessively. Johnson also exhibited echolalia, the involuntary repetition of others' words. On one occasion, after snapping at his close friend, the diarist Hester Thrale, she gently replied, "Oh, dear good man!" Later, he was found curled in his armchair, half-asleep, whispering over and over again: "Oh, dear good man."

Echolalia is a hallmark of Tourette's Syndrome, but it also appears in conditions such as aphasia, schizophrenia, and autism spectrum disorder (ASD). We first encountered echolalia in Chapter 3, where we discussed it as part of both typical language development and autism in children. Among autistic individuals, echolalia often functions as a form of self-stimulation, or "stimming," and as a coping mechanism during sensory overload. Albert Einstein, who was a late talker, reportedly displayed echolalic tendencies throughout his life, frequently repeating phrases two or three times, especially when he found them amusing. As noted earlier, people on the autism spectrum may also speak in ways that sound flat, robotic, or monotonous. A well-known example is Elon Musk, who has publicly identified as autistic and is often noted for his speech's lack of significant tonal variation, a feature sometimes referred to as "flat affect." In response to overwhelming situations, changes in routine, or communication challenges, some autistic people may suddenly scream, cry, or make unexpected vocalizations. Others have limited verbal abilities, or may not speak at all.

Research also points to a connection between autism and stuttering, with a higher prevalence of stuttering observed in autistic children, and also in those with epilepsy. As we explored in Chapter 3, stuttering (or stammering) is a speech disorder marked by disruptions in the flow of speech, including repetitions, prolongations of sounds, syllables, or words, and silent blocks, moments when a person tries to speak but no sound emerges. Around one percent of the global population stutters, though its exact cause remains unclear. Beyond developmental stuttering, it can stem from genetic factors, neurological differences, or environmental triggers such as anxiety, fatigue, time pressure, or self-consciousness. Stuttering is far more common in children, many of whom outgrow it naturally, though for some, it persists into adulthood.

From an early age, Joe Biden struggled with a pronounced stutter, enduring ridicule and bullying as a result. In school, classmates in Latin class mockingly dubbed him "Joe Impedimenta," while others nicknamed him "Dash," likening his halting speech to Morse code. Determined to overcome the disorder, Biden spent years practicing poetry, particularly the works of Ralph Waldo Emerson and William Butler Yeats, reciting verses in front of a mirror for hours at a time. Despite his speech impediment, he went on to become the first US president with a history of chronic stuttering. His speech patterns have often been misinterpreted as signs of senility or cognitive decline, leading critics to brand him "Sleepy Joe."

In reality, these features are consistent with stuttering. People who stutter may pause, substitute words, or slow their speech deliberately, as speaking quickly can worsen their symptoms. They may also adopt subtle physical behaviors, like blinking, closing their eyes, nodding, or leg tapping, to help manage the flow of their speech.

Spanish Ships I Cannot See, for They Are Not in Sight

Stuttering is closely related to a lesser-known speech disorder called cluttering. Cluttering affects the rate and rhythm of speech, making it sound abnormally fast, jerky, or disorganized. Unlike stuttering, which involves a breakdown in the motor execution of speech, cluttering is more about thought organization than articulation. A person may speak before fully forming their thoughts, resulting in fragmented or jumbled speech. Cluttering can also involve repeating words or collapsing them, omitting sounds so that, for example, *communication* becomes "commcation." Unlike those who stutter, who are often acutely aware of their dysfluency (as in Joe Biden's case), individuals with cluttering are frequently unaware of their irregular speech patterns. Winston Churchill may have experienced either stuttering or cluttering, though we know with certainty that he had a lifelong lisp, making it difficult for him to pronounce /s/.

As discussed in Chapter 3, lisps can stem from structural issues in the mouth, dental irregularities, cleft palate, or even hearing loss. In his youth, Churchill consulted the eminent speech specialist Dr. Felix Semon, who advised that "practice and perseverance are alone necessary." Churchill took this advice to heart and was often heard rehearsing tongue-twisters to correct his lisp, particularly: "Spanish ships I cannot see, for they are not in sight." Despite his speech challenges, Churchill became a legendary orator and one of Britain's most celebrated prime ministers, leading the country through World War II. Known for his wit, he even deliberately mispronounced *Nazi* as "nah-zee" as a mocking jab at the enemy. His distinctive speech became so familiar to the British public that, when his articulation improved, he had a special pair of dentures made to preserve his lisp during radio broadcasts. These dentures reportedly needed frequent repairs. Churchill had a habit of hurling them across the room in fits of rage.

In his later years, Churchill suffered a series of strokes, one of which led to *ataxia*. This is a condition caused by damage to the cerebellum, the part of the brain responsible for balance, coordination, and voluntary muscle movement. The stroke left him with slurred speech and facial drooping on the left side for several months. His condition was carefully concealed from the public and media at the time, in an effort to maintain morale. Remarkably, Churchill regained most of his fluency within two months. During a major speech at a Margate conference in 1953, however, a few attendees noticed his slurred words and unsteady gait, but chalked it up to drink. (Churchill was famously fond of alcoholic beverages, particularly brandy, whiskey, and champagne.) A few months later, he suffered another stroke while addressing guests at No. 10 Downing Street. In total, Churchill experienced eight strokes, the final one leaving him unable to speak in the last weeks of his life. The causes of his multiple strokes are believed to include a combination of lifestyle factors and family history. In the end, Churchill was granted a state funeral, an honor rarely extended to non-royals, marking the passing of a figure who had come to symbolize British resilience.

Ataxia is not to be confused with the similarly named *apraxia*. Both are neurological conditions, but they affect different parts of the brain and manifest in distinct ways. Verbal apraxia, for instance, originates in the cerebrum, the large, wrinkled mass at the top of the brain, while ataxia stems from damage to the cerebellum, which, as we mentioned above, governs balance and coordination. Unlike ataxia, which involves the loss of controlled muscle movement, apraxia is not a muscular problem. The muscles of the lips, tongue, and jaw function normally, but individuals with apraxia struggle to coordinate them for speech. They know exactly what they want to say, but there's a disconnect between the brain's speech plan and the motor commands required to carry it out.

Symptoms of apraxia include difficulty imitating sounds, mispronouncing words, and omitting sounds altogether, often resulting in unclear or distorted speech. As discussed in Chapter 3, apraxia of speech is typically a developmental disorder diagnosed in children, although it can also be acquired by adults. As seen in the case studies above, apraxia is often associated with Broca's aphasia, in which the person retains the desire and intent to speak but cannot articulate the words. Fortunately, speech, occupational, and physical therapies can now help many individuals with these conditions significantly improve their ability to communicate.

Dysarthria is another type of motor speech disorder. It makes clear speech difficult due to weakness or dysfunction in the muscles of the mouth and face, as well as the nerves or brain regions involved in speech production. People with dysarthria may speak in a way that sounds slurred, slow, mumbled, whispered, or unusually soft, due to limited movement of the tongue, lips, and jaw. Because dysarthria can also affect the respiratory system, it may alter vocal quality, resulting in speech that sounds nasal, hoarse, stuffy, or breathy.

This condition can have a range of causes, including brain damage from a stroke, head injury, or tumor. It also commonly arises from neurodegenerative disorders such as Parkinson's disease, multiple sclerosis, and amyotrophic lateral sclerosis (ALS), better known as motor neuron disease or Lou Gehrig's disease. (The condition was named after the famed New York Yankees player who was forced to retire in the 1930s after developing the illness. Gehrig had previously earned the nickname "The Iron Horse" for his strength and stamina.)

Amyotrophic lateral sclerosis is a progressive, fatal disease in which motor neurons degenerate and die, leading to muscle weakness and eventual paralysis. Those with ALS often struggle with swallowing, breathing, and speaking. One of the most well-known individuals with the disease was physicist Stephen Hawking, who was diagnosed in his early twenties. Over time, ALS gradually paralyzed him and caused dysarthria, giving his speech a slurred and slowed quality. In his forties, Hawking underwent a life-saving tracheotomy, a surgical procedure that opens the windpipe to assist with breathing. As a result, he permanently lost his natural voice.

The Little Painter Fellow

Speech perception disorders interfere with the ability to understand what others are saying. As discussed earlier, Wernicke's area plays a key role in processing incoming language, whether spoken, written, or signed. When this region is damaged, as in Wernicke's aphasia, comprehension becomes impaired. While not technically classified as a speech disorder, schizophrenia is another condition that can profoundly affect speech perception. As mentioned above, some people with schizophrenia may produce disorganized speech or word salad, but they also often struggle to understand and interpret spoken language. These difficulties are linked to abnormalities in the brain's auditory processing systems. Affected individuals may have trouble following complex sentences or distinguishing speech from background noise.

One of the most striking speech perception disturbances in schizophrenia is auditory hallucination, the experience of hearing voices that aren't actually present. These voices might comment on the person's actions, issue commands, or speak directly to them. They may be male or female, familiar or unfamiliar, and might speak in a different language or accent. Some whisper or shout; others are accompanied by sounds like humming, screeching, or banging. Often, these voices are hostile or disturbing, urging the person to harm themselves or others. Schizophrenia exists on a spectrum, and while hallucinations are common, not everyone with the condition experiences them.

Some modern scholars have tentatively diagnosed Vincent van Gogh with schizophrenia. What's certain is that he experienced episodes of psychosis, seizures, hallucinations, and delusions, which he described as "unbearable." Once nicknamed *'t schildermenneke* ("the little painter fellow"), van Gogh found painting to be a therapeutic outlet for his psychiatric turmoil, though he was unable to work amid his most intense episodes. During a heated quarrel with fellow artist Paul Gauguin, van Gogh reportedly believed he heard a voice command: "Kill him!" He raised a razor to attack Gauguin, but at the last moment, turned the blade on himself. In the infamous act of self-mutilation that followed, van Gogh severed his left earlobe.

More recently, serial killer David Berkowitz, the notorious "Son of Sam," claimed that a dog's voice told him to kill. But hearing voices isn't always pathological. Research suggests that some people who regularly hear voices, yet live otherwise ordinary lives, may have brains that are especially tuned to detect patterns. In one study, these individuals were more likely to detect meaning in distorted sounds, ones that others didn't notice, and their brains showed increased activity in areas linked to attention and signal detection. This supports a growing theory known as *predictive processing*: the idea that the brain doesn't just take in the world, it actively predicts what it expects to find, shaping what we hear, see, and feel. For some, that means hearing voices in the noise. It's not necessarily a sign of mental illness but a fascinating glimpse into how powerful, and sometimes peculiar, the human brain really is.

Individuals with schizophrenia often experience auditory processing deficits, difficulties that also occur in auditory processing disorder (APD). This disorder affects the brain's ability to process and make sense of sounds, particularly in challenging environments like noisy rooms or when distinguishing between similar sounds. Importantly, APD is not a form of hearing loss; rather, it's a breakdown in how the brain interprets auditory information. Of course, hearing impairment and deafness can significantly impact both the use and understanding of spoken language. Without sufficient auditory input, whether from others or their own voice, Deaf individuals may have difficulty accurately producing speech sounds. Deafness also limits the ability to comprehend spoken language, even when assistive devices are used. Hearing loss can be inherited or arise from a variety of causes, including head trauma, aging, prolonged exposure to loud noise, or even certain chemicals.

Ludwig van Beethoven began to notice hearing difficulties in his mid-twenties, and by his forties, he was profoundly deaf. The exact cause of his deafness remains uncertain, but modern analysis of a preserved lock of his hair points to lead poisoning, likely from his habit of drinking wine contaminated with lead. (At the time, lead was commonly added to wine as a sweetener, preservative, and to enhance its flavor and color.) Today, we know that lead exposure can damage the auditory system and impair language processing.

Despite his deafness, Beethoven continued to communicate with friends, family, and colleagues, sometimes verbally, but increasingly through sketchbooks and pocket notebooks. Remarkably, his disability didn't halt his composing. He wrote music in his mind and committed it to paper, relying on innovative methods to "hear" through touch. He is said to have held a pencil in his mouth and pressed it against the piano to sense the vibrations of the notes. There's also evidence that he sawed the legs off his pianos, allowing the sound to resonate through the floor and into his body as he composed. By the time he wrote his iconic *Symphony No. 9*, Beethoven was completely deaf.

Rather than hearing language, many Deaf individuals primarily *see* it. They perceive language visually, often through lip reading or, more commonly, sign language. Instead of processing spoken words, they interpret meaning through hand movements, facial expressions, and body language. Some Deaf people report thinking in visual images or signs, much as hearing individuals might think in spoken words. How a Deaf person perceives and processes language depends on factors such as the age at which they lost their hearing, their early communication environment, and their exposure to sign language. (For a deeper discussion of how sign language is acquired, see Chapter 3.)

In Beethoven's case, there is no evidence that he knew or used sign language, unsurprising, given that it was not widely recognized or systematized during his lifetime. Nonetheless, sign languages had existed for centuries. The first book on the subject was published in 1620 by Juan Pablo de Bonet, and historical accounts suggest that Deaf people have used gestural communication since ancient times. We might remember that in *Cratylus*, Plato has Socrates remark that Deaf or nonverbal individuals "make signs with the hands, head, and the rest of the body," a striking early acknowledgment of visual language.

In Beethoven's time, deafness carried a significant social stigma, prompting many, Beethoven included, to conceal their hearing loss. Nearly a century later, in 1880, an international conference in Milan declared oral education superior to manual or sign-based instruction. This decision led to the widespread banning of sign language in Deaf schools, a devastating setback that affected the education, self-expression, and quality of life of Deaf individuals for generations. Progress came in the 1970s, when linguist William Stokoe provided compelling evidence that sign language is a fully developed language in its own right, complete with its own structure, grammar, vocabulary, and even regional dialects. Since then, sign languages have continued to evolve and gain recognition, finally earning their place alongside spoken languages. Today, sign language is not only used by Deaf individuals but also by their families, friends, and many others, including people with speech and language difficulties due to autism, Down syndrome, cerebral palsy, or aphasia.

The Little Bronco

Signing is language, though it also falls under the broader category of augmentative and alternative communication (AAC), the many ways people communicate beyond speech. This augmentation includes tools, devices, systems, and strategies that support or replace spoken language. These range from high-tech speech-generating devices to low-tech methods like Beethoven's notebooks, which he used for written conversations after losing his hearing, or the alphabet cards crafted by Lenin's wife so he could communicate following his debilitating strokes.

One of the most extraordinary examples of alternative communication is Helen Keller. Born in 1880, the same year as the Milan conference that banned sign language in schools, Keller became deaf and blind at just nineteen months old after a severe illness. While her family doctor called it "brain fever," modern historians suspect it was likely rubella, scarlet fever, or meningitis. As she was still a toddler, her language development hadn't advanced much beyond babbling and a few words. In her memoirs, Keller described the profound isolation of her early childhood, likening it to being alone "at sea in a dense fog."

As a toddler who couldn't see or hear, and understandably frustrated, Keller expressed herself through tantrums. She kicked and screamed, hurled objects, and struck those around her. Her unruly behavior earned her the nickname "the Little Bronco." Everything changed when she was seven years old and met a new teacher, Anne Sullivan, who would unlock the door to language. Sullivan was no stranger to alternative communication herself; she had contracted trachoma at age five, a painful eye disease that left her partially blind.

One day, she led Keller to a water pump, placed the child's hand under the stream, and spelled the word *water* into her other palm. The breakthrough was immediate. Within months, Keller had learned to fingerspell, and her vocabulary quickly expanded to hundreds of words and simple sentences. The two became lifelong companions. In time, Keller mastered multiple communication methods, including reading lips by touch, reading and writing in Braille and raised type, and even speaking aloud. She went on to become not only a symbol of perseverance but one of the most influential and tireless advocates for people with disabilities.

Assisted communication has come a long way. Today, modern assistive technologies include smartphone and tablet apps, eye-gaze systems, and speech-generating devices. When physicist Stephen Hawking developed motor neuron disease, he retained his vision and hearing, but gradually lost the ability to produce intelligible speech. His voice became slurred and nasal, and after his life-saving tracheotomy, he could no longer speak at all. To communicate, Hawking turned to technology. He began using "the Equalizer," a computer program that allowed him to select words and phrases on a screen. Mounted to his wheelchair, the system was operated via a hand switch, which fed selections into a speech synthesizer. Though the synthesized voice had an American accent, Hawking embraced it, saying he had grown to identify with it. Using his computer interface, he was able to browse the Internet, write emails, and compose speeches, all at a rate of roughly fifteen words per minute.

As Hawking's condition progressed, he eventually lost the use of his hands and was at risk of developing locked-in syndrome. This is a state of near-total paralysis in which a person remains fully conscious and able to think but is unable to move or speak, communicating only through eye movements. To maintain communication, Hawking began using a switch attached to his glasses that detected subtle movements in his cheek muscles. Later, he relied on raising his eyebrows and blinking to control his speech-generating device. An infrared sensor mounted on his glasses detected these blinks, enabling him to express up to ten words per minute. The system also incorporated eye-tracking technology, allowing him to "point" at items on a screen, and used predictive software that adapted to his writing style over time.

When Hawking was diagnosed with ALS at the age of twenty-one, doctors gave him only a few years to live. Yet he defied the odds, living to seventy-six, and never letting his disability define him. A celebrated scientist and public intellectual, Hawking authored ten books and published hundreds of academic papers throughout his remarkable career.

The Little Lion

Many conditions can affect not just speech production and processing, but reading as well. For people who are blind or visually impaired, reading typically relies on auditory or tactile alternatives, such as audiobooks, text-to-speech software, or Braille. Braille reading is generally slower than reading print, as it depends on tactile sensitivity to interpret raised dot patterns, making quick skimming difficult. On average, adults read Braille at about 70–100 words per minute, roughly a third the speed of print reading. However, some experienced readers can exceed 200 words per minute, and AI-powered Braille-reading robots can achieve speeds of up to 315 words per minute. Successful Braille reading often depends on using both hands and maintaining strong tactile sensitivity in the fingers. In extraordinary cases, individuals who lack hand function have learned to read Braille using their lips, or even their tongue.

People who are born deaf often face significant challenges when learning to read, primarily because they don't have access to the sounds of spoken language. Without hearing words, they miss out on developing phonological awareness, the ability to recognize how letters correspond to sounds, which is a crucial foundation for decoding written text. (For a refresher, revisit Chapter 3.) In effect, they are learning to read a language they haven't naturally acquired through speech. As discussed in the previous chapter, not all Deaf readers experience an "inner voice" when reading silently. Instead, they might visualize signs or concepts rather than hearing the words in their minds.

Wernicke's aphasia, while an acquired condition rather than a developmental one, can also interfere with reading. Like deafness, it may disrupt silent reading, particularly because it impairs language comprehension. A person with Wernicke's aphasia might read aloud fluently, with natural rhythm and intonation, but have difficulty understanding what they're reading. They may substitute incorrect words or even insert made-up ones, leading to further confusion as they process the text.

Some forms of aphasia affect more than speech, they can impair the ability to read entirely. This condition is known as *alexia*, or word blindness: the acquired loss of the ability to recognize written words, even those once familiar. Remarkably, our understanding of this kind of impairment dates back to antiquity. Hippocrates was the first to describe a patient who had lost the "memory for letters" and noted that speech disorders were often accompanied by paralysis on the opposite side of the body from the brain injury (because the brain's hemispheres control movement contralaterally).

Often caused by stroke, brain trauma, lesions, or infection, alexia typically results from damage to the left fusiform gyrus, sometimes called the *visual word form area*, which plays a crucial role in reading. In many cases, individuals with alexia can still write and spell yet are unable to read what they've just written. For example, a person might compose a full sentence by hand but be unable to recognize a single word of it just moments later.

Soviet propaganda once showed photographs of Vladimir Lenin reading books and newspapers at his Gorki estate, but in reality, after suffering multiple strokes, he had developed alexia. According to his speech therapist, Lenin's "ability to read aloud was substantially damaged, as was his ability to recognize letters, words, and sentences." This contrast between public image and private reality underscores how neurological impairments were often hidden or downplayed, especially in political figures, reflecting broader societal discomfort with acknowledging cognitive decline.

As we saw in the previous chapter, skilled readers don't read one letter at a time, they recognize whole words at a glance, taking in multiple letters simultaneously. Spelling out each letter would slow us to a crawl. But that's exactly what happens in a rare form of alexia known as *letter-by-letter reading*. In this condition, people can no longer recognize words as complete units; instead, they painstakingly identify and sound out each letter, one at a time. It's as exhausting as it sounds, and it drastically reduces reading speed. This condition is usually linked to damage in the visual word form area, the part of the brain responsible for word recognition.

Interestingly, alexia can look quite different depending on the writing system. Take Japanese, for instance. The language combines *kana* (symbols representing syllables) and *kanji* (characters that convey meaning). These are processed in different regions of the brain, and alexia can selectively impair one system or the other. Some Japanese readers with alexia lose the ability to read kana but can still read kanji; others lose kanji recognition but retain kana. A small number lose both, demonstrating how deeply intertwined language and the brain really are.

Word blindness is used to describe alexia, a lesser-known condition, but it has also been applied to a much more common one. *Dyslexia* is arguably the best-known language processing disorder. In the 1870s, German physician

Adolf Kussmaul observed patients who could speak and write normally but struggled to read. He called this puzzling difficulty *Wortblindheit*, or "word blindness." His work influenced ophthalmologist Rudolf Berlin, who noticed that while these individuals had trouble with printed text, their vision was perfectly intact. They weren't literally blind, just "word blind." Berlin coined a new term: *dyslexia*, from the Greek for "difficulty with words."

Importantly, early doctors recognized that dyslexia was not the result of low intelligence or poor education. In 1896, English physician William Pringle Morgan described the curious case of fourteen-year-old Percy: "the eldest son of intelligent parents, the second child of a family of seven. He has always been a bright and intelligent boy, quick at games, and in no way inferior to others of his age. His great difficulty has been – and is now – his inability to learn to read." Morgan concluded that this was likely due to a "congenital defect," and he was right. Dyslexia is most often a developmental disorder, present from birth and closely tied to how the brain is wired. But in some cases, it is acquired later in life, typically as a result of brain injury, stroke, or degenerative disease. Dyslexia is also remarkably common, affecting an estimated 7 to 20 percent of the population. And it tends to run in families; if one parent has dyslexia, their child has a 30 to 50 percent chance of inheriting it.

Symptoms of dyslexia often include trouble with spelling and difficulty distinguishing letters that look or sound alike. In the nineteenth century, Percy, mentioned above, drew attention for his creative spellings: writing *scone* for *song*, *scojock* for *subject*, *wiehout* for *without*, and even misspelling his own name as *Precy*.

A core difficulty in dyslexia is phonological awareness, the ability to hear and manipulate the sounds in words, and to connect those sounds with written letters. (This issue also appears in some people with Down syndrome.) But the most defining feature of dyslexia is trouble with reading. People with the condition often read slowly and make frequent mistakes, especially when reading aloud. They might reverse letters or misread words, for instance, reading *now* as *won*, or *left* as *felt*. Letters like 'b' and 'd', or 'p' and 'q', may be processed incorrectly or inconsistently. Words can blur together, spaces may seem to disappear, and reading silently becomes especially challenging, with comprehension often affected.

Many people with dyslexia find they understand and remember material better when they hear it, rather than read it. Brain imaging studies support this difference. Unlike typical readers, who primarily engage regions in the left hemisphere associated with language (such as the left temporal and occipitotemporal cortex), people with dyslexia tend to rely more on areas in the right hemisphere when reading. This neurological shift helps explain why reading can feel more effortful, and why tools like audiobooks can make such a difference.

Dyslexia is often accompanied by attention difficulties, making it hard to maintain focus and easy to become distracted. In fact, dyslexia and attention deficit hyperactivity disorder (ADHD) frequently co-occur and share some overlapping traits. Attention deficit hyperactivity disorder is marked by difficulties with sustaining attention, hyperactivity, and impulsivity, factors that can seriously interfere with reading. These challenges can make it hard to concentrate on a text, follow the thread of a narrative, or absorb meaning from what's being read. This disorder can also affect working memory, making it difficult to hold onto and process information from one moment to the next.

Other developmental conditions, like ASD, can also impact reading. Many children with autism can read fluently and have strong language skills, but they may struggle with comprehension, especially when it comes to grasping meaning beyond the literal. For example, they might find it hard to summarize a story, understand the connections between ideas, or interpret characters' perspectives, emotions, and intentions.

In the previous chapter, we explored the McGurk Effect, a striking example of how our senses work together to shape perception. Interestingly, research shows that autistic individuals tend to experience a weaker version of this effect. When presented with conflicting visual and auditory speech cues, they're less likely to perceive the illusory blended sound. This suggests differences in how visual and auditory information are integrated during speech perception, possibly linked to difficulties in reading facial expressions like joy, anger, or sadness.

Another fascinating trait associated with autism is *hyperlexia*, a condition where children develop advanced reading abilities, often before they can even speak. These children sometimes show a deep, even obsessive, fascination with letters and numbers. While we can't retroactively diagnose historical figures, some have speculated that Alexander Hamilton might have been hyperlexic. He reportedly learned to read before acquiring fluent speech, and as an adult, his prolific writing was legendary. Nicknamed "the little lion," Hamilton poured his energy into an astonishing volume of letters, essays, speeches, and reports, driven by a lifelong intensity that might, today, be seen through a different lens.

All Work and No Play Makes Jack a Dull Boy

Alexander Hamilton has also been suspected of having *hypergraphia*, a rare condition characterized by an overwhelming compulsion to write or draw, often excessively. One biographer noted that Hamilton wrote as if he were "running out of time," a description that echoes the urgency and intensity typical of hypergraphia. People with this condition frequently keep exhaustive journals, meticulously documenting the details of their daily lives, and often feel a constant need to put thoughts onto the page.

Another historical figure thought to exhibit signs of hypergraphia is Charles Lutwidge Dodgson, better known by his pen name Lewis Carroll. In addition to writing *Alice's Adventures in Wonderland* and nearly twenty other books, Carroll penned more than 98,000 letters, and maintained a thirteen-volume diary. He also kept a comprehensive record of every letter he sent or received over his lifetime. His writing was playful and inventive, often infused with riddles, puns, and ciphers, some composed backward or in rebus form, where images stand in for words (such as a pumpkin next to the symbol π to represent "pumpkin pie").

Carroll was so driven by bursts of nighttime inspiration that he invented a tool called the *nyctograph*, a stencil-like card that allowed him to write in the dark without needing to light a candle. He also lived with a stutter for most of his life. According to popular lore, the dodo bird in *Alice in Wonderland* was a self-referential nod, inspired by his stammering pronunciation of "Do-do-Dodgson." Both Hamilton and Carroll demonstrate how learning and neurological differences, whether in reading, speech, or the drive to write, can shape not only how people experience the world, but how they leave their mark on it. These conditions, while sometimes seen as limitations, can also fuel extraordinary creativity, insight, and output.

Hypergraphia can be a symptom of temporal lobe changes, especially in cases of epilepsy. It has been speculated that Lewis Carroll may have experienced this condition. Hypergraphia is particularly associated with Geschwind syndrome, a cluster of behavioral traits sometimes seen in people with temporal lobe epilepsy. This syndrome includes hypergraphia, hyper-religiosity, emotional intensity, and a tendency toward philosophical or mystical thinking. Some researchers believe that Vincent van Gogh exhibited many of these features. Over the course of his short life, van Gogh created nearly 2,000 artworks and wrote more than 900 letters, most addressed to his brother Theo. These letters offer a vivid portrait of his creative process and deteriorating mental health. Often, they included small drawings of the paintings he was working on, which he referred to as "scratches."

But hypergraphia doesn't always manifest as poetic letters or literary masterpieces. In some cases, it can present as disorganized and incoherent writing, devoid of grammar or structure. This form is sometimes known as *graphorrhea*, and it has been linked to schizophrenia or the manic phases of bipolar disorder. Graphorrhea is frequently accompanied by *logorrhea*, excessive and uncontrollable speech. This isn't just being overly talkative; it can involve a rapid torrent of fragmented, nonsensical language, not unlike word salad. Some literary characters appear to mirror these symptoms. The frenzied monologues of Shakespearean fools such as Feste in *Twelfth Night* and the stream-of-consciousness style in James Joyce's *Ulysses* can resemble logorrhea (though these are, of course, intentional literary devices, not clinical symptoms).

Lewis Carroll had a particular fondness for inventing words, as seen in his iconic nonsense poem *Jabberwocky*, which begins: "'Twas brillig, and the slithy toves did gyre and gimble in the wabe." (The surreal logic and linguistic playfulness of this verse echo, in a way, Noam Chomsky's famous syntactically correct but semantically nonsensical sentence "Colorless green ideas sleep furiously.") A few of Carroll's whimsical coinages have entered the lexicon, including *chortle*, a blend of *chuckle* and *snort*, and *galumph*, meaning to move in a clumsy, triumphant manner, a mash-up of *gallop* and *triumph*.

Hypergraphia can sometimes resemble this same kind of linguistic freewheeling, though often in more chaotic or compulsive forms. It may involve made-up words, erratic scribbles, or frantic streams of thought, as well as obsessive lists or doodles. An iconic pop culture example appears in *The Shining*, where author Jack Torrance, holed up with his family in a remote hotel, appears to be writing diligently, overcoming his writer's block. In reality, he's descending into madness. His wife eventually discovers his "manuscript," a stack of pages repeating a single chilling line: "All work and no play makes Jack a dull boy."

In extreme cases, people with hypergraphia will write on whatever surface is available, walls, mirrors, even toilet paper. A parody of this appears in *The Simpsons* Halloween special "The Shinning," where a deranged Homer scrawls across the walls, "No beer and no TV make Homer go crazy."

Lost for Words

As we've seen, many people today have poor handwriting, but *dysgraphia* is something more serious. It's a learning disability that affects a person's ability to write, not just legibly, but coherently and consistently. Dysgraphia is most often identified in children, especially those with ASD or ADHD, though it can also develop later in life.

Symptoms include illegible handwriting, frequent spelling mistakes, reversed letters or numbers, writing words backward, or scrambling the order of letters. In these ways, dysgraphia overlaps with dyslexia. But while dyslexia primarily affects language processing, dysgraphia involves fine motor control and the physical act of writing. As a result, it can extend beyond handwriting to include difficulties with drawing, tracing, painting, using utensils, doing puzzles, or handling small objects. For children, these challenges are often misread as laziness or carelessness, which can erode self-esteem and lead to anxiety. Occupational therapy is often helpful in improving both handwriting and overall motor coordination, offering practical tools to navigate a world that still depends heavily on written communication.

Dysgraphia can make it difficult to think and write simultaneously, especially during tasks that require creativity, like storytelling. British author Agatha Christie is widely believed to have had dysgraphia. She once described herself as "the slow one in the family" and admitted that "both writing and spelling were a pain to me." Despite being an avid and capable reader, Christie struggled with spelling, arithmetic, foreign languages, and the physical act of writing.

The mastermind behind Hercule Poirot and Miss Marple often outlined her plots in notebooks, but her handwriting was so poor that even she sometimes couldn't decipher it. To work around this, she began dictating her novels into a machine called a Dictaphone, and a secretary would later transcribe the recordings into manuscripts. She also carried a small typewriter with her everywhere and used a hunt-and-peck method, joking that it helped her bypass her troublesome handwriting. Christie's challenges with writing didn't hold her back. In fact, she went on to author more than sixty novels and became the best-selling novelist in history, surpassed only by the Bible and Shakespeare.

Dysgraphia is typically a developmental disorder, while the related condition *agraphia* is acquired later in life. Agraphia is the loss of the ability to write or communicate through writing, distinct from illiteracy, where the ability was never developed in the first place. Its symptoms range from mild to profound and may include difficulty spelling, selecting the correct letters, or forming them legibly. People with agraphia often write erratically, misusing lines and margins, writing too fast or too slowly, or losing the ability to write altogether.

Agraphia is usually caused by neurological damage, such as brain injury, stroke, tumor, or degenerative conditions like dementia or Alzheimer's disease. While it can occur on its own, it most often coexists with alexia, the inability to read. In addition to alexia, Vladimir Lenin developed agraphia in the final years of his life, following several of his strokes. No longer able to read or write, he relied on his personal secretary, Lydia Fotiyeva, to transcribe his words. During this period, he dictated his famous "Testament," a trio of essays warning of corruption within the

Communist Party and cautioning against the rise of certain figures, most notably Joseph Stalin, who was poised to take over from the ailing leader. Not long after, Lenin suffered a third stroke that left him paralyzed and nonverbal. He died the following year.

Agraphia can also affect musicians in a uniquely specialized way. *Musical agraphia*, sometimes classified under the broader term *amusia*, is a condition in which a person loses the ability to write musical notation. They can no longer translate what they hear into written musical symbols, even if their ability to play, sing, or mentally imagine music remains intact.

This rare and tragic affliction befell Maurice Ravel, the celebrated French composer, conductor, and pianist, best known for his hypnotic orchestral piece *Boléro*. At the height of his career, Ravel developed a progressive neurological condition that robbed him of the ability to read and write music, though his musical sensibility remained disturbingly intact. In his final years, he could still hear and appreciate music, but no longer recognized his own compositions. After listening to a recording of his string quartet, he reportedly remarked, "That was really very good. Remind me of the composer's name." On another occasion, attending a concert of his piano works, Ravel applauded enthusiastically, mistakenly thinking the audience's ovation was meant for the colleague sitting beside him.

Although some have speculated that Ravel suffered from Alzheimer's disease or another form of dementia, no autopsy was performed, and the precise nature of his illness remains unknown, an unsolved mystery as haunting as his final notes.

The Last Word

In this chapter, we've explored a range of language disorders and how they impact the ability to use, understand, read, and write language. We've examined their symptoms, causes, and potential treatments. What becomes clear is that language loss can occur in many different ways, and for many different reasons.

Fortunately, the brain is not static. *Neuroplasticity* plays a key role in atypical language by allowing the brain to reorganize and form new pathways when typical language areas are disrupted or underdeveloped. Whether due to injury, developmental disorders, or unusual learning conditions, it supports the brain's ability to compensate, adapt, and reroute language processing in remarkable ways.

It's a sobering thought that figures like Louis Victor Leborgne, the Marquise de Dampierre, and Charles Baudelaire might have lived very different lives with access to today's medical knowledge, assistive technology, and therapeutic interventions. Speech and occupational therapy, in particular, could have dramatically improved both their communication and their quality of life.

As we leave behind the topic of language lost, we turn to language gained. Specifically: second language acquisition. How do we learn a language beyond our mother tongue? How does one language shape and influence another? And how is language learning beneficial for us, not just linguistically, but in social and cognitive ways?

6

How Do We Learn Other Languages?

Roughly half of the world's population, some four billion people, are bilingual. While bilingualism is widespread globally, it's more common in some regions than others. A familiar joke captures the contrast: "What do you call someone who speaks two languages? Bilingual. What do you call someone who speaks only one? American." As with many jokes, there's a grain of truth in it. In Europe, more than half the population speaks at least two languages. In Canada, around 30 percent are bilingual. In the United States, that number drops to about 20 percent. Still, language learning is steadily gaining momentum around the world, spurred by immigration, globalization, and a growing recognition of the social, cognitive, and economic benefits of speaking more than one language.

In this chapter, we explore how people learn languages beyond their mother tongue, the language acquired naturally in early childhood. How does learning a second language differ from learning a first? What kinds of challenges do learners typically face? We delve into the intricacies of translation, and contrast the fantastical solutions of science fiction, like the babel fish or the TARDIS, with the real-world capabilities and limitations of artificial intelligence. We also examine the fascinating cases of polyglot savants, both genuine and questionable, and revisit those rare individuals who suddenly begin speaking with a foreign accent, or even in an entirely new language. Finally, we consider what the science says about the powerful cognitive and social advantages of learning another language.

The One-Man Tower of Babel

According to the 1998 edition of the *Guinness Book of World Records*, Ziad Youssef Fazah held the title of the world's greatest living *polyglot*, a person who speaks multiple languages. (In everyday usage, *linguist* is often used the same way.) The word polyglot comes from the Greek *polyglōttos*, meaning "many-tongued." Dubbed the "One-Man Tower of Babel," the Liberian-born Fazah claimed he could speak, read, and understand an astonishing fifty-nine languages.

Language scientists refer to the native or mother tongue as the *first language*, while any others learned later, regardless of whether they're second, third, or fifty-eighth, are grouped under the umbrella of *second languages*, because they are languages learned in addition to the first. The term *bilingualism* describes the ability to speak two languages, while *multilingualism* (or *plurilingualism*, for lovers of linguistic tongue-twisters) refers to speaking several. These terms also apply to entire communities or nations where multiple languages are actively used.

For example, Canada officially recognizes both English and French, with French especially prominent in Quebec, Ontario, and Montreal. In New Zealand, English, Māori, and New Zealand Sign Language all hold official status. An official language is one designated for use in government, education, and public life, symbolizing a language's cultural and historical importance. Some nations, such as the United Kingdom and Australia, have never declared an official language, although English remains the de facto language spoken by the majority. At the other extreme, Bolivia recognizes thirty-seven official languages, India has twenty-two, and South Africa twelve. But a high number of official languages doesn't necessarily mean the average citizen is multilingual.

Being bilingual or multilingual means having fluency in two or more languages, fluency here referring to the ability to read, speak, and understand a language with ease and accuracy. Many multilingual individuals can switch between their languages effortlessly, depending on the context or conversation. A popular fictional example is Dr. Gregory House from the television show *House*, who impressively navigates between English, Spanish, Russian, Portuguese, Hindi, and Mandarin when communicating with patients. This kind of *code-switching* showcases the mental agility and cultural awareness that often accompany multilingualism. (And more on this soon.)

But while bilingualism is increasingly common around the world, true polyglots are exceptionally rare. Throughout history, a few extraordinary individuals have claimed staggering linguistic abilities. Cardinal Giuseppe Mezzofanti, born in 1774, reportedly spoke thirty-eight languages. The tenth-century polymath Al-Farabi was said to know seventy. Hans Conon von der Gabelentz, a nineteenth-century German linguist, published work on eighty languages. The most ambitious claim, however, comes from Sir John Bowring, Governor of Hong Kong in the 1850s, who was reputed to know 200 languages. In modern times, record-holder Ziad Fazah's native language was Arabic, but it's worth asking: Just how fluent was he really in the other fifty-eight languages he claimed to know?

His talents were put to the test in 1997 on a Chilean television show, *Viva el Lunes*. During a live segment, Fazah was asked basic questions in a variety of languages, including Russian ("What day of the week is it?"), Greek ("How many days will you stay in Chile?"), and Hindi (to translate the show's title, which means "Long live Mondays" – a cheeky jab at the Monday blues). Unfortunately, he failed to answer these simple questions correctly, along with several others, except for the one posed in his native Arabic. The incident cast serious doubt on the depth of his linguistic knowledge, and some time later, his name quietly disappeared from future editions of the *Guinness Book of World Records*. While this public test may have been humiliating, it also highlights an important distinction: knowing *about* a language isn't the same as truly *speaking* it.

One of the most extraordinary living examples of a true polyglot is Christopher Taylor, a UK-born savant with a remarkable talent for learning languages. Savant syndrome is a rare condition in which individuals with intellectual or developmental disabilities display profound abilities in a specific domain: mathematics, music, or, in Christopher's case, languages. Diagnosed with brain damage at just six weeks old, Christopher experienced significant delays in walking and talking. Yet by the age of three, he had developed a voracious appetite for factual material – reading dictionaries, telephone books, technical manuals, and guides to flags and foreign currencies with intense focus. His reading ability is striking: Not only can he read in the standard fashion, but also upside down and sideways, with equal ease.

Although Christopher lives in a care facility and cannot manage basic daily tasks – he struggles with dressing, grooming, and housework – his linguistic abilities are astonishing. He can read, write, translate, and converse in fifteen to twenty languages, including Danish, Dutch, Finnish, German, Modern Greek, Hindi, Italian, Norwegian, Polish, Portuguese, Russian, Spanish, Swedish, Turkish, and Welsh. His fluency ranges from full conversational command to basic understanding, but in every case, his learning is largely self-driven. Christopher absorbs languages through introductory "teach yourself" books, lessons, and interactions with native speakers, and he picks up new languages with astonishing speed. When invited to appear on a television show in the Netherlands, for instance, he was advised to brush up on his rudimentary Dutch. Armed with just a grammar book and a dictionary, Christopher immersed himself for a few days and became almost fluent by the time of the broadcast. In a controlled study, he not only picked up the North African language Berber with impressive speed but also mastered "Epun," an artificial language invented by the researchers purely for the experiment.

Probably the Oddest Thing in the Universe

Douglas Adams' cult classic *The Hitchhiker's Guide to the Galaxy* introduces readers to the babel fish – a small, bright yellow, leech-like creature described as "probably the oddest thing in the universe." When inserted into the ear, it instantly translates any spoken language into the listener's native tongue by converting sound waves into brain waves. With a babel fish in your ear, you could understand any language in the galaxy, effortlessly. As you might have guessed, its name is a playful nod to the Tower of Babel story we encountered earlier in the book.

The babel fish has since inspired the name of a real-world translation tool, one of many. Today, we have a wealth of language-learning apps and machine translation services at our fingertips, from Babbel and Duolingo to Google Translate. Alongside them are countless ads promising to teach you a new language in just a month, a few weeks, or even a single day. If only it were that easy. If bilingualism came as naturally to us as it does to Christopher Taylor, or were as simple as popping a tiny yellow fish into our ear, the world would be full of fluent polyglots. But the reality is different. Language learning is a slow, incremental process that demands time, dedication, effort, and patience. There's no shortcut or secret trick to fast-track fluency.

So, how do we actually learn a second language? There are countless pathways, ranging from informal exposure at home, like picking it up from family members, to structured learning through private tutors, flashcards, books, and language apps. More formal approaches include attending classes or enrolling in language schools. Traditional methods often conjure up images of students droning through drills, parroting vocabulary and phrases in the hope of committing them to memory. While repetition has its place, particularly for mastering basic expressions, it does little to develop real fluency.

Modern language learning emphasizes active engagement over passive memorization. It encourages learners to participate, interact, and use the language in meaningful contexts. One of the most effective methods, supported by research, is immersion, where the learner is surrounded by the target language in a naturalistic setting. Immersion can happen in a classroom or, ideally, while living in a country where the language is spoken. It's the linguistic equivalent of being thrown in the deep end: Learners are immersed in both language and culture, alongside native speakers, and "bathed" in real-world communication. The goal is to foster intuitive understanding, mimicking the way children acquire their first language, not by studying grammar rules in isolation but by experiencing the language in action.

A closely related language-learning strategy is the natural approach, which emphasizes comprehension before production. In this method, learners are first exposed to large amounts of language input, spoken or written, before being expected to speak or write themselves. The idea is that language acquisition happens most effectively through meaningful communication and understanding, rather than through the rote memorization of grammar rules. Consistent exposure to the target language is believed to be a key driver of progress.

The challenge, of course, is that many learners lack regular access to native speakers or immersive environments. Not everyone has the opportunity to study abroad or spend a summer in Paris polishing their French. Fortunately, research shows that simulated immersion, creating immersive experiences in everyday contexts, can also be highly effective. These might include joining online courses, participating in internet forums, listening to music, watching films and television, or even playing video games in the target language.

One compelling study involved a group of Albanian-speaking women in Kosovo who regularly watched subtitled Turkish soap operas over a period of one to two years. None of them had taken a single Turkish class, yet they were able to pass intermediate-level listening and reading exams in the language. Anecdotal evidence supports this too. Gene Simmons, the KISS vocalist and bassist, was born Chaim Witz in Israel and moved to the United States at the age of eight. His first language was Hebrew, but he taught himself English by reading comic books and watching television, mimicking the crisp, authoritative accent of broadcaster Walter Cronkite. Whether through soap operas or rock stars, the message is clear: Meaningful exposure to language in real contexts, even pop culture, can be a powerful way to learn.

Regardless of the method we choose, the underlying process of language acquisition tends to follow a consistent pattern. There are several predictable stages in second language acquisition, many of which mirror the stages of first language development. In fact, learning a second language often draws on the structures and strategies already established by the first, building upon existing linguistic knowledge to make sense of a new system. The first of these stages is known as the *pre-production* phase, typically lasting around six months. During this time, learners focus on listening and observation. They begin to internalize the sounds, rhythms, and structures of the new language, often without speaking much, if at all. As we'll see, this period is similar to the "silent phase" seen in early childhood language development.

Like a first language, a second language is primarily processed in the left hemisphere of the brain, especially in the two key regions we've discussed previously: Broca's area, which is associated with speech production, and Wernicke's area, which supports language comprehension. However, emerging research has revealed that the right hemisphere also plays an essential role in acquiring a new language, especially in detecting and processing unfamiliar sounds. This right-brain activity helps learners distinguish subtle phonetic differences, adjust to novel sound patterns, and attune to the unique intonation and stress of the target language. In other words, learning a second language isn't simply a matter of reusing old circuits, it also calls on new ones, especially when we encounter sounds and structures that don't exist in our native tongue.

During this period, which is also called the silent or receptive phase, learners may accumulate a vocabulary of up to five hundred words, even though they haven't yet begun to speak. This stage resembles the early preverbal and babbling phases of first language acquisition, where comprehension begins to outpace production. Communication is typically nonverbal: Learners rely on gestures like pointing, nodding, and drawing to express themselves and to follow basic instructions.

The next stage, *early production*, usually emerges between six and twelve months of exposure. By this point, learners often have a receptive and active vocabulary of around one thousand words. They begin to produce simple speech, one- or two-word phrases, and often fall back on short, memorized chunks of language. These may be used incorrectly at times, but that's entirely normal. Errors are frequent and expected, just as they are when children begin speaking their first language. As we'll soon see, mistakes aren't signs of failure; they're essential milestones on the path to fluency.

The next stage, known as *speech emergence*, typically develops after one to three years of exposure to the target language. At this point, learners have built a vocabulary of up to three thousand words and can read, write, and understand simple sentences. They begin to ask questions, participate in short conversations, and express themselves with increasing confidence. Comprehension has improved significantly, and, as with first language development, it continues to outpace verbal production. Learners at this stage may still struggle with aspects of language that go beyond the literal: Homophones, slang, idioms, jokes, and figurative expressions often remain confusing. Grammatical and pronunciation errors are still common, but they serve as valuable learning tools. Mistakes aren't setbacks, they're part of the process, helping the learner refine their understanding over time.

With continued practice and exposure, learners progress toward *fluency*. Fluency isn't a fixed point, but a spectrum, from basic conversational ability to near-native command. In the stage known as *intermediate fluency*, learners typically understand up to six thousand words. Their comprehension is strong, errors are less frequent, and they feel far more comfortable engaging in spoken conversation. The final stage, *advanced fluency*, represents true proficiency. At this level, the learner demonstrates excellent comprehension, speaks and writes with confidence, and uses the language naturally and effectively. Grammatical accuracy is typically consistent, though subtle pronunciation differences may still reveal their non-native origins. For most learners, reaching this stage is a long journey, but it's the point at which the second language becomes not just something they've learned but something they live in.

One influential theory draws a key distinction between *acquiring* a language and *learning* it. According to this view, acquisition is a natural, subconscious process that occurs through exposure. It involves developing an intuitive, implicit understanding of how a language works, gained not through formal study but by observing and imitating patterns in everyday use, often without even realizing it.

In contrast, *learning* refers to a conscious, deliberate process: the formal study of grammar rules, vocabulary, and language conventions. This type of explicit knowledge requires focused attention and mental effort, and it's typically acquired through instruction or structured practice. Unlike acquired language, which is used automatically, learned language is retrieved consciously, its rules applied to monitor or "edit" speech, either during or after communication. This monitoring function resembles the self-regulation stage of speech production discussed earlier in Chapter 4. Both implicit and explicit knowledge contribute to second language use, working in tandem to support communication. However, it's implicit knowledge, the kind built through exposure and use, that is often credited with true fluency.

How long does it take to become fluent in another language? The answer is complex. In some respects, learning a second language parallels the process of acquiring a first. In others, it diverges significantly. Second language learners are often expected to progress far more quickly than they did with their mother tongue. Children typically take nearly two years to string together two-word phrases, while adults can manage this within just a few months.

And yet, paradoxically, mastering a second language can take far longer. Most people acquire their native language by the age of five, but even with that internal template in place, reaching fluency in a second language may take just as long, or even longer. It's not uncommon for the process to stretch over a decade or more. As we've seen, language learning is a life-long endeavor. Just as we continue to expand and refine our first language throughout life, the same is true for any additional languages we take on.

Unlike first language acquisition, which follows relatively predictable developmental milestones, second language learning doesn't unfold at a fixed pace. While most infants begin babbling by six to eight months and speak their first word around age one, there is no universal timeline for second language learners, child or adult. The commonly described stages of acquisition serve as useful guidelines, but they are not rigid benchmarks. Every learner is different, with individual needs, learning styles, and rates of progress. And beyond that, language learning is shaped by a host of external factors. Let's take a closer look at some of these key influences now.

The Younger, the Better?

Many factors can influence how successfully someone learns a second language, and one of the most widely studied is age. A learner's age can affect not just how quickly they pick up a new language but also how well they ultimately master it. So, how do adults compare to children when it comes to second language learning? To explore this, let's revisit the Critical Period Hypothesis, or the idea of sensitive periods, which we discussed back in Chapter 3. This theory suggests that there's a developmental window during childhood when the brain is especially receptive to language input. Once that window closes, acquiring a first language becomes far more difficult. Researchers believe these sensitive periods extend to second language learning as well. In other words, there may be an optimal window in which children can absorb an additional language more easily and with greater potential for native-like fluency.

We might remember that newborns are capable of distinguishing between multiple languages and, contrary to popular belief, they are not "confused" by multilingual input. This supports the widespread belief that when it comes to second language acquisition, the younger the learner, the better.

That said, the exact boundaries of this sensitive period are still a matter of debate. Some researchers argue it spans from birth to around age four or five. Others extend it to age nine or ten, while many suggest it may last until puberty, or even into the teenage years. There's also growing evidence that there may be distinct sensitive periods for different aspects of language, such as pronunciation, grammar, or vocabulary. So, while the brain's flexibility clearly changes with age, the story is more nuanced than a simple early-versus-late divide.

There are both cognitive and social reasons why children tend to learn languages more easily, or at least differently, than adults. A second language is primarily processed in the left hemisphere of the brain, particularly in Broca's and Wernicke's areas, where the native language is also stored. But in children, the second language is often integrated more closely with the first, forming a unified neural network. Adults, by contrast, are more likely to develop separate pathways for each language, which can make switching between them more effortful.

One major factor is the brain's plasticity in early life. During childhood, the brain is highly adaptable and can quickly internalize new language patterns and structures. This flexibility, known as neuroplasticity and mentioned in the previous chapter, allows children to acquire language in a way that often appears effortless. But neuroplasticity diminishes with age, and as a result, learning a new language later in life typically requires more time and effort. Genie's case is often cited to illustrate this. Her right hemisphere partly compensated for the underdeveloped language areas in her left hemisphere caused by early deprivation. (Her language abilities, however, remained limited because she missed the sensitive period for development.)

Children tend to learn language implicitly. They absorb it naturally through immersion, social interaction, and repetition, often without consciously thinking about grammar or syntax. For example, a toddler picks up sentence patterns just by hearing and using them every day. Adults, on the other hand, usually rely more on explicit learning, studying rules, memorizing vocabulary, and using deliberate strategies to understand the language. For instance, an adult learner might spend time memorizing verb conjugations or practicing grammar exercises. Both methods can lead to fluency, but they engage the brain in distinctly different ways.

Social factors also help explain why younger learners often pick up new languages more quickly. One major difference is inhibition. Children tend to be less self-conscious than adults and are more willing to take risks, including making mistakes when speaking. They'll stumble through unfamiliar words and grammar without much concern for how they sound. Adults, by contrast, are often more hesitant and cautious speakers. They're acutely aware of their mistakes – mispronunciations, awkward phrasing, grammatical slips – and this awareness can make them hold back. But mistakes are not signs of inadequacy; they're an essential part of the learning process. Unfortunately, there's a persistent misconception that grammatical errors or strong accents reflect lower intelligence. Non-native speakers are sometimes mocked or unfairly judged, which only heightens adult learners' fear of making mistakes, or of not being understood at all.

This inhibition isn't just social; it's also cognitive. The adult brain's more developed prefrontal cortex, responsible for self-monitoring and judgment, can become a double-edged sword. While it helps with planning and reflection, it also fuels self-doubt, over-analysis, and embarrassment. These mental hurdles can interfere with spontaneous speech and block deeper engagement with the language. In this way, successful language learning demands a kind of bravery. It requires learners to tolerate uncertainty, laugh at their own mistakes, and push through discomfort. Not surprisingly, risk-takers, those who are willing to speak up, experiment, and occasionally get it wrong, tend to progress faster.

Achieving native-like fluency is significantly more difficult for adults, who often face challenges with vocabulary, grammar, and especially pronunciation, particularly when the second language differs greatly from their first. Of these, accent is one of the most powerful markers of nativeness. The ability to produce native-like pronunciation is closely tied to the age at which language learning begins. Children are far more adept than adults at acquiring a near-native accent. If exposed to a second language during the sensitive period, they're more likely to absorb its sounds and rhythms effortlessly, without being heavily influenced by the phonological patterns of their mother tongue. Adults, by contrast, often struggle to shed the pronunciation habits of their first language. A native-like accent may be the most difficult feature to master, or, conversely, the hardest to lose.

This ties back to an idea we explored in Chapter 1: Native speakers often perceive themselves as accentless, assuming that it's only others who "have an accent." Of course, everyone has an accent, what varies is whether it matches the dominant local variety. Speaking with a first-language accent instantly identifies someone as a non-native speaker, which can shape how they're perceived, regardless of their fluency. The British sitcom *'Allo 'Allo!* played with this dynamic to great comedic effect. Set in Nazi-occupied France, it features Officer Crabtree, a bumbling British agent posing as a French police officer. His most distinctive trait is his hilariously mangled French accent, particularly his vowel distortions, his catchphrase "Good moaning!" being a prime example. His speech is riddled with double entendres like "I have my dirty to do" (for "I have my duty to do"), and his far-fetched explanation for his accent: "I was raised in Nipples" (meaning Naples). Despite his linguistic blunders, Crabtree believes he speaks flawless French. Ironically, the actor who played him, Arthur Bostrom, actually *is* fluent in French.

Accents aren't just an obstacle for language learners, they can be tricky for actors too. To meet the demands of a role, many actors work with dialect coaches who train them in the subtle nuances of pronunciation, rhythm, and intonation, helping them adopt a convincing accent. More often than not, this involves mastering a different variety of English, which is considerably easier than learning an entirely new language from scratch. Take, for example, Australian actress Nicole Kidman, who has convincingly portrayed American, English, Irish, and Scottish characters across numerous films. Some actors, however, embrace their distinctive accents as part of their public persona. Among those well known for their unmistakable non-native English accents are Austrian-born bodybuilder and actor Arnold Schwarzenegger, and martial artist-actors Jean-Claude Van Damme (from Belgium) and Jackie Chan (from Hong Kong). Their accents remain consistent across roles, becoming part of their signature style.

Then there are native English speakers like Scottish actor Sean Connery, who famously held on to his native Edinburgh accent no matter the role, whether he was playing an Irish police officer, an English king, a Russian submarine captain, a New York beatnik poet, or even an Egyptian immortal with a Spanish name. These examples illustrate just how difficult it is to adopt a natural-sounding accent as a *late bilingual*, someone who learns a second language during adolescence or adulthood. There's a common assumption that immigrants will eventually "lose" their accents as they assimilate, adopting the pronunciation patterns of their new linguistic environment. But it's not that simple. Some do shift toward the dominant accent over time, a process known as *convergence*. Others may *diverge*, consciously or unconsciously retaining their original accent as a marker of cultural identity and belonging.

Not all "accents" are what they seem. As we saw in the previous chapter, some cases that sound like foreign accents are actually the result of a rare speech disorder known as foreign accent syndrome. In these unusual instances, a person's speech suddenly changes to the point where they sound as if they're speaking with a completely different accent, often one that seems "foreign" to listeners. This shift is typically caused by neurological damage from conditions such as dementia, stroke, multiple sclerosis, or traumatic brain injury. One of the more famous examples occurred in 1961, when voice actor Mel Blanc, the man behind Bugs Bunny, Porky Pig, and Daffy Duck, was in a near-fatal car crash on Sunset Boulevard in Los Angeles. He spent weeks in a coma. When he eventually regained consciousness, he could reportedly speak only in the voice of Bugs Bunny. Fortunately, the effect was temporary, and his normal speech returned within a few days. This is similar to the situation of George Michael that we looked at in the previous chapter, where a serious bout of pneumonia was followed by a brief but striking shift in his speech.

Other cases are more persistent. One American woman developed a British-sounding accent following routine jaw surgery, while a British woman began speaking with what resembled a French accent after experiencing a stroke. Foreign accent syndrome leads to a spontaneous and noticeable shift in a person's rhythm, pitch, and pronunciation, causing their native language to suddenly sound unfamiliar, even foreign, to others. But it's important to note that these new speech patterns don't reflect any actual regional or social accent. They aren't acquired through cultural exposure or imitation but rather emerge as a neurological side effect. What we hear as an accent is, in these occurrences, an illusion created by disrupted speech patterns.

In a few rare, documented cases, people spontaneously begin speaking a second language. A related condition, known as *foreign language syndrome*, involves temporarily switching from one's native language to another that the person, notably, has had some prior exposure to. In one recent case, a seventeen-year-old Dutch teenager underwent routine knee surgery and, upon waking, could speak only limited English, a language he had studied in school. By the next day, he had regained access to his native Dutch. This strange episode was later attributed to *emergence delirium*, a temporary state of confusion and disorientation that sometimes occurs as patients regain consciousness after anesthesia.

It's important to stress that these are neurological phenomena, not examples of true language acquisition. In folklore and religious contexts, however, stories of sudden linguistic ability have a long history. The term *xenoglossia* refers to the supposed spontaneous ability to speak or write in a language a person has never learned. In the *Book of Acts*, Luke describes how, on the Day of Pentecost, the disciples were filled with the Holy Spirit and suddenly began speaking in other tongues. In some modern Pentecostal and charismatic Christian traditions, worshippers engage in a similar practice known as *glossolalia*, or "speaking in tongues," a string of speechlike sounds that seem language-like but don't belong to any real or recognized language.

The Older, the Better?

In many respects, learning a second language earlier in life offers clear advantages. As we've noted, the saying "the younger, the better" often holds true when it comes to language acquisition. But there's an opposing view worth considering: "the older, the better." Age alone isn't a barrier to successful language learning. In fact, late bilinguals have distinct advantages of their own. While children may pick up a new language more quickly at first, adults can draw on well-developed cognitive abilities, such as reasoning, pattern recognition, and a broader existing vocabulary. These skills allow them to make faster progress once they begin actively using the language.

As mentioned previously, one common hurdle for language learners is everyday, colloquial speech. Unsurprisingly, adults often grasp idioms, metaphors, and nuanced expressions more easily than younger learners, though figurative language can be tricky for all, regardless of age. The 1970s British sitcom *Mind Your Language* humorously captured some of these challenges. The show followed a group of mature-age students navigating the peculiarities of English while attending an adult language school. In one memorable scene, the school principal encounters a student in the hallway and asks, "Are you in Mr. Brown's class?" The student earnestly replies, "No, I'm in the corridor." It's a perfect example of how literal interpretation, especially for adults who are new to the language, can lead to wonderfully comic misunderstandings.

Comedy aside, adults often benefit more from formal language classrooms thanks to their greater cognitive maturity and mental complexity. Another important factor is the learner's proficiency in their native language. Those who already have strong literacy skills, reading, writing, and speaking, in their first language are generally able to acquire a second language more quickly and effectively. Interestingly, the process also works in reverse. Learning a second language can actually sharpen a person's skills in their mother tongue. It encourages greater awareness of vocabulary, grammar, and sentence structure, often making the learner more reflective and analytical about how language works in general. As we've seen throughout this section, the sensitive period for language learning is not a rigid cutoff. While early exposure has clear benefits, adults are perfectly capable of achieving fluency through focused study, regular practice, and meaningful engagement with the language. That is, if they're motivated to do so.

This brings us to another major factor in second language learning: motivation. Motivation plays a vital role in language acquisition because it fuels the learner's desire to succeed. It shapes their level of enthusiasm, engagement, persistence, and ultimately, how far they'll go in mastering the language. Without sufficient motivation, even the most capable learner may struggle to overcome the inevitable challenges along the way. People are motivated to learn a second language for all kinds of reasons, from relocating abroad, as Gene Simmons did, to traveling, pursuing a personal interest, or advancing in their career. Some feel a strong pull to connect with their cultural roots by learning a heritage language. And of course, love can be a powerful motivator too. In the romantic comedy *Love Actually*, Colin Firth's character Jamie falls for Aurélia, a Portuguese woman he meets while staying in France. Determined to win her heart, he sets out to learn Portuguese. When he returns a few months later, he proposes – in endearingly flawed Portuguese. She accepts, and reveals that she has been learning English as well, "just in cases." It's a charming reminder that motivation, even when imperfectly expressed, can bridge more than just language barriers.

Others are motivated to learn a second language for cultural reasons. As a global language, English is widely studied so that learners can enjoy Anglophone television, movies, and music, and can participate more fully in online culture and social media. Conversely, many English speakers are drawn to learn Japanese in order to read manga or watch anime in its original form. These integrative motivations, such as a desire for belonging, identity, or deeper cultural connection, are often stronger and more enduring than purely instrumental goals like career advancement or travel.

This distinction is reflected in the film *Dances with Wolves*, in which Kevin Costner plays a Union soldier who gradually becomes part of a Lakota community. Captivated by the simplicity and spirit of their way of life, he learns the Lakota language as a step toward being accepted by the group. His language acquisition is fueled not by necessity but by a genuine desire to connect. This kind of interest in another culture can lead to near-native fluency, because learning a language is never just about vocabulary and grammar, it's about understanding the worldview behind the words. As the saying goes, language and culture are two sides of the same coin. And as we saw with the students in *Mind Your Language*, missing cultural cues can be just as much of a barrier as mispronouncing a word.

Motivation also works hand in hand with a learner's attitude toward the target language. A positive perception of the language, along with its culture and speakers, can significantly boost the desire to learn it. French, for instance, is often regarded as the *langue d'amour*, the language of love. It enjoys a long-standing reputation for elegance, refinement, and romance, bolstered by France's global associations with fine cuisine, haute couture, and celebrated literature. These cultural associations help make French one of the most popular second languages in the world.

Part of its appeal lies in its musicality: the flowing rhythm, nasal vowels, and soft consonants like /l/, /r/, /m/, and /n/ give it a distinctive charm. It's become a common trope that everything sounds better in French, even insults. In *The Matrix Reloaded*, the rogue program known as the Merovingian puts it bluntly: "I have sampled every language. French is my favorite – fantastic language, especially to curse with." He then launches into a string of obscenities that roughly translates into a nonsensical tirade, before concluding, "It's like wiping your arse with silk. I love it." Crude, perhaps, but a vivid illustration of just how powerful and seductive the *sound* of a language can be.

On the other hand, a negative attitude toward a language, whether it's perceived as difficult to learn, unpleasant sounding, or culturally unappealing, can significantly dampen motivation. German, for example, is often unfairly labeled as harsh, guttural, or aggressive. Irish comedian

Dylan Moran once quipped that German "sounds like a typewriter eating tinfoil being kicked down the stairs." This impression is partly due to its frequent use of "hard" consonants such as /k/, /g/, /ʃ/, and /pf/. Most German words begin with a consonant, and even those starting with a vowel are preceded by a glottal stop, a sound that can resemble a choke or cough, caused by a sudden closure in the vocal tract. (Revisit Chapter 1 if you want a refresher on phonology.)

Negative cultural stereotypes only reinforce this bias. German speakers are sometimes stereotyped as cold, rigid, or overly obsessed with order, caricatures that are not only unfair but deeply reductive. Lingering historical associations with World War II, Nazi Germany, and Hitler have also cast a long shadow over perceptions of the language. These views go back even further: In the sixteenth century, Holy Roman Emperor Charles V is said to have remarked, "I speak Spanish to God, Italian to women, French to men, and German to my horse." As we touched on in Chapter 1, these are not objective qualities of the languages themselves. They're stereotypes, rooted in culture and history. French isn't inherently romantic, just as German isn't inherently angry or aggressive. But these perceptions matter. Simply liking the way a language sounds, or disliking it, can powerfully shape our motivation to learn it, or not.

Finally, aptitude plays a significant role in second language learning. Like a natural ability for music, math, or sports, language aptitude refers to how readily someone can pick up a new language compared to others. Some people seem to have a natural "knack," "flair," or even a "gift" for languages. Christopher, the polyglot savant we met earlier, is an extraordinary example. Actress Nicole Kidman is often praised by directors for her "good ear" for accents, and language aptitude is a familiar trope in pop culture too. In *The Big Bang Theory*, Howard Wolowitz casually impresses women by picking up languages like French, Japanese, Russian, and Arabic, and even *Star Trek's* Klingon and Sindarin from *The Lord of the Rings*.

Of course, not everyone needs to be a savant or a sitcom polyglot to have strong language-learning potential. Aptitude varies from person to person, and while it's partly shaped by cognitive strengths (or weaknesses), it can also be nurtured with practice and perseverance. Ultimately, age, motivation, and aptitude work together, sometimes in harmony, some-times in tension, to determine how successful a person becomes at acquiring a second language.

In Two Minds

As we've seen, acquiring a second language is a slow, gradual process, one that can take years to fully achieve. It's also far from tidy. Rather than unfolding in a neat, linear progression, second language learning often follows a zigzag or even U-shaped path, marked by plateaus and occasional setbacks. Just like with first language acquisition, errors are a natural and expected part of the journey. In general, it's somewhat easier to learn a second language that's related to your native one. Languages within the same family often share vocabulary, grammar, and pronunciation patterns, which makes it easier to transfer knowledge from one to the other. For instance, Spanish speakers may find it less challenging to learn French or Italian because of their shared Latin roots. This is because learners tend to build on what they already know, using the structure of their first language as a foundation. But when the two languages are less closely related, that transfer of knowledge can get a little more complicated.

A common feature of second language acquisition is *language transfer*, when the learner's first language influences their use of a second. This can be helpful or hindering, but often it results in what's called *interference*, essentially, one language disrupting or getting in the way of learning another. Transfer can occur at any level of language, from accent and vocabulary to grammar. A classic example of phonological interference is when Japanese speakers confuse the English sounds /l/ and /r/, leading to "London" being pronounced as "Rondon." As we've discussed, this happens because Japanese doesn't distinguish between these two phonemes, so native speakers often don't even hear the difference. This challenge is humorously, if a little insensitively, portrayed in *Lethal Weapon 4*, when the crime boss "Uncle Benny" Chan offers Detective Riggs some food. "Flied lice?" Riggs quips. Chan snaps back: "It's fried rice, you plick."

But language transfer isn't all bad news. In fact, similarities between the structures of a learner's first and second languages can often aid the acquisition process. For example, some words across different languages are related by origin, like English *night*, French *nuit*, German *Nacht*, and Swedish *natt*. These are known as *cognates*, words that share a common etymological ancestor. Cognates are like linguistic cousins: They may look or sound slightly different, but they come from the same family tree. Because of their shared roots, they often resemble each other in spelling, pronunciation, and meaning, making them easier to recognize and learn. The closer two languages are genetically, the more of these helpful resemblances they're likely to share.

However, not all similar-looking words are truly related. *False cognates*, or more playfully, *false friends*, are words that appear to be related but actually have very different meanings. Take the English word *advertisement* and the French *avertissement*: They may look alike, but the latter means "warning" or "caution." Mistaking false friends can lead to confusion, miscommunication, or the occasional awkward moment. In French, *embarrassé* doesn't mean "embarrassed" but "pregnant," and in Spanish, *excitado* doesn't mean "excited" in the typical English sense, it means "aroused." These linguistic traps remind us that looking familiar doesn't always mean being familiar.

The more distantly related two languages are, the greater the likelihood of interference, especially in grammar. A study examining Turkish and Arabic speakers learning English found that the grammar of their native languages heavily shaped their use of the new one. An example from a Turkish student read, "Children can play in park," omitting the definite article *the*, which doesn't exist in Turkish. These learners also struggled with English pronouns like *she*, *he*, and *it*, since Turkish uses a single gender-neutral pronoun, *o*, for all three. In this light, the errors aren't random, they make sense. They're logical extensions of the learner's linguistic background.

Arabic-speaking students faced different challenges. Sentences like "They makes a big noise yesterday" reflect difficulties with verb tenses. Arabic has just three, compared to English's twelve. Word order was another stumbling block, with phrases like "the pen red" mirroring the

Arabic structure in which adjectives follow nouns. Arabic learners also tended to omit capital letters in writing. This is understandable, given that Arabic script doesn't distinguish between uppercase and lowercase letters. Directionality added yet another layer of complexity: While English is written left to right, Arabic flows right to left, creating confusion for learners switching between the two. Interestingly, this disorientation can go both ways. Arabic text is sometimes accidentally printed backwards in Western contexts, such as on signs or product packaging.

These are all examples of language transfer, where speakers carry prominent features of their first language into their second. It's a natural part of what linguists call *interlanguage*, a transitional form of language that blends elements of both the native and target languages. Interlanguage is also a kind of idiolect, or an individual's distinctive way of using language (a concept we explored back in Chapter 1). One of its hallmark features is overgeneralization, where a learner understands a rule but applies it too broadly. We've seen this before in first language development, when children say things like "goed" instead of "went," mistakenly applying the regular past-tense pattern to an irregular verb. Second language learners make similar errors, such as saying "deers" instead of "deer," assuming that all plurals follow the standard *-s* rule. These predictable mistakes arise before learners encounter the many irregular forms in English, words like *goose, moose, mice, wolves,* and *oxen,* which don't play by the usual rules.

Errors like these show that the learner is actively engaging with the language, testing out and applying grammatical rules. But if those errors go unnoticed or uncorrected, and the learner stops progressing, they may reach an end-state known as *fossilization*. This is when certain incorrect patterns become fixed in a person's speech, forming habits that are difficult, if not impossible, to undo. Just like a fossil, their language use is preserved in its current form, and no further progress is made. On the flip side, becoming fluent in a second language can sometimes lead to a decline in the first. This is known as *language attrition*, a gradual loss of native language skills due to lack of use. It's particularly common when the second language becomes dominant in daily life while the first language is confined to limited settings, like the home. One well-known example is the actress Mila Kunis, who was born in Ukraine and spoke Russian as her first language. After immigrating to the United States as a child, she became fluent in English, and later admitted that she now struggles with reading and writing in Russian due to disuse.

Livin' la Vida Loca

Interlanguage isn't just an individual phenomenon, it can take on a social life of its own. Within multilingual communities, shared interlanguages can evolve into a kind of hybrid communication system, where speakers regularly mix elements of both their native and second languages. One example is *Franglais*, a casual blend of French and English spoken in regions where the two languages overlap, such as parts of France and bilingual areas of Canada like Ontario and Montreal. As we saw earlier in this book, English has absorbed a huge number of French loanwords over the centuries. In Franglais, it's the opposite. English vocabulary is plugged into French grammatical structures, producing quirky hybrids like *bruncher* ("to brunch"), *une pompon girl* (a cheerleader), and *le footing* (jogging). Confusingly, *un jogging* refers not to the activity but to the clothes worn while jogging.

Other informal blends include *Hunglish* (Hungarian and English) and *Tinglish* (Thai and English). Tinglish typically uses English vocabulary with simplified Thai grammar, often producing shortened constructions like "no have" instead of "I don't have." Repetition is common too – phrases like "same same" or "near near" echo Thai reduplication patterns used for emphasis (*reo reo*, for example, means "fast" or "hurry up!"). English has something similar to reduplication in playful expressions like *hanky-panky, super-duper, easy-peasy*, or *cray-cray*. These mixed-language varieties are related to pidgins and creoles, serving as practical tools of communication in multilingual settings. They help speakers navigate cultural and linguistic boundaries, and adapt to environments where two or more languages are constantly in contact.

One of the most widely recognized interlanguage varieties is *Spanglish*, the hybrid blend of Spanish and English. While often used informally, the term Spanglish can carry pejorative connotations, depending on context, particularly when it's used to suggest that the speaker is using "incorrect" forms of either language. In reality, Spanglish reflects the dynamic linguistic creativity that emerges wherever two languages coexist closely. In the United States, where nearly 53 million people speak Spanish, 41 million of them as native speakers, Spanglish has become an everyday reality. Spanish is the fastest-growing language in the country, and Spanglish flourishes in communities where English and Spanish speakers interact frequently. It's especially prevalent in states like California, Texas, and Florida, and can be heard across homes, schools, workplaces, and media.

Spanglish is often characterized by clever wordplay and linguistic blending. For example, English words are adapted to Spanish grammar, as in *shoppear* ("to go shopping"), *emailear* ("to email"), and *Googlear* ("to Google"), where English nouns are affixed with the Spanish verb ending *-ar*. Some expressions lean into playful inventiveness, like *No problemo*, *smartphono*, or the cheeky *antibaby* for contraception. Spanglish is also deeply rooted in pop culture. Puerto Rican singer Ricky Martin's global hit "Livin' la Vida Loca" ("living the crazy life") is an iconic example of this linguistic mix, as is Arnold Schwarzenegger's iconic farewell in *Terminator 2*: "Hasta la vista, baby." Over time, phrases like these have entered the broader cultural lexicon. As long as Spanish continues to grow alongside English in the US, Spanglish will evolve with it, shaped by the people who live at the intersection of two linguistic worlds.

Technically, expressions like *livin' la vida loca* are examples of a linguistic phenomenon known as *code-switching*, the practice of alternating between two or more languages within a single utterance, sentence, or conversation. Bilingual and multilingual speakers often shift fluidly between languages, drawing on words, phrases, and grammatical structures from each. This isn't a sign of confusion; it's a sign of linguistic agility. A common form of code-switching involves swapping languages when using *discourse particles*, short phrases added to the end of a sentence to convey tone, emphasis, or mood. In Singaporean English, or Singlish, for instance, speakers often tack on *lah* for flavor: "The price is too high for me, lah!" While this kind of switching was once referred to as *code-mixing*, a term that wrongly suggested disorganization or error, research now recognizes it as a marker of proficiency and sophisticated language control. (Using swear words naturally in a second language can be a marker of fluency, too.)

Code-switching also shows up in pop culture and advertising. Taco Bell, for example, blends English and Spanish in its slogan *Live Más* ("Live More") and in the catchphrase of its famous talking chihuahua: *Yo quiero Taco Bell!* ("I want Taco Bell!"). This strategic code-switching is designed to appeal to different demographics and to give the brand a sense of cultural authenticity (however debatable that claim might be).

Code-switching provides a window into the way bilinguals process and produce language. Rather than switching one language off and the other on, both languages are partially active in the brain at all times, even when only one is being spoken. This creates a constant competition for selection during speech, requiring a high degree of cognitive control to activate the intended language while suppressing interference from the other. The result is a remarkable ability to switch fluidly between languages based on context, audience, or emotion.

Speakers code-switch for all kinds of reasons: to express identity, to conceal meaning from others, to access a word or phrase that comes more easily in one language, or simply because one language has just the right word, the *chef's kiss*, for the moment. In the classic 1950s sitcom *I Love Lucy*, code-switching was often used to comedic effect. Lucy's Cuban-born husband, Ricky Ricardo, famously slipped into rapid-fire Spanish whenever he was angry, usually leaving Lucy (and the audience) in the dark. Sometimes he'd toss in just a single well-chosen word. In one scene, when Lucy pleads, "Ricky, why can't you just let me go to the show with the girls?" he retorts, "Because, Lucy, you are my wife and you should be home taking care of the house, not running around like a *loquita* with your friends!" Here, *loquita*, Spanish for "crazy girl," delivers a punch that wouldn't land quite the same way in English.

The show's use of code-switching not only highlighted cultural differences but also poked fun at the perceived gaps in communication, playing on mid-century stereotypes of "broken" English while inadvertently demonstrating the linguistic richness of bilingual expression.

My Hovercraft Is Full of Eels

Interlanguage is a natural part of what happens when two languages come into contact. While code-switching demands significant cognitive control, both interlanguage and code-switching are often misunderstood or unfairly judged by native speakers. Non-native speech is frequently labeled as "broken," "butchered," or even a "bastardization" of the target language, terms that carry heavy social and cultural baggage. But such judgments overlook the linguistic complexity involved in navigating multiple languages and the inevitable influence of one language on another. Interlanguage also shows up in translation, where the interference of one language on another can result in unexpected, and sometimes comical, outcomes. As mentioned earlier in the book, one notorious example is what's colloquially (and often offensively) called Engrish, a term used to mock nonstandard Asian English, playing on the stereotype of Japanese speakers confusing /l/ and /r/ sounds.

In some East Asian countries, English is frequently used on signs, menus, and product packaging, both for practical communication and as a marker of trendiness or international appeal. However, these translations are often machine-generated, rushed, or produced by non-native speakers, resulting in English that ranges from mildly awkward to completely bewildering. Entire websites and Reddit threads are dedicated to documenting these mistranslations. One viral example involves a store sign in Chinese characters that correctly reads "Fresh Supermarket," but whose English translation appears as "Very Suspicious Supermarket." The intended phrase may have been "Auspicious Supermarket," a nod to the strong cultural value placed on good fortune in Chinese tradition. Sometimes the mistranslations are more tongue-in-cheek. The fashion label Superdry splashes Japanese characters across its clothing, but many of the phrases are nonsensical or grammatically bizarre to native Japanese readers. As it turns out, Superdry is a British company, and the Japanese text was machine-generated as part of a branding strategy that parodied the very idea of Engrish. It's a case of linguistic interference turned into ironic aesthetic.

In the early stages of language acquisition, learners often turn to translation apps like Google Translate, which use artificial intelligence to convert written and spoken language between different tongues. While these tools can be helpful, they're no substitute for actual language learning. They don't teach grammar, nuance, or cultural context, crucial elements of fluency that go far beyond word-for-word translation.

Still, these programs are useful for achieving basic comprehension and getting a message across. They're widely used online, particularly on social media, where quick, automatic translations are the norm. Travelers, who usually aim for convenience rather than fluency, often rely on these apps to navigate foreign languages. But as the old saying goes, much is lost in translation. For those with limited exposure to the target language, this can lead to frequent errors in pronunciation, grammar, or meaning. And while translation apps may help someone produce a coherent phrase, communication is a two-way street. One major limitation is receptive language: understanding what's said in return. A user might manage to speak or type a question, but without listening comprehension, they may have no idea how to interpret the response.

A cringeworthy scene in *National Lampoon's European Vacation* captures the pitfalls of overconfidence in translation technology while also playing on well-worn stereotypes of culturally insensitive Americans and haughty French servers. The Griswold family finds themselves in a busy Parisian restaurant, looking awkward in matching berets their father, Clark, insisted they wear. To communicate, Clark pulls out a primitive translation device and promptly addresses their waiter as *garçon*. (Literally "boy," this term is outdated and considered condescending, roughly equivalent to calling a man *servant*.) The server quickly clocks them as American tourists and, realizing they don't understand a word of French, proceeds to insult them to their faces, his stream of abuse cloaked in a polite, even cheerful tone. When Clark orders a Coca-Cola, the waiter dubs it "American champagne." Asked for wine, he sneers, "I'll bring you some dishwater. You won't know the difference." He then makes lewd comments about Clark's wife and daughter, none of which the family understands. Clark, oblivious, beams at the seemingly friendly exchange and cheerfully thanks the waiter, who smiles and replies with a venomous *Va te faire foutre!* – French for "fuck you." Clark turns to his family, pleased: "Nice guy, huh? You see, kids, people appreciate tourists making an effort to speak their language." The scene is played for laughs, but it underscores a real gap between producing language and understanding it, and how blind trust in technology or surface-level communication can result in spectacular misunderstandings.

Modern machine translation can both translate text and interpret spoken language, making communication easier for people who don't share a common language or lingua franca. However, human translation generally remains superior. Although it takes longer, human translators provide greater accuracy and a deeper understanding of cultural context, subtle nuances, and the often-elusive meaning behind words.

Slang, in particular, poses a significant challenge for translators. Its informal, rapidly evolving nature depends heavily on region and context, making it difficult to capture in another language. One famous example often cited in language classes involves former US President John F. Kennedy's 1963 speech in Berlin. Speaking in front of the Berlin Wall, Kennedy declared, *Ich bin ein Berliner* ("I am a Berliner") to express solidarity with the people of the divided city. Widespread legend has it that Kennedy's words were a grammatical blunder: because *Berliner* is also slang for a jelly-filled doughnut, many German teachers in the US have taught that he inadvertently called himself a pastry. In reality, the phrase was carefully composed by a native German speaker and was perfectly appropriate in the context. (In statements of nationality, German often leaves off the *ein*, but in Kennedy's statement, including it was appropriate as a deliberate expression of solidarity.) Moreover, while *Berliner* can mean the pastry in some parts of Germany, in Berlin itself the doughnut is known as *ein Pfannkuchen*. Kennedy's declaration remains a powerful symbol of unity, not confectionery confusion.

While human translation generally surpasses machine efforts, it can still falter when the translator lacks fluency. A classic example comes from the 1990s Japanese video game *Zero Wing*, which became infamous for the awkwardly phrased line "All your base are belong to us." This mistranslation quickly turned into an internet meme. It later emerged that the game's English translation was handled internally by a member of the design team rather than a professional translator. The game's creator, Tatsuya Uemura, apologized for the translator's "really terrible" English skills.

Such cautionary tales highlight the critical importance of accurate translation, especially when different writing systems are involved, and nowhere is this more visible than in tattoos. In the movie *Alpha Dog*, Justin Timberlake portrays Frankie "Nuts" Ballenbacher, a drug dealer whose toughness is symbolized by Chinese characters tattooed on his left bicep. However, fans fluent in Chinese quickly noticed that the characters actually read "ice skating," somewhat undermining his rough image. Fortunately for Timberlake, the tattoos were temporary. Translation blunders have also plagued advertising campaigns. In the 1980s, Mercedes-Benz entered the Chinese market under the name *bensi*, which unfortunately translates to "rush to die." Recognizing the mistake, the company later rebranded itself as *benchi*, meaning "run quickly," a much more fitting name for a luxury car brand. This example underscores how even the most established global brands must navigate the complexities of language and culture carefully. A name that works perfectly in one language can carry unintended – and sometimes disastrous – meanings in another. It serves as a reminder that successful communication goes far beyond direct translation, requiring deep cultural insight and sensitivity.

Long before machine translation existed, travelers relied on phrasebooks filled with everyday words and essential expressions: how to greet someone, order in a restaurant, or navigate public transport. Locals are often eager to help, and, fortunately for English speakers, many people in popular tourist destinations can speak at least a little English. While some travelers still use these guides, they have largely been replaced by modern apps. Phrasebooks can be helpful but are often outdated in terms of culture and slang, or worse, riddled with errors.

A classic Monty Python sketch hilariously highlights the pitfalls of relying on poorly translated phrasebooks. A Hungarian tourist enters a tobacconist and haltingly reads from his English phrasebook, "I will not buy this record, it is scratched." The clerk corrects him, "No, this is a tobacconist." The customer then replies, "Ah! I will not buy this *tobacconist*, it is scratched!" The clerk eventually realizes the man wants to buy cigarettes. Things quickly spiral: When the customer asks for a box of matches, the phrasebook instructs him to say "My hovercraft is full of eels." The conversation deteriorates further when the tourist inadvertently propositions the clerk with "Do you want to come back to my place?" Borrowing the phrasebook, the clerk attempts to communicate the cost, but his Hungarian translation is so offensive it earns him a punch in the face. A policeman steps in, but the customer's attempt to explain only results in him complimenting the officer on his "beautiful thighs." After being arrested, the tourist indignantly exclaims, "My nipples explode with delight!" The scene cuts to a courtroom, where the phrasebook's publisher faces trial. Attempting to conceal his guilt, he proclaims, "I wish to plead incompetence."

Just like the babel fish, science fiction often imagines clever ways to sidestep the very real challenges of translation between human languages, and sometimes extraterrestrial ones. In the *Star Wars* universe, C-3PO is a humanoid robot programmed for etiquette and translation, famously fluent in over six million forms of communication. In *Doctor Who*, the incumbent Time Lord and their companion travel through space and time aboard the TARDIS, a ship equipped with a "translation matrix" that renders nearly every language in the universe instantly intelligible. The TARDIS doesn't just translate speech, it transmits understanding telepathically, so that everyone hears others speaking their own language.

But even this sci-fi solution has its limitations. In the episode "Fires of Pompeii," the Doctor and his companion land in ancient Pompeii and attempt to warn the locals of the impending eruption of Mount Vesuvius. Unfortunately, Latin at that time lacked a word for "volcano," the concept simply didn't exist, so their warnings fell on confused ears. *Star Trek* also introduced a universal translator, or "UT," a device that could interpret alien speech in real time, converting it seamlessly into the user's native tongue. Whether implanted, handheld, or built into the starship's systems, the translator made intergalactic diplomacy, and screenwriting, a lot easier.

This kind of technology was once purely the stuff of science fiction, until recently. Google's Pixel Buds, for example, use Google Translate to provide live translation in more than a hundred languages. When a sentence is spoken, it's translated into the target language and read aloud. The app is powered by AI and built on deep learning. Earlier versions of translation tools worked by translating each word individually, then applying grammatical rules to piece together a sentence, often resulting in stiff, fragmented language. Neural networks, by contrast, process entire sentences at once, predicting the most likely translation based on large language models (LLMs), massive datasets of previously translated text. Trained on many hours of speech, these systems use machine learning to recognize linguistic patterns and deliver far more natural results.

In practice, however, live translation still has its flaws. The app struggles with unfamiliar vocabulary, strong regional accents, and interference from overlapping conversations and noisy environments. Idioms, other metaphor, and slang often trip it up too. LLMs are also heavily biased toward Western languages and cultures. Despite these bugs, the gap between science fiction and reality is closing fast. AI translation continues to improve, but it hasn't replaced real multilingualism. Human interpreters don't need to worry about being out of work just yet. It may be some time before artificial intelligence reaches human-level fluency, and even longer before we get anything resembling a fully functional universal translator. In *Star Trek*, after all, it's not invented until the late twenty-second century.

Gray Matters

Machine translation is a helpful tool in many contexts, especially as the technology continues to evolve, but it's still no substitute for learning a second language. Beyond the practical advantages of speaking another tongue, there are significant cognitive benefits as well. What actually happens to our brains when we learn a new language?

Earlier in the chapter, we explored how age influences second language acquisition. Age also affects the way language learning shapes the brain on a physical level. Our brains are made up of neurons and dendrites, the connections between neurons, collectively known as "gray matter." Studies show that early bilinguals tend to have more gray matter than monolinguals, indicating a denser neural network. This increased density is associated with improved attention, memory, and executive function.

Bilingualism also enhances the brain's "white matter," the system of nerve fibers that connects the four lobes of the brain and facilitates communication between regions. Research has found that bilingual individuals tend to have greater white matter integrity than monolinguals, which contributes to faster processing and stronger cognitive performance overall. In short, learning another language doesn't just open up new worlds of communication, it literally strengthens the architecture of the brain.

Late bilinguals also enjoy many of the neurological benefits associated with learning a second language. Engaging with new vocabulary, grammar, and sounds creates fresh neural pathways and strengthens existing connections within the brain. These links are reinforced through regular practice and by building on prior knowledge. Language learning is arguably one of the most demanding, yet rewarding, mental tasks we can take on. It's a powerful way to exercise our brains. For older learners, it offers significant cognitive protection, helping to guard against dementia, Alzheimer's disease, and other forms of age-related neurological decline. Bilingualism has also been shown to enhance what's known as *cognitive reserve*, the brain's ability to compensate for damage or degeneration without showing noticeable impairments. In this way, speaking more than one language acts as a kind of mental buffer, preserving brain health well into old age.

These physical changes are accompanied by improvements in a range of mental abilities and social skills. Learning a new language has been linked to enhanced academic performance, even beyond communication. Language learners tend to outperform their monolingual peers across various subjects, including core areas like mathematics and science. Language learning also boosts concentration and attention span. Research shows that acquiring a second language improves alertness and focus, making it easier to tune out distractions, an asset for everyone, but particularly beneficial for individuals with attention deficit hyperactivity disorder. Language learning can also strengthen memory by engaging recall and memorization skills, such as learning new vocabulary and grammatical rules.

Studying a new language also strengthens executive function, the set of cognitive skills that includes working memory, flexible thinking, problem-solving, and decision-making. It appears to enhance creativity and imagination, perhaps due to the mental processes involved: translation, code-switching, disciplined study, and the openness required to learn and adapt. Research shows that language learning fosters open-mindedness and empathy, helping us to step into someone else's shoes and see the world from another perspective. This, in turn, can lead to improved communication skills in everyday life. Ultimately, learning another language enriches our personal, social, and professional relationships, and makes us more capable, thoughtful, and connected human beings.

In a world that often feels divided, being able to speak across languages is more than just a skill, it's an essential step toward greater understanding and unity.

The Last Word

In this chapter, we explored the stages of second language acquisition, how they mirror and diverge from the way we learn our first, and the predictable missteps that arise along the way, from mother-tongue interference to the influence of age, aptitude, and motivation on fluency. We delved into linguistic phenomena like interlanguage and code-switching, as seen through the lens of pop culture, social tropes, and stereotypes. We met rare individuals like polyglot savant Christopher, and examined unusual language-related conditions, such as foreign language syndrome. We considered the rise of artificial intelligence and machine translation, along with their many possibilities and current limitations.

And finally, we reflected on the remarkable cognitive and social benefits of learning another language: a deeply enriching way to stretch the brain and open the mind.

Learning a new language is never simple, but it is always rewarding. It deepens our understanding of how language works, reveals unfamiliar perspectives, and fosters empathy across borders.

In the end, every new language is a doorway to another world – offering a glimpse into new cultures and worldviews, and reminding us of our extraordinary human capacity to connect.

Conclusions
In Other Words

Beyond Words has been a journey into the fascinating world of psycholinguistics: the study of language and the mind. While the name suggests a blend of linguistics and psychology, the reality is much richer. Psycholinguistics draws on philosophy, cognitive science, neuroscience, and more, weaving together insights from across disciplines. Along the way, we've explored how we acquire our first language, how we learn others, how we make sense of what we hear and say, and what happens when these processes falter. Foundational to this were the big questions: *What is language?* And *where did it come from?* By starting with the nature and origins of language itself, we laid the groundwork for understanding all that followed. At first, it might seem surprising that so many different areas fall under the same umbrella. But as the story unfolded, the pieces came together to reveal a bigger picture: a deeper understanding of how we learn, use, and occasionally lose language.

Psycholinguistics might be a relatively new field, but its story starts much earlier. We traced its beginnings all the way back to ancient Egypt and Greece, where early ideas about language first appeared in medical writings and in the musings of philosophers like Plato. Along the way, we met some of the major figures who helped shape the field, from William Jones and Wilhelm Wundt to Noam Chomsky and Susan Curtiss. Their efforts laid the groundwork for the questions and theories we're still exploring today. Of course, not all of the early ideas held up. Some, like Franz Gall's phrenology or Wolfgang von Kempelen's "Chess Turk," strayed into pseudoscience. But those moments are part of the story too. We've looked at key discoveries, accidental breakthroughs, bold theories, and the many ways people have tried to understand how language works. And like any living science, psycholinguistics is full of lively disagreement and debates, some of which are still going strong.

In the first chapter, we started with what seemed like a simple question: What exactly is language? As it turns out, the answer is anything but simple. We quickly discovered that language is far more than just a system of communication. It's a rich, layered phenomenon that touches nearly every aspect of human life. We unpacked the differences between signs and symbols, considered the arbitrary nature of language, and dived into the big question of linguistic relativity, whether language shapes thought or vice versa (or whether both might be true). We saw how linguists define language in terms of smaller building blocks, from individual sounds to full sentences, all governed by grammatical rules.

From there, we explored the nuances of languages and dialects, social and regional, standard and nonstandard, and how these reflect identity and culture. We looked beyond speech to writing too, tracing the diversity of writing systems around the world, from ancient Egyptian hieroglyphs to Australian Aboriginal message sticks. And we clarified that spelling and writing are not the same thing. Language, we also saw, isn't just spoken or written, it's signed as well. Sign languages are full, complex systems in their own right, complete with regional variation and cultural depth.

We wrapped up that chapter by zooming in on the body and brain, examining how the vocal tract works, how specific areas of the brain coordinate language, and how discoveries like the FOXP2 gene and the structure of the hyoid bone have deepened our understanding of how humans speak, and what happens when things go wrong.

In the second chapter, we made a bold claim: Language is the greatest invention of humankind, yes, even more impressive than sliced bread. That naturally raised some big questions: Where did language come from? When did it emerge? And how exactly did it all begin? We dug into the origins of language in *Homo sapiens* and considered whether earlier hominins like *Homo habilis* or our close cousins the Neanderthals might have had some capacity for language too. From there, we marveled at the evolution of language learning and the development of over 7,000 living languages spoken around the world today, even as we acknowledged the many that have disappeared along the way.

We saw that the puzzle of language origins has intrigued minds as brilliant as Charles Darwin's, who proposed that speech might have evolved from gestures, music, dance, or even imitative sounds like *buzz* and *hiss*. We traced the history of early spoken and written languages, learning that while speech likely predates writing by tens of thousands of years, or even more, Sumerian cuneiform still holds the title as the oldest known written language. And we explored the still-controversial question of whether there was a single "original" language.

The chapter also brought us to attempts, some groundbreaking, others more quixotic, to teach human language to nonhuman animals. We looked at famous experiments with apes like Koko the gorilla and Nim Chimpsky, along with efforts involving parrots, dogs, and even horses. Finally, we took a look at the remarkable communication systems in the animal kingdom, from the dances of honeybees to the color-coded signals of chameleons, showing that while human language may be unique, we are far from alone in our desire to be understood.

After defining language and exploring its possible origins, we turned in Chapter 3 to how we acquire it. We revisited some of history's earliest, and most ethically questionable, language deprivation experiments, from ancient Egypt to medieval Europe, in search of answers to what language, if any, children develop without exposure. This opened the door to heartbreaking real-life cases of so-called "feral" or wild children, like Victor of Aveyron and Genie, whose tragic lives offered rare insight into first language acquisition, and its limits.

From there, we dived into one of the biggest debates in the field: Is language learned through experience, or are we born with it? We met the opposing views of B. F. Skinner and Noam Chomsky, the latter of whom famously proposed the idea of an inborn "language acquisition device." This led us to the Critical Period Hypothesis and the notion that there are sensitive developmental windows for language, something also observed in other species like songbirds and sheep.

We charted the stages of typical language development, from prenatal exposure and early babbling to toddler word bursts and childhood milestones. Along the way, we found out why "baby talk" isn't silly, it's actually helpful, and how children's adorable linguistic missteps ("goed" instead of "went") show they're hard at work figuring out the rules. We also explored atypical language development in children with autism, cerebral palsy, and deafness, and how Deaf children naturally acquire sign language. In the end, we saw that no two children take exactly the same path, and that learning a language isn't something we outgrow, it's a lifelong process.

In Chapter 4, we explored how we produce and comprehend language, from speaking and listening to reading and writing. We unpacked the intricate mental processes behind everyday communication, including how we retrieve words from our mental dictionaries and recognize them in context. Along the way, we encountered fascinating experiments like the McGurk Effect, the Ganong Effect, and the Stroop Effect, which reveal just how complex and sometimes deceptive our perceptions can be. Surprisingly, we also learned that certain animals, like chinchillas and quail, perceive elements of human speech in ways not too different from us.

We dipped into some of the field's more controversial theories, like motor theory and mirror neurons, and saw that even fluent speakers regularly make mistakes. We looked at common speech errors, from classic malapropisms to the famously scrambled spoonerisms, and how these slips offer insight into the workings of the mind. Our investigation into reading showed how much our eyes and inner voices coordinate behind the scenes, and how easily garden path sentences can lead us astray. We also explored curious phenomena like the Mandela Effect and "typoglycemia," where our brains autocorrect jumbled text without us realizing it. Finally, we turned to writing itself, how it relies on cognitive, linguistic, and motor skills, and revisited the debate over handwriting versus typing. Despite how central writing is to modern life, we ended with a sobering reminder: Literacy remains an ongoing global challenge.

In Chapter 5, we shifted our focus from how people use language to how they lose it. This wasn't about everyday slips of the tongue or common errors, rather we explored what happens when language is disrupted by disability, disease, disorder, or brain injury. Our journey began in ancient Egypt with the earliest known case of language loss due to brain trauma, then leapt forward to the groundbreaking discoveries of Broca's and Wernicke's areas. We explored the different forms of aphasia and their effects on language use and comprehension, illustrated by famous cases like "Tan" and well-known figures such as Vladimir Lenin and Charles Baudelaire.

We examined a range of language disorders, along with their symptoms, causes, and treatments. These included Samuel Johnson's Tourette's Syndrome, Winston Churchill's lisp, and Beethoven's deafness. We also looked at how language loss can be met with alternative modes of communication, from Helen Keller's use of Braille to Stephen Hawking's pioneering speech-generating devices. We revisited the long-standing debate over sign language, including misguided efforts to suppress it, despite its vital role in communication.

From there, we turned to reading disorders, especially forms of so-called "word blindness," such as alexia and dyslexia, and considered writing impairments like Agatha Christie's dysgraphia. We also examined claims that Alexander Hamilton and Lewis Carroll may have shown signs of hypergraphia, the compulsion to write excessively. The chapter closed with a poignant reflection: Many of those who struggled with these conditions in the past might have received meaningful help had they lived in a time with today's scientific knowledge.

In the final chapter, we explored how we acquire second languages, those we learn in addition to our mother tongue. We saw that this process shares many similarities with first language acquisition, but also comes with its own challenges and surprises. Along the way, we encountered bilinguals, multilinguals, and some astonishing tales of polyglots (both genuine and questionable). We broke down the stages of second language learning and the various approaches people take, from immersion to instruction. We returned to the Critical Period Hypothesis, this time to consider how sensitive periods influence our ability to pick up new languages, both in childhood and later in life. This led us to reflect on the pros and cons of being an early versus late bilingual, especially when it comes to mastering pronunciation and accent.

We also touched on unusual cases like foreign accent syndrome and foreign language syndrome, and examined how motivation, mindset, and natural ability play a part in success. As always, mistakes proved to be a crucial part of the journey. We looked at what happens in the minds of bilinguals, including the development of interlanguage and the phenomenon of code-switching. Then we turned to translation, both human and machine, and considered its triumphs and blunders, in everything from viral memes to sci-fi fantasies like the babel fish or the TARDIS. And finally, we saw how learning a second language doesn't just expand our communication, it changes our brains, boosting cognitive abilities and deepening social understanding.

This book has asked some big questions about language: what it is, where it came from, how we acquire it, use it, and sometimes lose it. Searching for answers has led us down more than a few rabbit holes (and the occasional garden path). For me, writing it has meant walking a tightrope: balancing the depth and accuracy expected in scholarly research with the goal of enticing curious readers to share in the wonder of this endlessly fascinating subject. I hope we've managed to strike that balance. Ideally without too many tears, or headaches.

Our journey, however, has sparked even more questions. That's just how science works. This adventure has opened up new paths to explore, reminding us that the story of psycholinguistics is far from over. While history helps us understand where the field stands today, the real excitement lies in where it's heading next. Psycholinguistics has expanded dramatically in recent years, and it remains a vibrant, fast-evolving area of research. So, where do we go from here?

Looking ahead, the future of psycholinguistics promises exciting new frontiers, especially in neuroscience and artificial intelligence. Advances in brain imaging and cognitive science will deepen our understanding of how language is processed at the neural level, offering better tools to diagnose and treat conditions that impair speech and communication. Each new insight reminds us that language isn't just stored in the brain, it *is* the brain at work.

At the same time, artificial intelligence will continue to refine its models of human language use, shedding light on how we acquire, interpret, and produce language. How we teach machines to use language may, in turn, teach us more about ourselves. Meanwhile, AI will increasingly become a part of our daily interactions. From virtual assistants to customer service bots, it's already shaping how we communicate, work, and even form relationships.

As these fields evolve, psycholinguistics will remain at the heart of our quest to understand what language reveals about the mind. Returning to our jigsaw puzzle analogy, every discovery adds another piece to the puzzle. And while the full picture is still emerging, with each piece we come closer to grasping the rich, intricate workings of how we learn, use, and sometimes lose language.

It's a story still unfolding, one that brings us closer to understanding language, and, ultimately, ourselves.

Further Reading

Introduction

Aitchison, Jean. 2011. *The Articulate Mammal: An Introduction to Psycholinguistics.* Routledge.

Altmann, Gerry T. 2006. History of psycholinguistics. In K. Brown (ed.), *Encyclopedia of Language and Linguistics* (Vol. 1). Elsevier.

Breasted, J. H. 1930. *The Edwin Smith Surgical Papyrus* (Vols. 1–2). University of Chicago Press.

Darwin, Charles. 1998 (1872). *The Expression of the Emotions in Man and Animals.* Oxford University Press.

Galton, Francis. 1869. *Hereditary Genius: An Inquiry into Its Laws and Consequences.* Macmillan.

Hippocrates. 1849. *On the Sacred Disease* (trans. Francis Adams). In *The Genuine Works of Hippocrates* (Vol. 1, pp. 318–334). Sydenham Society. (Original c.400 BCE.)

Kantor, Jacob R. 1936. *An Objective Psychology of Grammar.* Principia Press.

Kempelen, Wolfgang von. 1791. *Mechanismus der menschlichen Sprache nebst Beschreibung seiner sprechenden Maschine.* J. B. Degen.

Levelt, William. 2012. *A History of Psycholinguistics: The Pre-Chomskyan Era.* Oxford University Press.

Locke, John. 1975 (1690). *An Essay Concerning Human Understanding* (ed. P. H. Nidditch). Clarendon Press.

Plato. 2007. *Republic* (trans. D. Lee). Penguin Books. (Original c.380 BCE.)

Rousseau, Jean-Jacques. 1979 (1762). *Emile: Or, On Education* (trans. A. Bloom). Basic Books.

Scovel, Thomas. 1998. *Psycholinguistics.* Oxford University Press.

Skinner, B. F. 1957. *Verbal Behavior.* Appleton-Century-Crofts.

Wundt, Wilhelm M. 1900. *Völkerpsychologie: T. 1-2. Die Sprache* (Vol. 1, no. 2). Verlag von Wilhelm Engelmann.

Chapter 1

Aristotle. n.d. On interpretation (trans. E. M. Edghill). In J. A. Smith and W. D. Ross (eds.), *The Works of Aristotle* (Vol. 1). Clarendon Press. (Original work written c.350 BCE.)

Auvenshine, R. C. and Pettit, N. J. 2020. The hyoid bone: An overview. *Cranio* 38(1): 6–14. https://doi.org/10.1080/08869634.2018.1487501.

Bloomfield, Leonard. 1933. *Language*. Henry Holt & Co.

Boas, Franz (ed.). 1911. *Handbook of American Indian Languages* (Vol. 1). Government Printing Office.

Bolinger, Dwight. 1975. *Aspects of Language*. Harcourt Brace Jovanovich.

Carr, Philip. 2019. *English Phonetics and Phonology: An Introduction*. John Wiley & Sons.

Chomsky, Noam. 2009 (1957). *Syntactic Structures*. De Gruyter.

Chomsky, Noam. 2013. Lecture I: What Is language? *The Journal of Philosophy* 110(12): 645–662. http://www.jstor.org/stable/43820808.

Craig, Holly and Washington, Julie A. 2013. Recent research on the language and literacy skills of African American students in the early years. In David K. Dickinson and Susan B. Neuman (eds.), *Handbook of Early Literacy Research* (Vol. 2). Guilford Press.

Crowley, Terry. 1990. *Beach-la-Mar to Bislama: The Emergence of a National Language in Vanuatu*. Clarendon Press.

Crystal, David. 2013. *Spell It Out: The Curious, Enthralling and Extraordinary Story of English Spelling*. St. Martin's Press.

Dąbrowska Ewa. 2020. How writing changes language. In A. Mauranen and S. Vetchinnikova (eds.), *Language Change: The Impact of English as a Lingua Franca* (pp. 75–94). Cambridge University Press.

Derrida, Jacques. 2016 (1967). *Of Grammatology*. Johns Hopkins University Press.

Escobar, Anna Maria and Mufwene, Salikoko. 2022. *The Cambridge Handbook of Language Contact*. Cambridge University Press.

Evans, Vyvyan. 2014. *The Language Myth: Why Language Is Not an Instinct*. Cambridge University Press.

Hauser, Marc D., Chomsky, Noam, and Fitch, W. Tecumseh. 2010. The faculty of language: What is it, who has it, and how did it evolve? In R. K. Larson, V. Déprez, and H. Yamakido (eds.), *The Evolution of Human Language: Biolinguistic Perspectives*. Approaches to the Evolution of Language (pp. 14–42). Cambridge University Press.

Hill, Joseph C., Lillo-Martin, Diane C., and Wood, Sandra K. 2019. *Sign Languages: Structures and Contexts*. Routledge.

Jackendoff, Ray. 2002. *Foundations of Language: Brain, Meaning, Grammar, Evolution*. Oxford University Press.

Levinson, Stephen C. 2003. *Space in Language and Cognition: Explorations in Cognitive Diversity*. Cambridge University Press.

Levisen, Carsten. 2012. *Cultural Semantics and Social Cognition: A Case Study on the Danish Universe of Meaning*. De Gruyter Mouton.

Napoli, Donna J. and Lee-Schoenfeld, Vera. 2010. *Language Matters: A Guide to Everyday Questions about Language.* Oxford University Press.

Nunan, David. 2012. *What Is This Thing Called Language?* Palgrave Macmillan.

Orwell, George. 1949. *1984.* Secker & Warburg.

Pennington, Martha C. 2014. *Phonology in English Language Teaching: An International Approach.* Routledge.

Plato. 1995. *Phaedrus* (eds. A. Nehamas and P. Woodruff). Hackett. (Original work written 370 BCE.)

Pullum, Geoffrey K. 1991. *The Great Eskimo Vocabulary Hoax and Other Irreverent Essays on the Study of Language.* University of Chicago Press.

Rickford, John R. 2007. *Spoken Soul: The Story of Black English.* John Wiley & Sons.

Sapir, Edward. 1921. *Language: An Introduction to the Study of Speech.* Harcourt, Brace & Co.

de Saussure, Ferdinand. 2013 (1916). *Course in General Linguistics.* Bloomsbury Publishing.

Steinmetz, Sol. 2008. *Semantic Antics: How and Why Words Change Meaning.* Random House.

Trask, R. L. 2007. *Language and Linguistics: The Key Concepts.* Routledge.

Trudgill, Peter. 2016. *Dialect Matters: Respecting Vernacular Language.* Cambridge University Press.

Twain, Mark. 1889. *A Tramp Abroad.* Chatto & Windus.

Whorf, Benjamin. 1956. Science and linguistics. In John Carroll (ed.), *Language, Thought and Reality: Selected Writings of Benjamin Lee Whorf* (pp. 207–219). MIT Press.

Wittgenstein, Ludwig. 1953. *Philosophical Investigations* (trans. G. E. M. Anscombe). Blackwell.

Wodehouse, P. G. 2013 (1934). *Thank You, Jeeves.* W. W. Norton.

YIVO Bleter. 1944. Volume 23, Number 3, May–June issue.

Yule, George. 2010. *The Study of Language.* Cambridge University Press.

Chapter 2

Bickerton, Derek. 2009. *Adam's Tongue: How Humans Made Language, How Language Made Humans.* Farrar, Straus and Giroux.

Botha, Rudolf. 2024. Did *Homo erectus* have language? The seafaring inference. *Cambridge Archaeological Journal* 35(1): 31–37. https://doi.org/10.1017/S0959774324000118.

Burridge, Kate. 2011. *Gift of the Gob: Morsels of English Language History.* HarperCollins Australia.

Chomsky, Noam. 1986. *Knowledge of Language: Its Nature, Origin, and Use.* Praeger.

Conde-Valverde, M., Martínez, I., Quam, R. M., Rosa, M., Velez, A. D., Lorenzo, C., et al. 2021. Neanderthals and *Homo sapiens* had similar auditory and speech capacities. *Nature Ecology and Evolution* 5(5): 609–615. https://doi.org/10.1038/s41559-021-01391-6.

Coulmas, Florian. 2003. *Writing Systems: An Introduction to Their Linguistic Analysis.* Cambridge University Press.

Creasman, Pearce Paul and Wilkinson, Richard H. 2017. *Pharaoh's Land and Beyond: Ancient Egypt and Its Neighbors.* Oxford University Press.

Darwin, Charles. 2019 (1871). *The Descent of Man: Selection in Relation to Sex.* Max Bollinger.

Ekström, Axel G. 2023. Viki's first words: A comparative phonetics case study. *International Journal of Primatology* 44: 249–253. https://doi.org/10.1007/s10764-023-00350-1.

Falk, Dean. 2009. *Finding Our Tongues: Mothers, Infants and the Origins of Language.* Basic Books.

Fisher, Simon E. 2019. Human genetics: The evolving story of FOXP2. *Current Biology* 29(2): R65–R67. https://doi.org/10.1016/j.cub.2018.11.047.

Gillespie-Lynch, Kristen, Greenfield, Patricia M., Lyn, Heidi, and Savage-Rumbaugh, Sue. 2014. Gestural and symbolic development among apes and humans: Support for a multimodal theory of language evolution. *Frontiers in Psychology* 5: Article 1228. https://doi.org/10.3389/fpsyg.2014.01228.

Girard-Buttoz, Cédric, Zaccarella, Emiliano, Bortolato, Tatiana, et al. 2022. Chimpanzees produce diverse vocal sequences with ordered and recombinatorial properties. *Communications Biology* 5: 410. https://doi.org/10.1038/s42003-022-03350-8.

Herrel, Anthony and Tolley, Krystal A. 2014. *The Biology of Chameleons.* University of California Press.

Hillert, Dieter G. 2015. On the evolving biology of language. *Frontiers in Psychology* 6: 1796. https://doi.org/10.3389/fpsyg.2015.01796.

Hobaiter, Catherine and Byrne, Richard W. 2014. The meanings of chimpanzee gestures. *Current Biology* 24(14): 1596–1600. https://doi.org/10.1016/j.cub.2014.05.066.

Jespersen, Otto. 1922. *Language: Its Nature, Development and Origin.* Allen & Unwin.

Kaminski, J. and Nitzschner, M. 2013. Do dogs get the point? A review of dog-human communication ability. *Learning and Motivation* 44(4): 294–302. https://doi.org/10.1016/j.lmot.2013.05.001.

Kellogg, Winthrop N. and Kellogg, Luella A. 1933. *The Ape and the Child: A Comparative Study of the Environmental Influence upon Early Behavior.* Hafner.

Kelly, Piers. 2020. Australian message sticks: Old questions, new directions. *Journal of Material Culture* 25(2): 133–152. https://doi.org/10.1177/1359183519858375.

Kenneally, Christine. 2007. *The First Word: The Search for the Origins of Language.* Viking Press.

Klein, Richard G. 2017. Language and human evolution. *Journal of Neurolinguistics* 43 Part B: 204–221. https://doi.org/10.1016/j.jneuroling.2016.11.004.

Köhler, Wolfgang. 1929. *Gestalt Psychology.* Liveright.

Leroux, Maël and Townsend, Simon W. 2020. Call combinations in great apes and the evolution of syntax. *Animal Behavior and Cognition* 7(2): 131–139. https://doi.org/10.26451/abc.07.02.07.2020.

Meyer, Heinrich August Eduard. 1846. *Manners and Customs of the Aborigines of the Encounter Bay tribe, South Australia.* George Dehane.

Müller, Max Friedrich. 1864. *Lectures on the Science of Language.* 2nd series. Longmans.

Olkowicz, Seweryn, Kocourek, Martin, Lučan, Radek K., et al. 2016. Birds have primate-like numbers of neurons in the forebrain. *Proceedings of the National Academy of Science USA* 113(26): 7255–7260. https://doi.org/10.1073/pnas.1517131113.

Ouattara, Karim, Lemasson, Alban, and Zuberbühler, Klaus. 2009. Campbell's monkeys concatenate vocalizations into context-specific call sequences. *Proceedings of the National Academy of Science USA* 106(51): 22026–22031. https://doi.org/10.1073/pnas.0908118106.

Pinker, Steven and Jackendoff, Ray. 2005. The faculty of language: What's special about it? *Cognition* 95(2): 201–236. https://doi.org/10.1016/j.cognition.2004.08.004.

Price, Tabitha, Wadewitz, Philip, Cheney, Dorothy et al. 2015. Vervets revisited: A quantitative analysis of alarm call structure and context specificity. *Scientific Reports* 5: 13220. https://doi.org/10.1038/srep13220.

Reidenberg, Joy S. and Laitman, Jeffrey T. 2018. Anatomy of underwater sound production with a focus on ultrasonic vocalization in toothed whales including dolphins and porpoises. In S. M. Brudzynski (ed.), *Handbook of Behavioral Neuroscience.* Elsevier. https://doi.org/10.1016/B978-0-12-809600-0.00047-0.

Ruse, Michael. 2013. *The Cambridge Encyclopedia of Darwin and Evolutionary Thought.* Cambridge University Press.

Stollznow, Karen. 2014. *Language Myths, Mysteries and Magic.* Palgrave Macmillan.

Terrace, Herbert S. 1979. *Nim.* Knopf.

Woodard, Roger D. 2004. *The Cambridge Encyclopedia of the World's Ancient Languages.* Cambridge University Press.

Woods, Christopher, Teeter, Emily, and Emberling, Geoff (eds.) 2010. *Visible Language: Inventions of Writing in the Ancient Middle East and Beyond.* Oriental Institute of the University of Chicago.

Yang, Zetian and Long, Michael A. 2025. Convergent vocal representations in parrot and human forebrain motor networks. *Nature* 640: 427–434. https://doi.org/10.1038/s41586-025-08695-8.

Chapter 3

Adani, Shir and Cepanec, Maya. 2019. Sex differences in early communication development: Behavioral and neurobiological indicators of more vulnerable communication system development in boys. *Croatian Medical Journal* 60(2): 141–149. https://doi.org/10.3325/cmj.2019.60.141.

Berko, Jean. 1958. The child's learning of English morphology. *Word* 14(3): 150–177. https://doi.org/10.1080/00437956.1958.11659661.

Bybee, Joan. 2010. *Language, Usage and Cognition*. Cambridge University Press.

Caesar, Julius. 2008. *The Gallic War* (trans. C. Hammond). Oxford University Press. (Original *c.*52 BCE.)

Catrou, François and Manucci, Niccalao. 1709. *The General History of the Mogol Empire, from Its Foundation by Tamerlane, to the Late Emperor Orangzeb: Extracted from the Memoirs of M Manouchi, a Venetian, and Chief Physitian to Orangzeb for Above Forty Years*. Jonah Bowyer.

Chomsky, Noam. 2015 (1957). *Syntactic Structures*. Martino Fine Books.

Colombelli-Négrel, Diane, Hauber, Mark E., Robertson, Jeremy, Sulloway, Frank J., Hoi, Herbert, Griggio, Matteo, and Kleindorfer, Sonia. 2012. Embryonic learning of vocal passwords in superb fairy-wrens reveals intruder cuckoo nestlings. *Current Biology* 22(22): 2155–2160. https://doi.org/10.1016/j.cub.2012.09.025.

Curtiss, Susan, Fromkin, Victoria, Krashen, Stephen, Rigler, David, and Rigler, Marilyn. 1974. The linguistic development of Genie. *Language* 50(3): 528–554. https://doi.org/10.2307/412222.

Dagognet, François. 2009. *Le docteur Itard entre l'énigme et l'échec*, preface by Jean Itard, Victor de l'Aveyron, éditions Allia.

Darwin, Charles. 2007 (1871). *The Descent of Man, and Selection in Relation to Sex*. Concise Edition and Commentary by Carl Zimmer. Penguin Books.

Darwin, Charles. 1977 (1877). Biographical sketch of an infant. *American Journal of Diseases of Children* 131(8): 909–912. https://doi.org/10.1001/archpedi.1977.02120210087019.

Goldschmidt, Richard. 1940. *The Material Basis of Evolution*. Yale University Press.

Herodotus. 2006 (5th century BCE). An account of Egypt. *Histories, 2.2.3. An Account of Egypt*. (trans G. C. Macaulay). https://www.gutenberg.org/files/2131/2131-h/2131-h.htm.

Holland, Alisha C. and Gazman, Zhamilya. 2023. Autobiographical memory and emotion. In Gesine Lenore Schiewer, Jeanette Altarriba, and Bee Chin Ng (eds.), *Language and Emotion* (Vol. 3, pp. 1399–1415). De Gruyter Brill.

Itard, Jean Mark Gaspard 1962. *The Wild Boy of Aveyron*. Appleton-Century-Crofts.

Kidd, Evan and Donnelly, Seamus. 2020. Individual differences in first language acquisition. *Annual Review of Linguistics* 6(1): 319–340. http://dx.doi.org/10.1146/annurev-linguistics-011619-030326.

Lenneberg, Eric. 1967. *Biological Foundations of Language*. Wiley.

Lindsay, Robert and Dalyell, John Graham. 1814. *The Chronicles of Scotland*. George Ramsay and Company.

Martin, Gary E., Klusek, Jessica, Estigarribia, Bruno, and Roberts, Joane E. 2009. Language characteristics of individuals with Down syndrome. *Topics in Language Disorders* 29(2): 112–132. https://doi.org/10.1097/tld.0b013e3181a71fe1.

May, Lilian, Byers-Heinlein, Krista, Gervain, Judit, and Werker, Janet F. 2011. Language and the newborn brain: Does prenatal language experience shape the neonate neural response to speech? *Frontiers in Psychology* 2: 222. https://doi.org/10.3389/fpsyg.2011.00222.

Mei, Cristina, Reilly, Sheena, Bickerton, Molly, Mensah, Fiona, Turner, Samantha, Kumaranayagam, Dhanooshini, et al. 2020. Speech in children with cerebral palsy. *Developmental Medicine & Child Neurology* 62(12): 1374–1382. https://doi.org/10.1111/dmcn.14592.

Navarro, Ester. 2022. What is theory of mind? A psychometric study of theory of mind and intelligence. *Cognitive Psychology*, 136: 101495. https://doi.org/10.1016/j.cogpsych.2022.101495.

Penfield, Wilder and Roberts, Lamar. 1959. *Speech and Brain Mechanisms*. Princeton University Press.

Pinker, Steven. 1994. *The Language Instinct*. W. Morrow.

Salimbene di Adam. n.d. On Frederick II, 13th Century. *Medieval Sourcebook*. Fordham University. https://sourcebooks.web.fordham.edu/source/salimbene1.asp.

Steensma, David P. 2005. Down syndrome in Down House: Trisomy 21, GATA1 mutations, and Charles Darwin. *Blood* 105(6): 2614–2616. https://doi.org/10.1182/blood-2004-10-3974.

Takei, Wataru. 2001. How do deaf infants attain first signs? *Developmental Science* 4(1): 71–78. https://doi.org/10.1111/1467-7687.00150.

Tolkien, J. R. R. 1954–1955. *The Lord of the Rings*. George Allen & Unwin.

Tomasello, Michael. 2003. *Constructing a Language: A Usage-Based Theory of Language Acquisition*. Harvard University Press.

Treiman, Rebecca and Kessler, Brett. 2014. *How Children Learn to Write Words*. Oxford University Press.

Tsang, Christine D. 2012. Behavioral methodologies in infant language acquisition. In Norbert M. Seel (ed.), *Encyclopedia of the Sciences of Learning* (pp. 434–436). Springer. https://doi.org/10.1007/978-1-4419-1428-6_399.

Chapter 4

Altmann, Gerry T. M. 1997. *The Ascent of Babel: An Exploration of Language, Mind, and Understanding.* Oxford University Press.

Colby, Sarah E. and McMurray, Bob. 2023. Efficiency of spoken word recognition slows across the adult lifespan. *Cognition* 240: 105588. https://doi.org/10.1016/j.cognition.2023.105588.

Costa, Albert, Strijkers, Kristof, Martin, Clara, and Thierry, Guillaume. 2009. The time course of word retrieval revealed by event-related brain potentials during overt speech. *Proceedings of the National Academy of Sciences USA* 106(50): 21442–21446. https://doi.org/10.1073/pnas.0908921106.

Coulmas, Florian. 2003. *Writing Systems: An Introduction to Their Linguistic Analysis.* Cambridge University Press.

Dave, Arjun. 2022. Hand writing versus keyboard writing: Effect on word recall. *International Peer Reviewed E Journal of English Language & Literature Studies – ISSN: 2583–5963* 4(2): 1–30. https://doi.org/10.58213/ell.v4i2.50.

Davis, Matt. n.d. *Cmabrigde.* MRC Cognition and Brain Sciences Unit, University of Cambridge. https://www.mrc-cbu.cam.ac.uk/personal/matt.davis/Cmabrigde/.

Dell, Gary S. 1995. Speaking and misspeaking. In Lila R. Gleitman, Mark Liberman, and Daniel N. Osherson (eds.), *An Invitation to Cognitive Science* (Vol. 1: Language, pp. 183–208). MIT Press.

Diehl, R. L. and Kluender, K. R. 1987. On the categorization of speech sounds. In S. Harnad (ed.), *Categorical Perception: The Groundwork of Cognition* (pp. 226–253). Cambridge University Press.

Fogassi, Leonardo and Ferrari, Pier Francesco. 2004. Mirror neurons, gestures and language evolution. *Interaction Studies* 5(3): 345–363. http://dx.doi.org/10.1075/is.5.3.03fog.

Fowler, C. A. and Rosenblum, L. D. 1990. Duplex perception: A comparison of monosyllables and slamming doors. *Journal of Experimental Psychology: Human Perception and Performance* 16(4): 742–754. https://doi.org/10.1037//0096-1523.16.4.742.

Fromkin, Victoria A. 1980. *Errors in Linguistic Performance: Slips of the Tongue, Ear, Pen and Hand.* Academic Press.

Ganong III, William F. 1978. A word advantage in phoneme boundary experiments. *Journal of the Acoustical Society of America* 63(S1): S20–S20. https://doi.org/10.1121/1.2016541.

Hayes, John R. and Flower, Linda S. 1980. Identifying the organization of writing processes. In Lee W. Gregg and Erwin R. Steinberg (eds.), *Cognitive Processes in Writing* (pp. 3–30). Lawrence Erlbaum Associates.

Kennison, Sheila M. 2013. *Introduction to Language Development.* Sage.

Kimura, Doreen. 1961. Cerebral dominance and the perception of verbal stimuli. *Canadian Journal of Psychology* 15(3): 166–171. https://psycnet.apa.org/doi/10.1037/h0083219.

Kluender, Keith R., Diehl, Randy L., and Killeen, Peter R. 1987. Japanese quail can learn phonetic categories. *Science* 237(4819): 1195–1197. https://doi.org/10.1126/science.3629235.

Kuhl, Patricia K. and Miller, James D. 1975. Speech perception by the chinchilla: Voiced–voiceless distinction in alveolar plosive consonants. *Science* 190(4209): 69–72. https://doi.org/10.1126/science.1166301.

Levelt, Willem J. 1993. *Speaking: From Intention to Articulation*. MIT Press.

Levelt, Willem J. 2001. Spoken word production: A theory of lexical access. *Proceedings of the National Academy of Sciences* 98(23): 13464–13471. https://doi.org/10.1073/pnas.231459498.

Levelt, Willem J., Roelofs, Ardi, and Meyer, Antje S. 1999. A theory of lexical access in speech production. *Behavioral and Brain Sciences* 22(1): 1–38. doi:10.1017/S0140525X99001776.

Liberman, Alvin M. and Mattingly, Ignatius G. 1985. The motor theory of speech perception revised. *Cognition* 21(1): 1–36. https://doi.org/10.1016/0010-0277(85)90021-6.

McCusker, Leo X., Gough, Philip B., and Bias, Randolphe G. 1981. Word recognition inside out and outside in. *Journal of Experimental Psychology: Human Perception and Performance* 7(3): 538–551. https://psycnet.apa.org/doi/10.1037/0096-1523.7.3.538.

McGurk, Harry and MacDonald, John. 1976. Hearing lips and seeing voices. *Nature* 264(5588): 746–748. https://doi.org/10.1038/264746a0.

Motley, Michael. T. and Baars, Bernard J. 1979. Effects of cognitive set upon laboratory induced verbal (Freudian) slips. *Journal of Speech and Hearing Research* 22(3): 421–432. https://doi.org/10.1044/jshr.2203.421.

Pelczarski, Kristin M. and Yaruss, J. Scott. 2014. Phonological encoding of young children who stutter. *Journal of Fluency Disorders* 39: 12–24. https://doi.org/10.1016/j.jfludis.2013.10.003.

Rawlinson, Graham E. 1976. The significance of letter position in word recognition. Unpublished PhD thesis, Psychology Department, University of Nottingham, UK.

Rayner, Keith. 2009. The 35th Sir Frederick Bartlett lecture: Eye movements and attention in reading, scene perception, and visual search. *Quarterly Journal of Experimental Psychology* 62(8): 1457–1506. https://doi.org/10.1080/17470210902816461.

Rayner, Keith, White, Sarah J., Johnson, Rebecca L., and Liversedge, Simon P. 2006. Raeding wrods with jubmled lettres: There is a cost. *Psychological Science* 17(3): 192–193. https://doi.org/10.1111/j.1467-9280.2006.01684.x.

Rayner, Keith, Pollatsek, Alexander, Ashby, Jane, and Clifton Jr, Charles. 2012. *Psychology of Reading*. Psychology Press.

Roux, Franck-Emmanuel, Draper, Louisa, Köpke, Barbara, and Démonet, Jean-François. 2010. Who actually read Exner? Returning to the source of the frontal "writing centre" hypothesis. *Cortex* 46(9): 1204–1210. https://doi.org/10.1016/j.cortex.2010.03.001.

Shi, Yungfen and Xie, Yuhong. 2017. Viewpoint in garden path sentence: A functional approach. *Open Journal of Modern Linguistics* 7: 33–40. https://doi.org/10.4236/OJML.2017.71003.

Spilling, Eivor F., Rønneberg, Vibeke, Rogne, Wenke M., Roeser, Jens, and Torrance, Mark. 2023. Writing by hand or digitally in first grade: Effects on rate of learning to compose text. *Computers & Education* 198: 104755. https://psycnet.apa.org/doi/10.1016/j.compedu.2023.104755.

Sticht, Thomas. 2022. Adult literacy and basic education in the United States. In *Oxford Research Encyclopedia of Education*. https://doi.org/10.1093/acrefore/9780190264093.013.1744.

Stroop, John R. 1935. Studies of interference in serial verbal reactions. *Journal of Experimental Psychology* 18(6): 643–662. https://doi.org/10.1037/h0054651.

Traxler, Matthew J. 2011. *Introduction to Psycholinguistics: Understanding Language Science*. Wiley-Blackwell.

Traxler, Matthew J. and Gernsbacher, Morton A. (eds.). 2011. *Handbook of Psycholinguistics*. Elsevier.

van Drempt, Nadege, McCluskey, Annie, and Lannin, Natasha A. 2011. A review of factors that influence adult handwriting performance. *Australian Occupations Therapy Journal* 58(5): 321–328. https://doi.org/10.1111/j.1440-1630.2011.00960.x.

Vitevitch, Michael S. and Luce, Paul A. 2016. Phonological neighborhood effects in spoken word perception and production. *Annual Review of Linguistics* 2(1): 75–94. https://doi.org/10.1146/annurev-linguist-030514-124832.

Warren, Richard M. and Obusek, Charles. 1971. Speech perception and phonemic restorations. *Perception & Psychophysics* 9: 358–363. https://psycnet.apa.org/doi/10.3758/BF03212667.

Chapter 5

Acharya, Aninda B. and Wroten, Michael. 2024. Wernicke Aphasia. In StatPearls [Internet]. Treasure Island (FL): StatPearls Publishing. https://www.ncbi.nlm.nih.gov/books/NBK441951/.

Ahmad, Abdullah, Jagdhane, Nitin, Ademmer, Karin, and Choudhari, Kishor. 2024. Carl Wernicke of "Wernicke's Area": A historical review. *World Neurosurgery* 185: 225–233. https://doi.org/10.1016/j.wneu.2024.02.103.

Alderson-Day, Ben, Lima, César F., Evans, Samuel, Krishnan, Saloni, Shanmugalingam, Pradheep, Fernyhough, Charles, and Scott, Sophie K. 2017. Distinct processing of ambiguous speech in people with non-clinical auditory verbal hallucinations. *Brain* 140(9): 2475–2489. https://doi.org/10.1093/brain/awx206.

Baig, Mirza M. Z. and Ahmad, Mudassar M. 2018. Crossing over the communicative barrier: Case of Helen Keller's developmental disability and language learnability. *Kashmir Journal of Language Research* 21(1): 157–167.

Biden, Joe. 2007. *Promises to Keep: On Life and Politics*. Random House.

Brookshire, Robert H. and McNeil, Malcom R. 2014. *Introduction to Neurogenic Communication Disorders*. Elsevier Health Sciences.

Chernow, Ron. 2005. *Alexander Hamilton*. Penguin.

Cohen, Laurent, Henry, Carole, Dehaene, Stanislas, Martinaud, Olivier, Lehéricy, Stéphane, Lemer, Cathy, and Ferrieux, Sophie. 2004. The pathophysiology of letter-by-letter reading. *Neuropsychologia*. 42(13): 1768–1780. https://doi.org/10.1016/j.neuropsychologia.2004.04.018.

Darvesh, Sultan, Cash, Megan K., Martin, Earl, and Engelhardt, Eliasz. 2024. Expressive amusia and aphasia: The story of Maurice Ravel. *Dementia & Neuropsychologia* 18: e20230108. https://doi.org/10.1590/1980-5764-dn-2023-0108.

Dieguez, Sebastian and Bogousslavsky, Julien. 2007. Baudelaire's aphasia: From poetry to cursing. *Frontiers of Neurology and Neuroscience* 22: 121–149. https://doi.org/10.1159/000102876.

Finger, Stanley. 1994. *Origins of Neuroscience: A History of Explorations into Brain Function*. Oxford University Press.

Grigorenko, Elena L., Klin, Ami, and Volkmar, Fred. 2003. Annotation: Hyperlexia: disability or superability? *Journal of Child Psychology and Psychiatry* 44(8): 1079–1091. https://doi.org/10.1111/1469-7610.00193.

Grzesiak-Witek, Danuta. 2017. Language trapped in the body: Why Stephen Hawking does not speak? Speech therapy for patients with ALS. *Społeczeństwo i Rodzina* 53(4): 106–120.

Isaacson, Walter. 2008. *Einstein: His Life and Universe*. Simon & Schuster.

Keller, Helen. 2005. *Story of My Life*. Penguin.

Kérchy, Anna. 2020. The acoustics of nonsense in Lewis Carroll's Alice tales. *International Research in Children's Literature* 13(Supplement): 175–190. https://doi.org/10.3366/ircl.2020.0345.

Kirby, Philip, Nation, Kate, Snowling, Margaret, and Whyte, William. 2020. The problem of dyslexia: Historical perspectives. *Oxford Review of Education* 46(4): 409–413. https://doi.org/10.1080/03054985.2020.1770020.

Kumari, Sativa, Spain, Rebecca, Mandel, Steven, and Sataloff, Robert T. 2014. The neurology of stuttering. In John Rubin, Robert T. Sataloff, and Gwen S. Korovin (eds.), *Diagnosis and Treatment of Voice Disorders* (pp. 153–164). Plural Publishing.

Langland-Hassan, Peter, Faries, Frank R., Richardson, Michael J., and Dietz, Aimee. 2015. Inner speech deficits in people with aphasia. *Frontiers in Psychology* 6: 528. https://doi.org/10.3389/fpsyg.2015.00528.

Lecours, André and Joanette, Yves. 1980. Linguistic and other psychological aspects of paroxysmal aphasia. *Brain and Language* 10(1): 1–23. https://doi.org/10.1016/0093-934x(80)90034-6.

Lee, Seung-Hwan., Chung, Young-Cho, Yang, Jong-Chul, Kim, Yong-Ku, and Suh, Kwang-Yoon. 2004. Abnormal speech perception in schizophrenia with auditory hallucinations. *Acta Neuropsychiatrica* 16(3): 154–159. https://doi.org/10.1111/j.0924-2708.2004.00071.x.

Little, Bethany, Gallagher, Peter, Zimmerer, Vitor, Varley, Rosemary, Douglas, Maggie, Spencer, Helen, et al. 2019. Language in schizophrenia and aphasia: The relationship with non-verbal cognition and thought disorder. *Cognitive Neuropsychiatry* 24(6): 389–405. https://doi.org/10.1080/13546805.2019.1668758.

Miller, Amanda C., Keenan, Janice M., Betjemann, Rebecca S., Willcutt, Erik G., Pennington, Bruce F., and Olson, Richard K. 2013. Reading comprehension in children with ADHD: Cognitive underpinnings of the centrality deficit. *Journal of Abnormal Child Psychology* 41(3): 473–483. https://doi.org/10.1007/s10802-012-9686-8.

Minagar, Alireza, Ragheb, John, and Kelley, Roger E. 2003. The Edwin Smith Surgical Papyrus: Description and analysis of the earliest case of aphasia. *Journal of Medical Biography* 11(2): 114–117. https://doi.org/10.1177/096777200301100214.

Mohammed, Nasser, Narayan, Vinayak, Patra, Devi P. and Nanda, Anil. 2018. Louis Victor Leborgne ("Tan"). *World Neurosurgery* 114: 121–125. https://doi.org/10.1016/j.wneu.2018.02.021.

Moores, Donald F. 2010. Partners in progress: The 21st International Congress on Education of the Deaf and the repudiation of the 1880 Congress of Milan. *American Annals of the Deaf* 155(3): 309–310. https://doi.org/10.1353/aad.2010.0016.

Murray, T. J. 1979. Dr Samuel Johnson's movement disorder. *British Medical Journal* 1(6178): 1610–1614. https://doi.org/10.1136/bmj.1.6178.1610.

Nighoghossian, Norbert, Cho, Tae-Hee, and Mechtouff, Laura. 2021. Lenin's stroke. *Case Reports in Neurology* 13(2): 384–387. https://doi.org/10.1159/000515657.

Oyebode, Femi. 2013. Baudelaire and The Flowers of Evil. *Advances in Psychiatric Treatment* 19(1): 77–80. https://doi.org/10.1192/apt.bp.110.008391.

Randi, Judi, Newman, Tina, and Grigorenko, Elena L. 2010. Teaching children with autism to read for meaning: Challenges and possibilities. *Journal of Autism and Developmental Disorders* 40(7): 890–902. https://doi.org/10.1007/s10803-010-0938-6.

Raschle, Nora M., Chang, Maria, and Gaab, Nadine. 2011. Structural brain alterations associated with dyslexia predate reading onset. *Neuroimage* 57(3): 742–749. https://doi.org/10.1016/j.neuroimage.2010.09.055.

Ruben, Robert J. 2000. Redefining the survival of the fittest: Communication disorders in the 21st century. *Laryngoscope* 110(2 Pt 1): 241–245. https://doi.org/10.1097/00005537-200002010-00010.

Siegel, Linda S. 1988. Agatha Christie's learning disability. *Canadian Psychology / Psychologie canadienne* 29(2): 213–216. https://psycnet.apa.org/doi/10.1037/h0084531.

Stevens, Michael H., Jacobsen, Tcemarie, and Crofts, Alicia K. 2013. Lead and the deafness of Ludwig van Beethoven. *Laryngoscope* 123(11): 2854–2858. https://doi.org/10.1002/lary.24120.

Suzuki, Kyoko. 2022. Alexia and agraphia in Japanese. *Neurology and Clinical Neuroscience* 10(4): 191–197. https://doi.org/10.1111/ncn3.12610.

Tralbaut, Marc Edo. 1969. *Vincent Van Gogh.* Viking Press.

Traxler, Matthew J. 2011. *Introduction to Psycholinguistics: Understanding Language Science.* Wiley-Blackwell.

Ujiie, Y., Asai, T., Tanaka, A., Asakawa, K., and Wakabayashi, A. 2014. Autistic traits predict weaker visual influence in the McGurk effect. *Personality and Individual Differences* 60: S51–S52. https://doi.org/10.1016/j.paid.2013.07.211.

Voskuil, Piet. 2020. Vincent van Gogh and his illness. A reflection on a posthumous diagnostic exercise. *Epilepsy & Behavior* 111: 107258. https://doi.org/10.1016/j.yebeh.2020.107258.

Wagner, Richard K., Zirps, Fotena A., Edwards, Ashley A., Wood, Sarah G., Joyner, Rachel E., Becker, Betsy J., et al. 2020. The prevalence of dyslexia: A new approach to its estimation. *Journal of Learning Disabilities* 53(5): 354–365.

Walusinski, O. and Féray, J. C. 2020. The Marquise de Dampierre identified at last, the first described clinical case of Gilles de la Tourette syndrome. *Revue Neurologique* 176(10): 754–762. https://doi.org/10.1016/j.neurol.2020.01.353.

Ward, David and Scott, Kathleen S. (eds.). 2011. *Cluttering: A Handbook of Research, Intervention and Education.* Psychology Press.

Yurchak, Alexei. 2017. The canon and the mushroom: Lenin, sacredness, and Soviet collapse. *HAU: Journal of Ethnographic Theory* 7(2): 165–198. https://doi.org/10.14318/hau7.2.021.

Chapter 6

Abley, Mark. 2008. *The Prodigal Tongue: Dispatches from the Future of English.* Random House of Canada.

Adams, Douglas. 1995. *The Hitchhiker's Guide to the Galaxy.* Del Ray.

Alharbi, Sadeen, Alrazgan, Muna, Alrashed, Alanoud, Alnomasi, Turkiayh, Almojel, Raghad, Alharbi, Rima, et al. 2021. Automatic speech recognition: Systematic literature review. *IEEE Access* 9: 131858–131876. https://doi.org/10.1109/ACCESS.2021.3112535.

Anjomshoa, Leila and Sadighi, Firooz. 2015. The importance of motivation in second language acquisition. *International Journal on Studies in English Language and Literature* 3(2): 126–137.

Arenas, Aitor. 2024. Biological age and second language acquisition (SLA) over-time: A literature review. *Journal of Literature Language and Academic Studies* 3(1): 1–10. https://doi.org/10.56855/jllans.v3i01.1015.

Bak, Thomas H., Long, Madeleine R., Vega-Mendoza, Mariana and Sorace, Antonella. 2016. Novelty, challenge, and practice: The impact of intensive language learning on attentional functions. *PloS One* 11(4): e0153485. https://doi.org/10.1371/journal.pone.0153485.

Cano Fernández, Eva. 2021. *Language Phenomena in Second Language Acquisition: Between-Language Competition and Reverse Transfer*. Universidad Pontificia Comillas (Publicaciones).

Carroll, John B. and Sapon, Stanley M. 2002 (1959). *Modern Language Aptitude Test*. Second Language Testing.

Cummins, Jim. 2009. Bilingual and immersion programs. In Michael Long and Catherine Doughty (eds.), *The Handbook of Language Teaching* (pp. 161–181). Wiley-Blackwell.

Eichhoff, Jürgen. 1993. "Ich bin ein Berliner": A history and a linguistic clarification. *Monatshefte* 85: 71–80.

Ellis, Elizabeth M. 2016. *The Plurilingual TESOL Teacher: The Hidden Language Lives of TESOL Teachers and Why They Matter*. de Gruyter Mouton.

Ellis, Rod. 2015. Creativity and language learning. In Rodney H. Jones and Jack C. Richards (eds.), *Creativity in Language Teaching* (pp. 32–48). Routledge.

Eyman, Douglas. 2024. Translation and Chinese culture in video games. In Li Guo, Douglas Eyman, and Hongmei Sun (eds.), *Games and Play in Chinese and Sinophone Cultures*. University of Washington Press.

Granena, Gisela and Long, Mike (eds.). 2016. *Sensitive Periods, Language Aptitude, and Ultimate L2 Attainment* (Vol. 35). John Benjamins.

Grosjean, François. 2021. *Life as a Bilingual: Knowing and Using Two or More Languages*. Cambridge University Press.

Kazazogˇlu, Semin. 2020. The impact of L1 interference on foreign language writing: A contrastive error analysis. *Journal of Language and Linguistic Studies* 16(3): 1168–1188.

Kirschen, Bryan. 2013. Multilingual manipulation and humor in *I Love Lucy*. *Hispania* 96(4): 735–747. https://www.jstor.org/stable/23608523.

Krashen, Stephen D. 1981. *Second Language Acquisition and Second Language Learning*. Pergamon Press.

Krashen, Stephen D. and Terrell, Tracy D. 1983. *The Natural Approach: Language Acquisition in the Classroom*. Pergamon Press.

Li, Katarzyna. 2023. Age as a factor determining effectiveness of L2 acquisition. *Journal of Language Teaching* 3(9): 8–13. https://doi.org/10.54475/jlt.2023.021.

Li, Shaofeng and Zhao, Huijun. 2021. The methodology of the research on language aptitude: A systematic review. *Annual Review of Applied Linguistics* 41: 25–54. https://doi.org/10.1017/S0267190520000136.

McWhirter, Norris. 1997. *The Guinness Book of World Records*. Random House.

Mehmet, Ulker. 2019. The approach of learning a foreign language by watching TV series. *Educational Research and Reviews* 14(17): 608–617. https://doi.org/10.5897/ERR2019.3839.

Mercer, Sarah. 2016. Seeing the world through your eyes: Empathy in language learning and teaching. In Peter D. MacIntyre, Tammy Gregersen, and Sarah Mercer (eds.), *Positive Psychology in SLA* (pp. 91–111). Multilingual Matters.

Muñoz, Carmen, Pattemore, Anastasia and Avello, Daniela. 2024. Exploring repeated captioning viewing as a way to promote vocabulary learning: Time lag between repetitions and learner factors. *Computer Assisted Language Learning* 37(7): 1744–1770. https://doi.org/10.1080/09588221.2022.2113898.

Salamah, Husam K. Z., Mortier, Eva, Wassenberg, Renska, and Strik, Jacqueline. 2022. Lost in another language: A case report. *Journal of Medical Case Reports* 16(1): 25. https://doi.org/10.1186/s13256-021-03236-z.

Schroeder, Scott R. and Marian, Viorica. 2012. A bilingual advantage for episodic memory in older adults. *Journal of Cognitive Psychology* 24(5): 591–601. https://doi.org/10.1080/20445911.2012.669367.

Selinker, Larry. 1972. Interlanguage. *International Review of Applied Linguistics in Language Teaching* 10(1–4): 209–232. https://doi.org/10.1515/iral.1972.10.1-4.209.

Shwartz, Vered. 2025. *Lost in Automatic Translation: Navigating Life in English in the Age of Language Technologies*. Cambridge University Press.

Smith, Neilson Voyne and Tsimpli, Ianthi-Maria. 1995. *The Mind of a Savant: Language Learning and Modularity*. Wiley.

Stern, Yaakov, Barnes, Carol A., Grady, Cheryl, Jones, Richard N., and Raz, Naftali. 2019. Brain reserve, cognitive reserve, compensation, and maintenance: Operationalization, validity, and mechanisms of cognitive resilience. *Neurobiological Aging* 83: 124–129. https://doi.org/10.1016/j.neurobiolaging.2019.03.022.

Stollznow, Karen. 2014. *Language Myths, Mysteries and Magic*. Palgrave Macmillan.

Stollznow, Karen. 2020. *On the Offensive: Prejudice in Language Past and Present*. Cambridge University Press.

Vaddadi, Krishna M. and Thandava, Sreenivas. 2019. Cross-cultural marketing challenges in global environment. *International Journal of Economics and Management Studies* 6(12): 74–83. https://doi.org/10.14445/23939125/IJEMS-V6I12P109.

Zeanah, Charles H., Gunnar, Megan R., McCall, Robert B., Kreppner, Jana M., and Fox, Nathan A. 2011. Sensitive periods. *Monographs of the Society for Research in Child Development* 76(4): 147–162. https://doi.org/10.1111/j.1540-5834.2011.00631.x.

Index

1984, 14

acyrology, 109
Adams, Douglas, 165
ADHD. *See* attention deficit hyperactivity disorder (ADHD)
advanced fluency, 169
African American English (AAE), 26, 27, 28, 34
agraphia, 159, 160
AI, 8, 152, 191, 201
Aitchison, Jean, 1
Akbar the Great, 3, 73
Akkadian, 52, 53
alexia, 152, 153, 159, 199
Al-Farabi, 164
Alice's Adventures in Wonderland, 156
Allegory of the Cave, Plato, 3
'Allo 'Allo!, 173
allophones, 16
Alpha Dog, 189
Alzheimer's, 5, 109, 111, 139, 159, 160, 192
amelioration, 22
American Sign Language (ASL), 36, 59, 60, 98
amusia, 160
amyotrophic lateral sclerosis (ALS), 146, 151
An Objective Psychology of Grammar, 7
antidisestablishmentarianism, 18
Anu, 54
aphasia, 2, 102, 132, 133, 134, 135, 136, 137, 138, 139, 140, 142, 145, 146, 149, 152, 199
aphemie, 135
apraxia, 94, 145
Arabic, 23, 31, 37, 49, 52, 53, 71, 72, 75, 81, 98, 120, 164, 179, 181
Aramaic, 49, 52, 53
Aristotle, 6, 10, 66, 80
ASD. *See* autism spectrum disorder (ASD)

Astrid (foreign accent syndrome), 137
ataxia, 144, 145
attention deficit hyperactivity disorder (ADHD), 155, 158, 193
auditory processing disorder, 147
augmentative and alternative communication, 149
Australian Sign Language, 36
Australopithecus, 43
autism spectrum disorder (ASD), 94, 142, 155, 158

Babbitt, Raymond, 95
Babel, 50, 163, 166
babel fish, 162, 165, 166, 190, 200
Baudelaire, Charles, 8, 136, 140, 161, 199
Beethoven, Ludwig van, 148
Berenstain Bears, 124
Berkowitz, David, 147
Biden, Joe, 133, 143, 144
Big Bang Theory, 179
bilingual, 162, 184
bilingualism, 162, 163, 164, 166
Bislama, 29, 30, 33
A Bit of Fry & Laurie, 11, 21
Blanc, Mel, 174
Bloomfield, Leonard, 30
Boas, Franz, 14
Book of Acts, 175
Boss Baby, 81
Bowring, Sir John, 164
"The Boxer," 113
Brady Bunch, 92
Braille, 31, 152
British Sign Language, 36
Broca, Paul, 5, 134
Broca's area, 5, 39, 43, 117, 129, 138, 168
Brother John, 137
Bugs Bunny, 174

Burroughs, Edgar Rice, 75
Burroughs, William S., 126
Bush, George H. W., 106

Caesar, Julius, 91
Cain, Cassandra, 74
Cang Jie, 55
Canterbury Tales, 34, 35
Carroll, Lewis, 133, 156, 157, 199
categorical perception, 112, 118
Caxton, William, 33
cerebral palsy, 96
Chan, Jackie, 174
"The Chaos," 32
Chaucer, Geoffrey, 34
Chess Turk, 4, 103, 196
Chinese, 20, 23, 25, 31, 33, 52, 55, 114,
    186, 189
Chomsky, Noam, 7, 10, 21, 58, 60, 71, 78, 79,
    80, 81, 118, 157, 195, 197
Christie, Agatha, 159, 199
Churchill, Winston, 133, 144, 199
Clever Hans, 61, 65
Cockney, 17, 27, 37, 38
code-switching, 164, 184, 185, 186, 193, 200
conceptualization, 101
connected speech, 112
Connery, Sean, 174
convergence, 174
Cookie Monster, 86, 91, 92
coprolalia, 141
Costner, Kevin, 178
Coverdale, Miles, 34
Cratylus, 3, 35, 47, 149
Critical Period Hypothesis, 79, 171, 197, 199
Crocodile Dundee, 24
Cro-Magnon, 45
Cronkite, Walter, 167
cuneiform, 54, 55, 56, 197
Curtiss, Susan, 77, 79, 195

Daffy Duck, 174
Dagognet, François, 76
Dances with Wolves, 178
Darwin, Charles, 5, 48, 56, 65, 66, 80, 84, 85,
    95, 197
Darwin's theory of evolution, 44
de Bonet, Juan Pablo, 149
Derrida, Jacques, 30

Descent of Man, The, 56, 57, 65
di Adam, Salimbene, 72
Die Sprache, 7
discourse particles, 184
divergence, 174
Doctor Who, 190
Dogberryism, 109
Donders, Franz, 6, 102, 120
Douglas, Kirk, 140
Down, John Langdon, 96
Down syndrome, 95, 149, 154
Dravidian, 52
dysarthria, 145
dysfluency, 144
dysgraphia, 158, 159, 199
dyslexia, 89, 121, 132, 153, 154, 155, 158, 199

early bilingual phase, 178–184, 200
early production phase, 168
Eastman, George, 47
Ebonics, 26, 27
echolalia, 95, 142
Edwin Smith Surgical Papyrus, 2, 133, 140
Egypt, 2, 195, 197, 199
Egyptian Coptic, 53
Egyptian hieroglyphs, 30, 31, 55, 56, 120, 196
Elmo, 91, 92
emergence delirium, 175
Emile, or On Education, 5
Emperor Akbar, 3, 73, 98
Engrish, 16, 186, 187
Enmerkar, 55
Epun, 165
Etana, 54
Exner's area, 129
*Expression of the Emotions in Man and
    Animals, The*, 5

false cognates/friends, 181
Farsi, 53
Fawlty Towers, 113
Fazah, Ziad Youssef, 163, 164
Fehlleistungen, 106
Ferris Bueller's Day Off, 21
first language, 1, 29, 30, 36, 42, 52, 81, 93, 99,
    163, 166, 167, 168, 169, 170, 171, 173, 176,
    180, 182, 195, 197, 199
Firth, Colin, 177
fixation, 119

fluency, 169
fonts, 35, 121, 126
foreign accent syndrome, 137, 174, 175, 200
foreign language syndrome, 175, 193, 200
formulation, 101
fossilization, 182
fovea, 119
FOXP2, 40, 44, 94, 196
Franglais, 183
Frederick II, Holy Roman Emperor, 3, 72, 74
Freud, Sigmund, 106
Freudian slips, 106, 107
Fry, Stephen, 11, 21, 67
Futurama, 34
Fuzzy Logic Model, 114

Gabelentz, Hans Conon von der, 164
Gall, Franz Joseph, 4
Galton, Francis, 6, 80
Ganong effect, 114, 198
Garden of Eden, 49, 71
garden path sentences, 122, 198
Gardner, Allen and Beatrix, 59
Garfield, 101
Garner, Richard Lynch, 58
Gaspard Itard, Jean Marc, 76
Gauguin, Paul, 147
general auditory theory, 112
Genie (Wiley, Susan), 8, 76, 77, 79, 96, 98,
    99, 138, 172, 197
Geschwind syndrome, 157
glossolalia, 176
Gollum, 92
The Good, the Bad and the Ugly, 116
Google, 8, 103, 166, 184, 187, 191
graphorrhea, 157
Great Vowel Shift, 33
Greek, 1, 2, 3, 6, 15, 18, 19, 27, 30, 49, 51, 53,
    71, 72, 80, 154, 163, 164, 165
Guinness Book of World Records, 163, 164
Gutenberg. Johannes, 33
Guugu Yimithirr, 14

Hamilton, Alexander, 156, 199
Hanabiko (Koko), 59
Hawking, Stephen, 132, 146, 150, 199
Hayes, Keith and Catherine, 58
"Heart of Gold," 48
Hebrew, 3, 20, 49, 52, 53, 71, 72, 73, 98, 120, 167

Hello Kitty, 101
Hendrix, Jimi, 112
Hermes, 49
Hermogenes, 35, 47
Herodotus, 3, 71
Hinduism, 49
Hippocrates, 2, 3, 152
Hitchhiker's Guide to the Galaxy, The, 165
Hitler, Adolf, 66
Hogan, Paul, 24
Holy Roman Emperor Charles V, 179
Homo erectus, 43, 44
Homo habilis, 43, 197
Homo neanderthalensis, 44
Homo sapiens, 42, 43, 44, 45, 197
homographs, 113
homophones, 113, 169
Hoover, Herbert, 104
House, 164
Hunglish, 183
hyoid bone, 39, 44, 196
hypercorrection, 110
hypergraphia, 156, 157, 158, 199
hyperlexia, 155
hyper-religiosity, 157

I Love Lucy, 185
Iceman, 48
idiolect, 24, 182
illeism, 91
Inchkeith, 3, 72, 73
interlanguage, 182, 183, 186
intermediate fluency, 169
International Phonetic Alphabet (IPA), 16

James IV of Scotland (King), 3, 72
Java Man, 44
Johnson, Dr. Samuel, 142
joint attention, 85, 93
Jones, Terry, 140
Jones, William, 6, 51, 195
Joyce, James, 46, 157
Jungle Book, The, 75, 81

Kamala and Amala, 75, 98
kana, 153
kanji, 153
Kantor, Jacob, 7
Kath & Kim, 110

Keller, Helen, 132, 150, 199
Kellogg, Luella and Winthrop, 58
Kennedy, John F., 188
Khoisan, 84
Kidman, Nicole, 174, 179
Kipling, Rudyard, 75
Kish Tablet, 53, 54
Klingon, 179
Koko, 59, 61, 62, 63, 197

language acquisition device (LAD), 78, 79,
    80, 118, 197
language attrition, 111, 182
langue d'amour, 178
late bilingual phase, 174, 199
Latin, 6, 15, 20, 27, 30, 31, 34, 51, 53, 54, 71,
    72, 75, 98, 103, 143, 180, 190
Laurie, Hugh, 11, 21
Leborgne, Louis Victor, 134, 161
Lelong, Lazare, 134
Lenin, Vladimir Ilych, 8, 133, 135, 136, 139,
    150, 153, 159, 160, 199
Lenneberg, Eric, 79
Les Fleurs du Mal, 136
Lethal Weapon 4, 180
lethologica, 108
letter-by-letter reading, 153
Levisen, Carsten, 22
Lindsay, Robert, 72
livin' la vida loca, 183, 184
Locke, John, 6, 78, 80
logorrhea, 157
London Philological Society, 46
Look Who's Talking, 81
Lord of the Rings, The, 92, 179
Lou Gehrig's disease, 146. *See also*
    amyotrophic lateral sclerosis (ALS)
Love Actually, 177

malapropisms, 100, 109, 110, 198
Mandela Effect, 124, 198
Manucci, Niccolò, 73
Marquise de Dampierre, 141, 161
The Matrix Reloaded, 178
McGurk Effect, 116, 155, 198
*Mechanismus der menschlichen
    Sprache*, 4
Meno, 71
mental chronometry, 6, 102

mental lexicon, 101, 102, 114
Mesolithic era, 52
Mesopotamia, 52, 53, 55, 127
metathesis, 17, 34, 105
Mezzofanti, Cardinal Giuseppe, 164
Michael, George, 137, 175
Middle English, 23, 26, 34, 53
Mind Your Language, 176, 178
mirror neuron, 117
modernité, 136
mondegreen, 112
monogenesis, 49
Monty Python, 33, 140, 189
Monty Python and the Holy Grail, 33
Moran, Dylan, 179
Morgan, Pringle, 154
morphemes, 18, 22, 31
Morrison, Toni, 10
motherese, 89
motor theory, 116, 117, 198
Mount Vesuvius, 190
Much Ado about Nothing, 109
Müller, Max, 46, 57
multilingualism, 163, 164, 191
My Fair Lady, 17, 37

Napoleon, 4, 141
*National Lampoon's European
    Vacation*, 187
nature vs. nurture, 6, 7, 80
Neanderthals, 44, 45, 197
Nell, 73
neurodiversity, 75, 89, 94, 95, 98, 99, 121,
    132, 139, 142, 146, 147, 149, 153, 154, 155,
    157, 158, 198, 199
neuroplasticity, 161, 171
New Zealand Sign Language, 36, 163
Newspeak, 14
Nim Chimpsky, 60, 61, 197
nyctograph, 156

observer-expectancy effect, 62
Old English, 23, 26, 30, 33, 34
Olsen, Susan, 92, 93
On the Origin of Species, 56
On the Sacred Disease, 2
onomatopoeia, 13, 46
Orwell, George, 14
overextension, 90

overgeneralization, 90, 182
Oz, Frank, 91

parafovea, 119
paraphasias, 139
parapraxes, 106
parentese, 89
Paris Linguistic Society, 46
Patterson, Francine "Penny", 59
pejoration, 22
Penfield, Wilder, 79
Peppa Pig Syndrome, 87
perceptual span, 120
periphery, 119
personal vocabulary, 102
Pfungst, Oskar, 61
Phaedrus, 30
Pharaoh Psamtik, 3, 71, 77, 84
phonemes, 15, 18
phonological awareness, 88
phonotactics, 17
Phrygian, 3, 72
Pinker, Steven, 58, 79
Pirahã, 16, 30
Plato, 3, 6, 30, 35, 45, 47, 71, 78, 80, 149, 195
plurilingualism, 163
polygenesis, 49, 52
polyglot, 8, 162, 163, 164, 179, 193
Pompeii, 190
Porky Pig, 174
predictive processing, 147
pre-production phase, 168
presque vu, 108
Proto-Afroasiatic, 52
proto-language, 6, 42, 43, 51
proto-writing, 55
Psamtik I, 3, 71
psycholinguistics, 1, 3, 6, 7, 8, 195, 196, 200, 201
"Purple Haze," 112
Pygmalion, 17

Queen Victoria, 105

Rain Man, 95
Ravel, Maurice, 160
Received Pronunciation (RP), 28
receptive language, 66, 187
receptive phase, 168

regional dialects, 24, 149
The Republic, 3
right ear advantage, 113
Rindfleischetikettierungsüberwachungsauf gabenübertragungsgesetz, 19
The Rivals, 109
Roberts, Lamar, 79
Romulus and Remus, 75
Rousseau, Jean-Jacques, 5
Runny Babbit: A Billy Sook, 106
Russell, Bertrand, 71

saccades, 119
Sanichar, Dina, 75
Sanskrit, 6, 49, 51, 52, 53, 71
Sapir, Edward, 10, 14
Sapir-Whorf hypothesis, 14
Sarasvati, 49
Saussure, Ferdinand de, 7, 10, 30
schizophrenia, 147
Schleicher, August, 51
Schwarzenegger, Arnold, 174, 184
Scovel, Thomas, 1
second languages, 80, 163, 178, 181, 183, 199
Seinfeld, 108, 130
Semon, Dr. Felix, 144
Sesame Street, 91, 92, 114
Shaw, George Bernard, 17, 34
Sheridan, Richard Brinsley, 109
The Shining, 158
silent phase, 168
Silverstein, Shel, 106
Simmons, Gene, 167, 177
Simon and Garfunkel, 113
Simpson, Maggie, 83, 84
The Simpsons, 83, 158
Sindarin, 179
Singlish, 184
Skinner, B. F., 7, 78, 197
smooth pursuit eye movements, 119
Socrates, 30, 35, 71, 149
Sonnet 18, 126
Spanglish, 183, 184
speech emergence, 168
Spooner, Reverend William Archibald, 8, 104, 105, 108
Stalin, Joseph, 135, 160
Star Trek, 179, 190, 191

Star Wars, 190
Starmer, Keir, 107
Stroop Effect, 123
subvocalization, 123
Sumerian, 52, 53, 54, 55, 197
Symphony No. 9, 148

Taa language, 16
Taco Bell, 185
Tamil, 52
TARDIS, 162, 190, 200
Tarzan, 75, 81, 91
Taylor, Christopher, 164, 166
Taylor, Elizabeth, 84
telegraphic stage, 86
Terminator 2, 184
Terrace, Herbert S., 60
Thank You, Jeeves, 21
Theory of Mind, 88
Tiedemann, Dietrich, 5
Tier-Sprechschule, 66
Timberlake, Justin, 189
Tinglish, 183
tip-of-the-tongue phenomenon, 108
Tiwi, 51
Tolkien, J. R. R., 92
de la Tourette, Georges Gilles, 141
Tourette's Syndrome, 132
trisomy 21, 95
't schildermenneke, 147
Twain, Mark, 19
Twelfth Night, 157
The Twilight Zone, 73
two-word stage, 86
typoglycemia, 125

Ulysses, 46, 157
underextension, 90
Universal Grammar, 78, 80

Van Damme, Jean-Claude, 174
Van Gogh, Vincent, 147, 157
Van Orman Quine, Willard, 71
Vanuatu, 29
verbal apraxia, 145
Verbal Behavior, 7
The Vicar of Dibley, 104
Victor of Aveyron, 76, 98, 197
visual word form area, 153
Von Kempelen, Wolfgang, 4, 103, 196
Von Zell, Harry, 104

War and Peace, 118
Wa-Sania, 50
Webster, Noah, 35
Weinreich, Max, 27
Wernicke, Carl, 5, 138
Wernicke's aphasia, 138, 139, 152
Wernicke's area, 5, 39, 129, 138, 146, 168
West !Xoon, 16
Whorf, Benjamin, 14
Wiley, Susan, 76
Willis, Bruce, 140
Wittgenstein, Ludwig, 10, 14
Wodehouse, P. G., 21
word blindness, 152
word explosion, 87
word recognition, 112, 131, 153
word retrieval, 101, 102, 103, 139, 140
wug test, 87
Wundt, Wilhelm, 7, 195

xenoglossia, 175

Yanny vs. Laurel, 117
Young, Neil, 48

Zero Wing, 189
Zulu, 84

For EU product safety concerns, contact us at Calle de José Abascal, 56–1°,
28003 Madrid, Spain or eugpsr@cambridge.org.